THE
FORCE
OF
WITNESS

Irene Simmons, dress with calavera, for *Redressing Injustice* installation. Photo by author.

DISSIDENT ACTS A SERIES EDITED BY MACARENA GÓMEZ-BARRIS AND DIANA TAYLOR

THE FORCE OF WITNESS

CONTRA FEMINICIDE

OF

WITNESS

ROSA-LINDA FREGOSO

DUKE UNIVERSITY PRESS   DURHAM AND LONDON   2023

Project editor: Bird Williams
Designed by Matthew Tauch
Typeset in Arno Pro and Saira
by Westchester Publishing Services

Library of Congress Cataloging-in-Publication Data
Names: Fregoso, Rosa Linda, [date] author.
Title: The force of witness : contra feminicide / Rosa-Linda
Fregoso. Other titles: Dissident acts.
Description: Durham : Duke University Press, 2023. | Series:
Dis-sident acts| Includes bibliographical references and index.
Identifiers: LCCN 2022041435 (print)
LCCN 2022041436 (ebook)
ISBN 9781478019817 (paperback)
ISBN 9781478017103 (hardcover)
ISBN 9781478024385 (ebook)
Subjects: LCSH: Women—Crimes against—Mexico—Prevention. |
Women—Violence against—Mexico—Prevention. | Women—
Mexico—Social conditions—21st century. | Misogyny—Mexico. |
Collective memory—Mexico. | BISAC: SOCIAL SCIENCE / Women's
Studies | SOCIAL SCIENCE / Ethnic Studies / Caribbean & Latin
American Studies
Classification: LCC HV6250.4.W65 F745 2023 (print)
LCC HV 6250.4. W 65 (ebook)
DDC 362.88082—dc23/eng/20230110
LC record available at https://lccn.loc.gov/2022041435
LC ebook record available at https://lccn.loc.gov/2022041436

Cover art: Guillermo Scully, *Aquí Estamos* (2010).
Permission granted by Helena Scully Gargallo.
Photo by Chip Lord.

In loving memory of my sister, María Teresa "Terri" Araiza
—a warrior until the end (1956–2021)

Contents

Acknowledgments

Mil gracias to all who made this book possible. My ideas and arguments benefited from the thoughtful responses of audiences and colleagues at conferences, seminars, and community forums. I thank audiences who heard earlier versions of these chapters at the Observatório Nacional da Violência e Género in Lisbon, Portugal; Equal Rights Advocates in San Francisco, California; and Mujeres Unidas y Activas in Oakland, California. I am thankful to colleagues for their critical engagement with my work at the Center for the Study of Gender and Sexuality at the University of Chicago; La Red de Investigadoras por la Vida y Libertad de las Mujeres in Mexico City; the University of North Carolina School of Law; the University of California, Santa Barbara; Centro de Investigaciones y Estudios Superiores (CIESAS) in Mexico City; Colegio de la Frontera Norte, Ciudad Juárez, Chihuahua; Center for the Study of Gender and Sexualities at California State University, Los Angeles; Trinity College; Ohio State University; the University of Minnesota; Diplomado de Violencia Sexual y de Género, CIESAS, Oaxaca City, Oaxaca; University of California Humanities Institute in Mexico City; Özyegin University, Çekmeköy campus, Istanbul, Turkey; La Sapieza, Universita di Roma, Rome, Italy; Women, Gender and Sexuality Studies at the University of Washington, Seattle; University of Kentucky; Facultad de Ciencias Sociales de Comunicación, Universidad del País Vasco, Bilbao, Spain; University of California, Davis; Humanities Institute at Scripps College; Gender and Women's Studies at the University of Maryland, Baltimore County; and Centro de Derechos Humanos Hannah Arendt at the Universidad de Guerrero in Acapulco, Guerrero.

My thanks to graduate students and colleagues at the University of California, Santa Cruz. I am indebted to the Social Sciences Division at UCSC for their financial support. My enduring appreciation to Ryan Kendall, Jessica Ryan, Bird Williams, and the production staff at Duke University Press for their guidance and invaluable assistance. I am forever thankful to Ken Wissoker for believing in this project from its infancy and encouraging its completion. Thank you to the two readers at Duke University Press for their substantive, probing, and incisive comments. Mil gracias to my colleague Patricia Ravelo for locating Helena Gargallo Scully, the daughter of the late artist Guillermo Scully, and to Helena for granting me permission to use her father's artwork on the book's cover. As always, I am deeply grateful to Herman Gray for his lifelong love, support, and intellectual companionship. Miles y miles de gracias to the activists and artivists whose struggles for a world free of violence inspire us all. ¡Ni una más! y ¡Ni una menos!

Prelude

We'd chant once more, the names of the dead and
bear witness again and again, deeper and deeper,
to the anguish and suffering of that terrible place.
BERNIE GLASSMAN, *Bearing Witness*

This book began as a collection of essays on the topic of feminicide and disappearance on the Mexico-US border. Written over the course of ten years, each chapter attends to the necessity for remembering the horrors of feminicide and disappearance, and bearing witness to its devastating suffering and spirited resistance. At the heart of this book is a reading of witnessing that encourages both/and perspectives rather than an either/or interpretation.

The force of witness is the name given to the different modalities of feminist witness discussed in these pages. Witness is not solely an individual or an autonomous subject but a constellation of multiple social locations and practices. As conceptualized here, witness is constituted by interconnections and "social relatedness."[1] A force field of human thinking and doing, witness is multiply situated across deeply textured and heterogenous worlds.

Rather than an individual act or practice undertaken by a sovereign subject, the force of witness involves a collectivity forged on the basis of ethical and engaged planetary obligations and interdependency.[2] Instead of a universalist vision, witnessing emerges from pluriversal imaginaries. Each modality, endeavor, and presence of witness dealt with here is context specific, "linked with and contingent on the event witnessed." For "witnessing cannot be analyzed outside of its specific context, apart from its condition of possibility."[3] Witness affirms the dynamic, spirited connection between seen and unseen worlds.

Prior to my engagement with critical social theory related to trauma studies, memory studies, and the Holocaust, my understanding of witnessing was based on childhood memories. Growing up in a Catholic household in South Texas, I remember my parents railing against the door-to-door Christian acolytes, dressed in their Sunday best, as they knocked on doors, bearing the gift of *The Watchtower*. "Protestant fanatics," my mother would call them. They called themselves Jehovah's Witnesses.

My family's weekly viewing of the *Perry Mason* TV series introduced me to another notion of the witness: the eyewitness who was called to the witness stand, raised her right hand and pronounced the oath, "I swear to tell the truth, the whole truth, and nothing but the truth, so help me God." For years I believed that the religious and the courtroom witness were one and the same. Interestingly, these two modalities of witnessing remain intertwined, for the legal and religious traces of witness persist to this day in Occidental thought.

In social theory, to witness is both ethereal and tangible, abstract and substantial. Each form is context specific. *Witness* is a term of law and religion, history and psychoanalysis, conscious and unconscious processes. In law, philosophy, and epistemology, the eyewitness is privileged as the purveyor of "the most decisive proof of evidence in courtrooms," Shoshana Felman tells us.[4] This modernist, ocular-centric notion of firsthand seeing forms the basis of a truth known and remembered by the witness in a legal or juridical context. The witness as eyewitness is also central to the discursive realm of journalism and academic disciplines that rely on firsthand knowledge through experience as evidentiary basis for news stories, factual claims, and findings.[5] But just how reliable is the eyewitness? Does the witness testify to a truth recognizable as verifiable and factual? Or is there something unavailable as facts, inaccessible to verification, to her testimony?

"Some legal proof or the display of an object [this 'thing'] produced in evidence" is fraught, facilitated and complicated by the vicissitudes and oscillations of memory. As Jacques Derrida suggests, "This 'thing' is no longer present to him, of course, in the mode of perception at the moment when the attestation happens; but it is present to him, if he alleges this presence, as re-presented in the present of memory."[6] The witness's oath is for the truth as re-membered.

In his work as a psychoanalyst with Holocaust survivors, Dori Laub points us to the psychoanalytic context of the unconscious, to the realm of she who bears witness to a truth unavailable to its own speaker. He recounts the story of a survivor-witness to the uprising at Auschwitz who testified incorrectly before historians about the events of the day that Jewish prisoners blew up "three chimneys." The historians dismissed the woman as an unreliable witness (there was in fact only "one" chimney), yet for Laub the Auschwitz survivor bears witness to a "thing" unfamiliar: the unconscious truth and conditions of possibility of Jewish resistance. "She was testifying not simply to empirical historical facts," Laub explains, "but to the very secret of [Jewish] survival and of resistance to extermination."[7] She bears witness to "agency and resistance"[8]—to something that cannot be seen, to what James Baldwin calls "evidence of things not seen." On this basis, Kelly Oliver identifies the double sense of the term *witness*: "It is important to note that witnessing has both the juridical connotation of seeing with one's own eyes [the eyewitness] and the religious or now political connotation of testifying to that which cannot be seen, or bearing witness."[9]

In relation to the Holocaust experience, Laub identifies three distinct levels of witnessing: (1) "the level of being witness to oneself in the experience"; (2) "the level of being a witness to the testimony of others"; and (3) "the level of being a witness to the witnessing process."[10] In each of these instances, to witness is not an autonomous or stand-alone act but a "bonding" involving an interlocutor, a connection with (an)other: "Testimonies are not monologues," Laub continues; "they cannot take place in solitude. The witness is talking to *somebody*: to somebody they have been waiting for a long time."[11]

Oliver builds on this typology and connects the witnessing process to the formation of subjectivity. Witnessing is at the core of subjectivity, according to Oliver. But rather than conceive of subjectivity as a demand for "recognition and visibility," Oliver embraces a notion of "dis-identification" (to use José Muñoz's term).[12] As Oliver suggests, subjectivity is "relational and formed and sustained by address-ability (the ability to address others and be addressed by them) and response-ability (the ability to respond to others and oneself)."[13]

How to build on these understandings of *witness* in critical social theory, while at the same time going beyond the implied protagonist of the witness based on individual subjectivity? In light of the fact that in these cases, the witnessing process involves a restoration of "self-respect and a sense of one's self as an agent or a self," how do we contemplate its social related-ness?[14] In other words, how to envision witnessing beyond the logics of law and the modern state, and as different from a category, an identity, a subject, and its embeddedness in liberalism and the autonomous individual of Western humanism? How do we imagine witnessing as a pluriversal endeavor and presence?

The witness I write about in these pages figures as a countervailing force to the necropolitics or death force that for decades has brutalized the Mexico-US border region and spread to other parts of the hemisphere. The force of witness represents a collectivity that counters this death force with life, with the vitality of a life force of human and multispecies existence, and with the demands for life. "¡VIVAS LAS QUEREMOS!/WE WANT THEM ALIVE!" the mothers and their allies in the contra-feminicide movement chanted during the protest marches of the early twenty-first century.

As a countervailing force to the destruction of life, to witness involves an embodied form of resistance and refusal to the disciplining, symbolic and material annihilation, and objectifying logic of the "feminicide machine."[15] The force of witness counters the dehumanization of women's and femi-nized bodies, the extermination of poor, mestiza, Indigenous, Afro-descendant, and trans people.

As an embodied form of resistance and refusal constituted by social relatedness, the force of witness affirms and maintains a pluriversal, heter-ogenous stance contingent on events and circumstances. Unlike Western universalism, the theory of pluriversality opens our worldview to other possibilities for the human, ethics, and divergent imaginaries.[16]

Drawing from the contemplative traditions of Hinduism and Buddhism, historian and cultural critic Lata Mani considers witnessing to be a pluralistic and dynamic practice that can potentially expand our sensual engagement with the world: "Witnessing brings our attention to the inherently rela-tional nature of existence and perception. It helps us to actively experience the fact that the world is not external to us and discontinuous to us; we discover that the world is in us and we are of it."[17]

The force of witness involves a "letting go of the body as a 'unit'" (to quote Judith Butler) and putting aside an identity-based approach to the individual subjectivity of the witness, for an "interbeing" understanding of the human.[18] The subjectivity of interbeing is grounded in relations of soli-darity, just as the act of bearing witness is anchored in interbeing relations.

Interbeing is an/other version of the human distinct from the self-reliant individual of Western humanism; it is a relational being: the Mayan concept of In'Laketch—"you are my other self."[19]

To witness under countervailing forces, then, is not solely an individual act but an expansive orientation beyond human agency and species provincialism.[20] The force of witness connects with the feature that Cindy Holder and Jeff Corntassel refer to as "universal kinship"—an interrelatedness of humans to all other elements of the cosmos, living and nonliving beings, in the material and spirit worlds.[21]

As members of complex kinship networks and clan affiliations, one's interrelatedness and sense of belonging entail a multiplicity of duties and obligations to the social/collective. The force of witness involves an ethics of reciprocity, a "response-ability" (to use Oliver's formulation) whereby every human being (each of us) is obliged to contemplate and regard with compassion the suffering of others. The ethical, engaged labor of pluriversal witnessing entails planetary obligations and duties to something greater than the self.

In formulating an insurgent theory of communitarian feminism, Aymara feminist Julieta Paredes posits the dialectic between the individual and the collective, defined by social kinship network—"el ser humano es relacional."[22] This relational orientation of human life is central to Mesoamerican thinking of "the interconnectedness of everyone and everything in the universe, the intersubjective nature of men and women, interconnected with the earth, sky, plants, and planets."[23] Let us replace individuality with a "poetics of communality," to borrow from author and critic Cristina Rivera Garza.[24]

In *The Restless Dead*, Rivera Garza makes use of the Mesoamerican concept of communality vis-à-vis writing and other forms of labor.[25] This understanding of communality entails thinking beyond oneself and abandoning the notion of the individual. Building on the work of Mixe anthropologist Floriberto Díaz, Rivera Garza details how "shared labor, material reciprocity, and a relationship of mutual belonging with the earth are basic components of survival" in Mesoamerican thinking on communality.[26] In the Mixe conception and experience of communality, "tequio" in particular is a "practice of reciprocity based on forms of unpaid, obligatory service labor" that "connects nature with human beings in contexts of mutual belonging that radically oppose notions of property and dominion."[27]

For Indigenous communities throughout the Américas, claims on earth are situated in an epistemology grounded in the interconnectedness of all beings. These accounts of the complex interdependencies that allow the human to exist are central to Indigenousness as a worldview or way of relating to the cosmos as a living being with consciousness, including multispecies spirits who, as Susan A. Miller writes, "are real and powerful within the material world."[28] In an interconnected pluriverse, anchored in collective kinship and presumptive care for all things, witnessing is a life force inseparable from our duties, obligations, and response-ability to the community of interrelated beings. Witnessing expands our comprehension of interrelatedness.

Documentary filmmaker Lourdes Portillo brings this interrelatedness to bear in *Señorita Extraviada* (see chapter 3). The documentary's poetics at one level affirms a form of witnessing based on documenting the social suffering of feminicide and the force of resistance and agency on the part of mothers and families of the women and girls who were murdered and disappeared. At another level, witnessing in *Señorita Extraviada* is not just vision centered but multisensual, "part of a system of sensation and a space filled with the flesh of the world."[29] The documentary weaves together metaphorical images (storm clouds, desert landscapes, discarded shoes) with material (eyewitness) ones, touching visuality with musicality (and not simply soundtrack), into a multisensory poetics of witnessing whereby the interconnection of the senses creates a distinct conception of vision and space.

Portillo bears witness to the witnessing process. With *Señorita Extraviada* she connects the living and the dead through scenes of singular, stand-alone testimonial of a mother followed by a montage of photos of the dead and disappeared women and girls. Her imaging strategy conjures up their spirits and in so doing anchors the act of bearing witness in interbeing relations. This appearance of the living and the dead and disappeared as interconnected in a social kinship network composed of the dialectic between the individual and the collective creates a space for intersubjectivity.

The documentary is not just a portal for the experience of witnessing trauma. Bearing witness in this sense means more than what the eyes can see, beyond an image-based process, but is grounded in a communality of kinship and care. As witnesses to the witnesses, we (viewers) are all implicated in planetary kinship obligations and duties to something greater than the self. In inscribing this communality, *Señorita Extraviada* transforms viewers into a life force of witnesses who must now bear part of the burden of responding to feminicidal atrocities and demanding justice on the borderlands.

Felman and Laub called the Holocaust "an event without a witness," for the extermination of voices produced a "crisis of witnessing."[30] As a survivor of Auschwitz, Primo Levi asserts that he cannot be "one of the true witnesses" of the Holocaust: "The only real witness, whom Levi calls the integral witness, is he who has gone to the heart of horror."[31] Just as one cannot bear witness from inside the Holocaust, one cannot bear witness from inside feminicide and disappearance. One can bear witness to its tribulations and militant force of action—the vulnerability, agency, embodied forms of resistance and refusal on the part of the contra-feminicide/gender violence movement.

Witnessing, then, is not simply an identity or a category but a ground for critical solidarity and transformational alliances. In *Bearing Witness While Black*, Alissa V. Richardson defines Black witnessing as a "style of protest journalism" that serves "to document the human rights injustices against black people."[32] This form of "sousveillance" or reporting from below (as opposed to "surveillance") embodies a life force inspired by the claim to humanity: "Bearing witness while black is, after all, an act that is borne of a desire to be seen as human."[33]

In documenting the multiply overlapping struggles of the contra-feminicide movement in chapters 1 and 4, bearing witness exemplifies a potential antidote to the war on women and feminized bodies on the borderland. Just as Black witnessing makes an enduring claim "to be seen as human," so too does feminist witnessing on the border represent a countervailing force to the necropolitical targeting, objectification, and dehumanization of poor women and girls.

Feminist border witnessing takes the form of accompaniment, an act embedded in social relatedness (see chapter 4). In their inspiring book *Insubordinate Spaces*, Barbara Tomlinson and George Lipsitz define accompaniment as "a disposition, a sensibility, and a pattern of behavior . . . a commitment based on the cultivated capacity for making connections with others, identifying with them, and helping them."[34] The Latin roots of *accompaniment* "combine 'bringing together' (com) with 'breaking bread' (panis), connecting physical proximity, shared sustenance and reciprocity."[35] For Tomlinson and Lipsitz, accompaniment is an endeavor and an alliance based on informal networks of solidarity. Their formulation of accompaniment differs sharply from the paternalistic logic of "protective accompaniment" that has been "popularized by human rights discourse."[36]

We heard their screams of personal pain and their calls for solidarity, and so many of us came from elsewhere to accompany the activist-mothers on the border. As I detail in chapter 4, we did not come as the "unarmed bodyguards" that Mahoney and Eguren write about.[37] We did not come to monitor human rights violations and to protect the activist-mothers and human rights defenders, as in the paternalistic tradition of "protective accompaniment." Those who traveled to the border from the global North, global South, and from other parts of Mexico did not come as neutral, detached, and disinterested witnesses. We came to bear witness, as committed and engaged participants. We came to accompany and connect with the activists in Ciudad Juárez, to find common ground, and unite in their struggle for social change. Bearing witness as accompaniment is a form of entering into a relationship with the other, as Aymara people would say.

With regard to the both/and (rather than either/or) interpretation of its different modalities, *witness* is a term of the legal realm (to testify; to give evidence) as much as it is of politics (obligations; response-ability) or aesthetics (utopian, artistic imaginaries). Witnessing occurs in the social, cultural, and spiritual realms, so too in the space of law and the state. Two chapters (5 and 6) deal with witnessing in the conjuncture of legalism (state-centric justice) and politics (social justice). Each of these cases—the tribunal (chapter 5) and the expert witness (chapter 6)—bears witness to individual and collective trauma, as "witness to the trauma witness."

It is "impossible to testify from inside death," Felman reminds us. Like the Holocaust, feminicide and disappearance represent an "event-without-a-witness."[38] The women murdered and disappeared may have been annihilated as witnesses; however, their mothers and advocates took their place and testified before the Permanent Peoples' Tribunal (PPT). The mothers became speakers for the dead.

In contrast to official courtrooms, the quasi-juridical context of the PPT facilitates a space for an expanded discursive mode of witnessing, first in terms of an official, juridical mode of testifying to the facts of a historical occurrence (the details of the atrocity) and second, a personal, intimate mode of testifying to the truth of the mother/activist/witness's own suffering, trauma, and spirited resistance. In the expanded modality of testimonial discourse, the speaker provides verbal witness to the empirical/material annihilation of the witness (dead) and to the accumulated devastation and living pain of their loved ones, who call themselves the "living dead" (see chapter 5).

The judges of the tribunal are not neutral, detached, or unconcerned observers of the witnessing process but rather engaged and resolute participants in the struggle for human rights. Characterized as an innovation in law and politics, the PPT's vision of justice is a socially constituted one, emanating from popular consciousness, not from institutional, state-centric power. The tribunal affirms a moral and ethical obligation to the rights of people rather than a purely legalistic one. As committed and obliged witnesses to the witnesses, tribunal judges subvert the normative discourse and official context of the court of law, and in so doing affirm witnessing as a life force for the restoration of humanity and claims for social justice.

The process of witnessing within the confines of state-centric rights occurred in my role as an expert witness in gender asylum cases (see chapters 1 and 6). Here, too, the modality of "witness to the witness" opened up a space for alleviating the suffering of survivors of patriarchal violence. Rather than eschewing any association with the legal system, I learned from attorneys in gender asylum cases how to bear witness before a court of law in ways that did not compromise my feminist politics.

In petitions for gender asylum, the survivor bears witness through testimony (affidavit) to her own experience of trauma. As witness to the witness-survivor the role of the expert witness is to evaluate and attest to the veracity of the testimony and then determine the level of vulnerability (persecution) that the survivor faces if she were to return to her home country. This situation raises the paradoxical nature of bearing witness within the discursive framework of law in general and asylum petitions in particular.

The expert witness must attest to, evaluate, and interpret the testimony of the witness-survivor to trauma while simultaneously portraying the survivor as vulnerable victim. At first glance, this discursive strategy seems problematic because it appears to reinforce a paternalistic logic of passive women in need of protection, and, as Butler writes in another context, images of vulnerability and victimhood fix women "in a position of powerlessness and lack of agency."[39] Even so, in the ten years of working with legal teams for gender asylum, it became clear that attorneys are deploying vulnerability as a strategic concept and mobilizing it in the service of a greater political good, namely that of securing the right to existence for the petitioners and in some cases for their children. Attorneys for gender asylum witnesses-survivors cleverly addressed, engaged, and confronted the legal system and, in the process, insisted on social justice in the normative context of law and the state while they embraced an ethical response-ability to the suffering of witnesses-survivors of gender violence.

In their affidavits, the witnesses-survivors of gender violence testify with memories of pain, torture, and their abjection. The survivor thus assumes the position that Laub terms a "witness to [her]self," to her own experience of trauma.[40] If it is difficult for the listener (the witness of the witness) to hear or read the painful recollections, it can be even more harrowing for the survivor to recall her own experience of oppression and dehumanization. "The act of telling," writes Dori Laub, "might itself become severely traumatizing, if the price of speaking is *re-living*; not relief, but further retraumatization."[41]

It is in this context that Laub's words provide some comfort for, as the psychoanalyst explains, through the act of testifying, survivors of atrocities reclaim their "position as a witness," their agency as subject rather than object. As Laub suggests, "repossessing one's life story through testimony is a form of action, of charge, which [one] has to actually pass through, in order to continue and complete the process of survival after liberation."[42] Bearing witness, in other words, can potentially serve to repair the inner witness, heal, and rebuild one's humanity, self-respect, and a sense of oneself as agent. "The act of testifying restores subjectivity to the experience of objectification."[43]

Bearing witness to oneself or to one's inner self is not a solo act but is constituted through interconnection and social relatedness. There is, first of all, a relationship between the witness-survivor of gender violence and her interlocutor-witness who may be a therapist, a rights advocate, an attorney, or an expert witness. The witnessing process can, in addition, potentially constitute more than a dialogic encounter between the witness and an empathetic listener, the witness to the witness. If we envision the witnessing process as a form of "tequio"—a "practice of reciprocity" or "reciprocal help"[44]—then new possibilities emerge that transform the witness herself into a portal for solidarity, into a subject who avows her (our) planetary obligations and interdependency (see chapter 1).

．．．．．．．．．．．．．．．．．．．．

We gathered as border witnesses and participants in the political mobilization contra-feminicide. Some brought their expertise in grassroots modes of organizing; others their support and shelter for survivors of gender violence. Feminist researchers contributed their scholarship; journalists observed and documented the protests; artists depicted the unbearable violence and evoked utopian imaginaries of love, abolition, and nonviolence. We all arrived to honor the dead.

Some among us are witnesses to ourselves: survivors of gender violence; artists with childhood memories of sexual assault; activists who endured workplace harassment; males concerned about violence inflicted on their female kin. The life force of solidarity and resistance is often interconnected with one's own vulnerability, one's autobiographical encounter with the death force of violence. We came in the spirit of solidarity and communality, forging intersubjective relations that ground the act of bearing witness in human connections. The force of witness.

We are living in a world cleaved by multiple atrocities and senseless death. "We chant once more, the names of the dead and bear witness again and again, deeper and deeper, to the anguish and sorrow of that terrible place," Bernie Glassman declares.[45] We bear witness, not as a self-contained individual identity or body but as an embodied enactment of kinship obligations and response-ability to others. Multiply situated to dissolve individual subjectivity, witnessing is an act in which the body is "bound up and dependent on other bodies and networks of support."[46] We arrive as active, engaged, and committed participants in the struggle for social change. We step into someone else's footprints, walk beside them, nearby, alongside. The force of witness. Never alone.

1 Chronicles of Witness

The fear in her eyes was palpable as she glanced incessantly over her shoulders, as though aware that someone might overhear the conversation. At midday in this desolate corner of her neighborhood, an suv with opaque, tinted windows crept nearby, a pack of feral dogs barking at its wheels. Esmeralda Garza was hesitant to speak to me, a researcher from California.[1] The delicate weave of her speech filled with anxiety as she confided why she rarely left her home after dinner. "They're kidnapping girls at all hours of the day and night. In public places, stores, plazas, streets, markets. We're not safe. Anywhere."

Her body trembled despite the suffocating stillness of the summer day and the searing sun overhead. I understood at that very moment why feminists had coined the term *gender terrorism* to describe violence against women. This young woman from Ciudad Juárez was both terrified and terrorized. Terrorized because of her gender.

At the turn of the twentieth century, more than twenty years ago, Esmeralda's sister had disappeared, along with dozens of women and girls. Esmeralda could very well be the next victim. The killing and disappearance of women and girls on the US-Mexico border foreshadowed the alarming destiny of many more Mexicans and was the harbinger for increasingly common acts of inhumanity. What we witnessed in Ciudad Juárez during the 1990s was the canary in the coal mine for the violence of the years to come.

They began calling the killing of women and girls in Ciudad Juárez "feminicidio" two decades ago. The term came into widespread circulation in late 1998 when cases involving 137 women and girls murdered between 1993 and 1998 in the border city became major news. It was on the borderlands where feminist scholars gave the cruelties a name: feminicidio, which I translate as *feminicide*.[2] The first time someone uttered the word *feminicidio*, I misheard *genocidio* and felt it was appropriate.

Like its twin concept genocide, feminicide strips humanity from a particular social group by categorizing its members as less than human. Feminicide names violence by individuals and denounces governments that condone it. Feminicide marks a deadly differentiation between life and death. It is the violence of a distinction between those who matter and those who do not. Feminicide aims to deprecate and render killable humans classified as woman and those regarded as feminine, as feminized, irrespective of their biological assignment. Feminicide names the entanglement of dangerous bodies with endangered bodies. Dangerous bodies inflicting pain on endangered bodies.

My journey into the study of gender and sexual violence began in the summer of 1999, when filmmaker Lourdes Portillo called me to share ideas for her next documentary. I had just edited a book about her documentaries and we had become close friends.

"It'll be about the murders of the girls in Juárez," she explained. Portillo had decided to make the film after reading news reports in the Juárez newspapers and a later article in the *Nation* by Debbie Nathan about "the killings of maquiladora workers on the border," as the murders were referred to then.[3] Since the early 1990s, local feminists grouped under the 8 de marzo coalition had denounced gender violence on the Mexican border city, but their cries for justice had yet to attract national and international media attention.[4]

In 1999, I accompanied Portillo and her production team to the border and met mothers and sisters who shared horrifying stories about the murder of their loved ones: young women beaten and tortured before they were killed. Many had been raped or incinerated, some burned beyond recognition with acid.

Portillo and her film crew traveled often to Juárez, interviewing mothers and activists for her documentary, originally titled *Death Comes to the Maquilas*. A gifted storyteller, Portillo shared with me harrowing stories about armed men in unmarked SUVs stalking her production crew into the colonias, the neighborhoods where most of the victims had lived. In one instance, a vehicle with dark tinted windows parked all night outside the motel where Portillo and her crew were staying. On another occasion, as Portillo entered the local district attorney's office, she came face-to-face with a police officer whistling Tony Bennett's "I Left My Heart in San Francisco."

"I froze when I heard him do that," Portillo reported, "because I've become so paranoid. The scariest part about meeting him was that he called me by my family's nickname, 'Luli,' and asked me about La Precita (my neighborhood) in San Francisco. How did he know I lived there?"

After many trips to the border, Portillo completed her documentary in 2001, the year after I published my first article on feminicide in Ciudad Juárez, under the title "Voices without an Echo: The Global Gendered Apartheid," in which I critiqued the globalization and colonialist frameworks for interpreting gender violence in Mexico. By then the city had become known as the capital of feminicides, because violence against women was—and continues to be—a global phenomenon. My use of *apartheid* in the title signaled the extent to which state terror upholds a political system that differentiates by gender, dehumanizing women and denying them access to their full humanity, human rights, freedom, justice, and equality. In those early years, the majority of victims were poor mestizas and Indigenous women and girls, underscoring the severity of gender atrocities on par with racial injustices.

From my first trip to the border, I learned that feminicide is on the spectrum of the injuries inflicted on female and feminized bodies: incest and child molestation, being groped, stalked, sexually assaulted and raped, partner abuse, hunger, homelessness, illness, and incarceration. The most extreme of all these cruelties, feminicide gathers and disseminates so much pain to women, girls, and gender-nonconforming people across the Américas. Global pain. Feminist activists, to this day, evoke feminicide/feminicidio in their struggles to end the assorted cruelties agitating women's lives, devaluing female and feminized bodies and rendering women and trans people as disposable and killable.

A Few Small Nips (1935), an oil on canvas by Frida Kahlo, still chills my spine. The painting portrays the grisly scene of a man wearing a hat, with a menacing look, as he holds a gory knife and stands over the body of a woman lying on a blood-soaked bed. Her body displays multiple stab wounds, including a fatal one to the heart. Suspended above the room with dreary pink walls, two birds—a white dove and a black sparrow—lyrically stream a ribbon with the words "unos cuantos piquetitos" (a few small nips) across the mise-en-scène.

The painting was inspired by a story Kahlo read in the newspaper about a man who murdered his wife and justified his action by explaining to the judge, "But I only gave her a few small nips. It wasn't twenty stabs, Mister Judge." In the preliminary sketch, Kahlo provided even greater narrative details. Over the bed, a single dove suspends a ribbon with the words from a popular song, "Mi chata ya no me quiere" (My babe no longer loves me), suggesting the woman's infidelity. A young boy, perhaps their son, stands next to the man as witness to his gender crime. Tears trickle down the boy's cheeks.

I first encountered the painting in Martha Zamora's coffee table book *Frida Kahlo: The Brush of Anguish*, gifted to me thirty years ago by my husband, Herman. Over the years, I've seen Kahlo's works in traveling exhibitions and at the Dolores Olmedo Museum in Mexico City. Like no other work of art, *A Few Small Nips* stirred up repressed emotions buried deep within my psyche, which ultimately changed the trajectory of my research. For the past thirty years I have repeatedly returned to this nightmarish scenario. It plagues me and, in retrospect, I recognize how this haunting opened up a pathway into my study of gender and sexual violence. *A Few Small Nips* reminds me of our shared vulnerability to violence in everyday lives.

The woman in this painting could well have been me.

"Scratch a project, find a biography" is an oft-cited maxim in academia.

My first husband was a Vietnam veteran who returned from the war psychologically damaged and traumatized. In the four years we were together, I endured his verbal and physical cruelty, jealous rants about my virginity, and accusations of infidelity. One afternoon he held me hostage on the living room floor, a kitchen knife pressed up against my face, ordering me not to move or he'd kill me. I lay on the green shag rug, terrorized and terrified, as our eighteen-month-old daughter roamed the sparsely lit room, her sobs echoing mine. It wasn't until day turned to night that he finally got up, walked to the bedroom, and slammed the door shut.

I endured three more years of his violent outbursts. Slaps, shoves, and kicks, the name calling in barks like a drill sergeant, the breakups and reconciliations—too many to recall. I'd leave, and he'd beg me to come home, until one day I snapped. I couldn't heal the Vietnam War inside him. I had to save my daughter and my dignity.

At that time my ex-husband's behavior was known as "post-Vietnam syndrome," a psychological malady that later, in 1980, the DSM-III (*Diagnostic and Statistical Manual of Mental Disorders*, third edition) would label posttraumatic stress disorder, PTSD. In the early 1970s, little recourse to trauma treatment existed for Vietnam veterans, much less for the unnamed victims of the war: their partners and children. As a result, my fall-back position became to blame myself for fanning the flames of his post-Vietnam syndrome.

The Kahlo painting resonates with me so deeply because it conjures a greater truth: the cruel absurdity of misogynistic acts. Beneath the man's defense—"I only gave her a few small nips, Mister Judge"—we find the women-hating subtext of blaming the victim. "It's her fault. See what she did, she died on me?" "She shouldn't have done that; she shouldn't have bled to death." "They were just a few little nips with a knife and there she goes, dying on me."

It's the patriarchy that blames a survivor of rape for the injuries wreaked upon her: "Why did you go to the frat party in the first place?" "Why were you drinking with boys?" It's the same misogynistic logic that blamed the women in Ciudad Juárez for their own murders. "Why did she dress so provocatively?" "Why was she out late at night?" "Why did she go to that bar?" "Perhaps she led a double life, maquiladora worker by day, sex worker by night." In other words, her murder was her own fault.

Kahlo's painting renders the innumerable times women are blamed for the cruelty inflicted upon them by a masculinity so toxic that the perpetrator insists he is the one aggrieved: "It's not my fault—she made me do it!"

In the course of my study, I learned that the proclivity to act violently against females is not inherent or innate in males but rather is learned and enabled by heteropatriarchal institutions that sanction destructive force. My ex-husband's violence against me was the by-product of an imperialist war, authorized by a racist, capitalist government that sent a disproportionate number of young men of color like my ex-husband to fight an unjust war for profit. Years later, on the US-Mexico border, I witnessed another brutal example of state violence in a war against women that came to be known as feminicide.

On that first trip with Portillo to Ciudad Juárez, I befriended Clara Vega, a journalist who had written extensively about the murders and discovered evidence of government complicity.[5] She was one of the journalists in Mexico who "stand opposite of power"—contrapoder, to use Jorge Ramos's formulation.[6] When I asked Vega about the government's failure to stop the murders of women, she responded, "No investigan o encubren los datos [They don't investigate or they cover up the facts]. . . . Hay hombres poderosos involucrados en los asesinatos de mujeres [There are very powerful men behind the murders of women]." After years of receiving multiple death threats for her coverage of women's murders on the border, Vega and her family were ultimately forced to flee Mexico.

Vega's words about police abetment resonated deeply, triggering memories of my abusive first husband. One evening, early in our marriage, after enduring a beating, I locked myself in a bedroom and called the police. "My husband is going to kill me," I whispered to the dispatcher. A few minutes later, the police arrived, and my ex-husband greeted them, while I remained in the bedroom, anticipating that they'd ask to speak with me. I could hear their conversation through the bedroom window, the two cops standing on the front porch for several minutes having a friendly chat with my ex-husband. Not once did they inquire about me or ask to see if I'd been injured. My husband chuckled as he relayed, "We were just having an argument, but everything is fine now."

"Yes, we get those calls often," one of the cops responded. "Glad everything's okay. Y'all take care now." Frightened, but even more disgusted and enraged, I swore never to call the police again.

I don't equate the domestic violence I experienced with the atrocious cases of feminicide in Juárez, but I include it to trace the continuum of gender cruelty—from the least to the most extreme—in order to illustrate the pattern of state complicity with perpetrators of gender violence. There is a chain of terror connecting my past life, Frida Kahlo's painting, and the murders of women on the border.

Police indifference and complicity with perpetrators of gender violence is a deep structural problem occurring on both sides of the border—in South Texas and northern Mexico—and, for that matter, anywhere women's lives are deemed unworthy. What the journalist Clara Vega shared with me on that first trip to Juárez confirmed how deeply toxic masculinity is ingrained, permeating our social world, including the security forces that are purportedly trained to serve and protect. In aiding and abetting perpetrators, police exemplify and embody the systemic nature of state violence.

III

There is a continuing need to remember in order to never forget, since feminicides are now archived from public memory even as new carnage unfolds.
CYNTHIA BEJARANO, "Memory of Struggle in Ciudad Juárez"

In early fall 1999, I met the women who founded Voces sin Eco (Voices
without an Echo), the first organization of mothers-turned-activists,
whose signature campaign of painting black crosses over pink backgrounds on electrical poles throughout the city became the planetary
symbol of the contra-feminicide campaign. By the end of 1999, 162
women and girls had been brutally slaughtered in Juárez, and in most
cases they'd also been sexually assaulted. Hundreds more disappeared
in the span of six years (1993–1999).[7]

Even in those early days of the movement, when the pain and trauma of
losing a daughter under such horrific circumstances felt unfathomable, the
defiance exhibited by members of Voces sin Eco, coupled with their collective grace and dignified resilience, inspired scholars like me, who had never
witnessed violence against women on such a mass scale.

My research on gender and violence took an irreversible, notewor-
thy turn the day I witnessed a courageous young woman from Voces sin
Eco, Guillermina González, whose sister had been murdered in 1998,
denouncing a local state official before an audience of families and community members, journalists and academics. Guillermina's sister, Sagrario,
had been "raped, tortured, killed, and semi-buried in the desert mesa, ap-
proximately half a mile from her home in the Colonia Anapra."[8] Police
authorities had earlier made dismissive declarations to Mexico's Human
Rights Commission: "Many of the murdered women worked in factories
during the week and as prostitutes during the weekend in order to make
more money"; or "She visited a place where homosexuals and lesbians
gathered"; or "She liked dating different men and was an avid patron of
dance halls."[9]

Guillermina's response on this occasion was directed at a government
official who spoke at a forum to the local Juárez community and their supporters. When Guillermina heard him repeat the blame-the-victims-for-
their-own-deaths myth, alleging that if women had stayed home at night
they might still be alive, she stood up, widened her stance, pushed back her
shoulders, and chastised him in a forceful and unapologetic tone: "They are
not prostitutes; they are not statistics; but they do have a history!"[10]

The audience erupted in cheers. Joining the applause, I turned to face Guillermina, who remained standing, a defiant yet pained expression in her eyes. I could sense her grief and sorrow at the loss of so many young women in Ciudad Juárez (even if it wouldn't matter to me if her sister had been a sex worker).

As painful as it was to bear witness to Guillermina's suffering, it awakened in me an obligation and a duty to speak up and bring awareness to the atrocities in light of an official atmosphere of indifference and complacency. I felt a deep sense of responsibility to use my platform as a scholar to denounce the injustices. From that moment on, I decided to dedicate my research to the fight against gender and sexual violence in Mexico as a way to contribute to social change and social justice work. In the course of my research, I interviewed activist-mothers and their supporters working in activist and nongovernmental organizations (NGOs) and conducted archival research by combing through regional and national news coverage of feminicide and protests against gender and sexual violence in Mexico.

In the summer of 2001, Portillo hosted the first screening of her documentary *Señorita Extraviada* at the Roxie Theater in San Francisco and invited Guillermina and Felipe Nava, father of María Isabel Nava, whose corpse had been found during the filming, to speak. As representatives of Voces sin Eco, their fight for justice and the heartbreaking funeral of María Isabel were featured in the documentary. I served as translator for Guillermina during the question and answer session and afterward interviewed her about the ongoing local resistance and mobilization for justice.

I learned from Guillermina that the killings of women and girls had continued unabated. The activist-mothers remained firm in their demands for investigations and intervention into the feminicide cases, while corrupt local and state police dragged their feet and made excuses for their failure to solve the murders.[11] Police and local state officials fabricated lies and more lies to distort their ineptitude, indifference, and impunity for crimes against women's lives.

My determination deepened further when Cynthia Bejarano spoke about border activism at the UC Santa Cruz screening of Portillo's documentary. We had previously met at the Burials on the Border conference in 1999 at New Mexico State University. Twenty years my junior, Cynthia was equally determined to bring awareness to this human rights issue and serve the contra-feminicide movement with her work. A criminologist and professor at New Mexico State University, Cynthia had cofounded Amigos de las Mujeres de Juárez, an organization that provided logistic and financial support to the families of the murdered and disappeared women of Ciudad Juárez. Given her proximity to the border, Cynthia frequently participated in direct actions like vigils, protest marches, and demonstrations sponsored by local activists on both sides of the border. She had worked with Hilda Solis, then a congresswoman for the Thirty-Second District of California (later secretary of labor under President Obama, and currently councilwoman in Los Angeles), who was leading a congressional inquiry into the Ciudad Juárez feminicides.[12] We felt so united in our commitment that we decided to coauthor a collection of essays featuring collaborations between community activists, NGO and academic researchers, and feminist scholar-activists from Mexico, the United States, and Latin America. Cynthia's networking with local grassroots groups proved invaluable to this future book project.[13]

In the months that followed the release of *Señorita Extraviada*, I often accompanied Portillo to screenings of her documentary throughout the United States and abroad. We traveled to Spain in 2003 at the invitation of Judge Baltasar Garzón, who had achieved international acclaim for ordering the house arrest of General Augusto Pinochet in 1999, when the former Chilean dictator traveled to Britain for medical treatment. A prominent member of the Audiencia Nacional de España, Judge Garzón convened a seminar on gender violence at El Escorial featuring the feminicide in Juárez. He screened Portillo's documentary during a panel that he moderated. Seminar participants included the director of Amnesty International, the chief prosecutor of the International Criminal Court, and other international experts and activists in the area of human rights law. Besides expressing his support for the campaign against feminicide, Judge Garzón offered to take the case to the European Parliament.

At other times, Portillo and I spoke in public forums to audiences who were unaware of the feminicide in Juárez. I had by then embraced my role as a researcher and participant in contra-feminicide activism, which entailed raising awareness about gender violence in Mexico through my writings and public talks. During public presentations with Portillo, I provided a historical framework for the documentary and discussed its political and aesthetic merits as an activist film. I shared my preliminary observations as to the causes and consequences of the cruel policies of unprosecuted slayings and disappearances of women on the border. My understanding of "social movement struggles as generators of new knowledge" as well as the systemic nature of state violence in Mexico was beginning to take shape.[14]

Conducting research about feminicide in Juárez felt like walking through a dense fog of subterfuge only to emerge into a room of smoke and mirrors. In 1995, police arrested Egyptian chemist Adbel Latif Sharif Sharif, a convicted sex offender who worked as a consultant for a US maquiladora (assembly) plant, and charged him with the murder of one of the victims. As the murders continued in 1996, authorities responded to public outrage by families and women's rights activists and rounded up several other suspects, members of the gang Los Rebeldes, who confessed and were charged with six of the murders. Three years later, as the killings continued unabated, Los Choferes, a group of bus drivers transporting workers for the maquiladora industry, were arrested and confessed to five more killings.

Faced with myriad scenarios and suspects, police authorities opportunely fabricated an elaborate conspiracy between these two groups and the chemist Sharif who, according to authorities, had ordered the killing from his prison cell, paying $1,200 for each murder. Through his attorney, Sharif vehemently denied the charges. There was little substantive or material evidence to support the conspiracy allegations, and the Mexican Human Rights Commission shed further doubt on the government's theory, reporting that suspects were arrested without warrants and denied attorney representation, adding to the suspects' family members' accusations of police torture to elicit their confessions.[15]

Five years after rights groups started tracking feminicide in Ciudad Juárez, the National Commission for Human Rights issued a report charging gross irregularities and general negligence in state investigations, including the misidentification of corpses, failure to obtain expert tests on forensic evidence, failure to conduct autopsies or obtain semen analysis, failure to file written reports, and incompetence in keeping records of the rising tide of women's murders.[16] It became increasingly evident that the local government's failure to respond with diligence signaled their complicity with the perpetrators of gender violence.[17]

By the time I began my research in 1999, sensationalistic media accounts about the killings regularly utilized the stereotypical trope of serial sex killers. Urban legends about who was behind the killings proliferated: traffickers of illegal human organs kidnapping young women; an underground economy of pornography and snuff films; the Juniors (sons of the elite) killing women for sport; a satanic cult abducting women for occult rituals; and narco-traffickers practicing ritual human sacrifice prior to a smuggling operation. In light of the police's negligence and failure to conduct investigations, these conjectures were difficult to prove or disprove.[18]

Less lurid interpretations put forward theories about Mexican machismo behind the surge in gender violence: unemployed men envious of women workers; men expressing rage against poverty; men threatened by changing sex roles; abusive spouses or boyfriends murdering or disappearing their partners. The culprits were individualized and often portrayed as "deranged men from working classes or unhinged men from organized-crime ranks."[19]

Despite the obfuscation surrounding the culprits, the violent killings and disappearance of women and girls were undeniable, steering my research focus onto the systemic nature of state violence. State violence involves cruel policies and practices against social groups. It is rooted in a distinction between human worth and unworth, grievable and ungrievable lives, between those whose lives matter and those whose lives don't. The lives of poor and dark women in Ciudad Juárez did not matter. They had been stripped of their humanity and consigned to disposability. Women and girls had lost their human rights prior to and after losing their lives.

State violence is systemic when it permeates the entire system. Rather than referring only to overt violent action by representatives of the state, this violence manifests itself in indifference to women's and trans people's lives on the part of the police, security forces, state prosecutors, judges, politicians, and institutions. This disdain and dismissal of women's lives is political in nature. Feminicide in Ciudad Juárez could not be considered simply as the work of psychopaths. Instead of the aberration of a single individual or group, the murder and disappearance of women and trans people are (in Julia Monárrez's words) "politically motivated sexual violence" rooted in a system of heteropatriarchy.[20]

In Juárez, we find a new category of the persecuted, disposable human being, racially profiled mestizas or poor Indigenous women who are persecuted not "because of what they had done or thought" but, to rephrase Hannah Arendt, "because of what they unchangeably were—born into the wrong kind of race or wrong kind of class" and, in this case, the wrong kind of gender.[21]

The feminist mantra "the personal is political" takes on new significance in the context of violence in Mexico. Two decades ago I wrote, "One way to politicize violence against a class of women is to redefine it not as isolated or personal in nature, but as a weapon of war, a tool of political repression sanctioned by an undemocratic and repressive regime, in its war against poor and indigenous women."[22] The murders and disappearances of women and trans people in Mexico make evident the exercise of power across the social spectrum: the power of the state over civil society; rich over poor; white elite over Indigenous and mixed-race people; men over women; cisgender over queer and transgender people. It is a novel kind of dirty war, one waged by powerful forces against disposable female and feminized bodies. What feminists call the war against women should more aptly be renamed as the longest war.[23]

IV

Human indifference to cruelty is limitless. So too are the struggles against such indifference.

JOHN BERGER, *Bento's Sketchbook*

The war against women in Ciudad Juárez would not remain unchallenged. It incited mother-led struggles to end the indifference to cruelty against their daughters in the border city and activated a feminist resistance that mushroomed into a planetary movement against feminicide. This particular war against women unleashed an undercurrent that continues to instill consciousness and inspire subsequent generations of feminist activists.

Joined by other mother-based groups like Nuestras Hijas de Regreso a Casa (May Our Daughters Return Home) and Justicia para Nuestras Hijas (Justice for Our Daughters), the activist-mothers of Voces sin Eco and their feminist allies spoke even when everyone else remained silent and government authorities distorted what was happening to women in Chihuahua.

As the killings and disappearances continued into the new millennium, spreading throughout the region and to other parts of Mexico, it became apparent that impunity for the assassinations of women was both a consequence and an incitement for further feminicide and other forms of violence against women and trans people.

The discovery of eight female corpses in November 2001 at Campo Algodonero, an empty lot across from the maquiladora headquarters in a heavily trafficked boulevard of Ciudad Juárez, was the turning point in the struggle for justice. Similar to the first murders reported in the 1990s, the women's bodies exhibited signs of extensive torture and sexual assault. Outraged by the impunity and indisputable danger women confronted daily, 25,000 people attended a candlelight vigil at Campo Algodonero on December 16, 2001, organized by radio journalist Samira Izaguirre, also founder of Luz y Justicia. Like dozens of women's rights activists and journalists, Izaguirre received numerous death threats and later filed a petition for asylum in the United States.[24] The shocking discovery at the Campo Algodonero sparked a powerful convergence of local and international contra-feminicide activism.

A few weeks after the bodies were unearthed, women's rights activists in Chihuahua launched the campaign Ni Una Más (Not One More)—named after the slogan coined by the poet Susana Chávez, who was brutally assassinated in 2011. "¡Ni una más!" became the movement's anthem. We chanted "¡Ni una más! ¡Ni una más! ¡Ni una más!" repeatedly in public forums, during protest marches and demonstrations in front of local government offices. Activist-mothers held banners with images of their still-alive daughters invoking "¡Ni una más!" alongside the slogans "Las queremos vivas" (We want them alive) and "Vivas las llevaron, vivas las queremos" (Alive you took them, alive we want them).[25] These refrains chanted at marches, candlelight vigils, and public protests echoed the cries of the Mothers of the Plaza de Mayo in Argentina, who staged similar displays of sorrow and outrage, mourning and demands for justice for the disappearance of their sons and daughters during the country's Dirty War (1976–1983).

Spearheaded by Mujeres de Negro (Women Dressed in Black), a women's rights coalition based in Chihuahua City, the Ni Una Más campaign staged a protest march in 2002 as part of International Woman's Day events on March 8.[26] Over one hundred women (elderly, campesinas, factory workers, students, and professionals) dressed in black tunics and pink hats and walked 370 kilometers across the desert, from Chihuahua City to Ciudad Juárez, where they joined hundreds of protestors demanding an end to gender violence in the region.[27]

Mujeres de Negro called their march Exodus por la Vida (Exodus for Life), and for this event "they designed a large black cloth that could be worn simultaneously by some twenty women, as if they were wearing the same dress, with their pink-covered heads poking through holes in the fabric, which they wore as they marched down the 16 de Septiembre, a principal avenue in Ciudad Juárez."[28] The image of participants in Mujeres de Negro wearing a collective dress symbolized their unity on behalf of the Ni Una Más cause, despite their "deep political differences."[29] A few months later, on the International Day for the Elimination of Violence against Women (November 25), Mujeres de Negro led the mass mobilization of thousands of protestors marching through the streets of Mexico City, chanting "¡Ni una más!" as they demanded an end to impunity and violence against women in the state of Chihuahua.

Given my teaching and family commitments, I attended as many of these public acts of protest as possible. From Oakland, California, it was a short flight to El Paso, where I'd often join a group of US-based feminist scholar-activists working with activist-mothers and cross the border into Juárez. I initially joined the protests to express my solidarity with the struggle for justice, but as my trips became more frequent, I realized that I had myriad reasons to participate in the contra-feminicide movement.

In bearing witness to and participating in mass protests, we expressed our solidarity with a struggle for justice and embraced our responsibility to be active, steadfast participants in the social justice struggle. As a scholar who'd previously worked as a journalist, I used my platform to investigate, shed light on, and raise awareness about Mexico's number one human rights issue, writing articles on feminicide and speaking publicly in academic and community-based forums.

The connection I felt for the activist-mothers went beyond an expression of solidarity. It was a deeply felt bond rooted in my own experience as a mother. That well-worn cliché, "a mother's worst nightmare," had become a reality for the activist-mothers whom I met and interviewed. Hearing their stories, I'd find myself shaking uncontrollably, a leaden feeling in my gut at the thought of my daughter Xochitl being raped or murdered or disappeared as she was walking home from school or work. She, too, was young and vibrant, with years of life to live.

I vividly recall an interview with Luz María Álvarez, whose daughter Aracely had disappeared the year before.[30] When I gently asked, "How do you deal with not knowing the whereabouts of your daughter?," Luz María blinked to hold back tears and avoided eye contact with me before taking a deep breath, responding, "Every time I wash dishes, I look out the window and hope Aracely will appear, walking toward the house, with that big smile of hers."

I too inhaled deeply, my heart battering my ribcage as I imagined myself in her place, waiting for my daughter Xochitl to return after months of disappearance. Early on, I learned I had to keep these feelings of anguish to myself after sharing them with a human rights attorney representing one of the mothers. "If you're feeling so traumatized, how do you think the mothers feel?" the attorney remarked in a biting tone. But the trauma many of us who join the contra-feminicide movement feel is real. It's called bystander

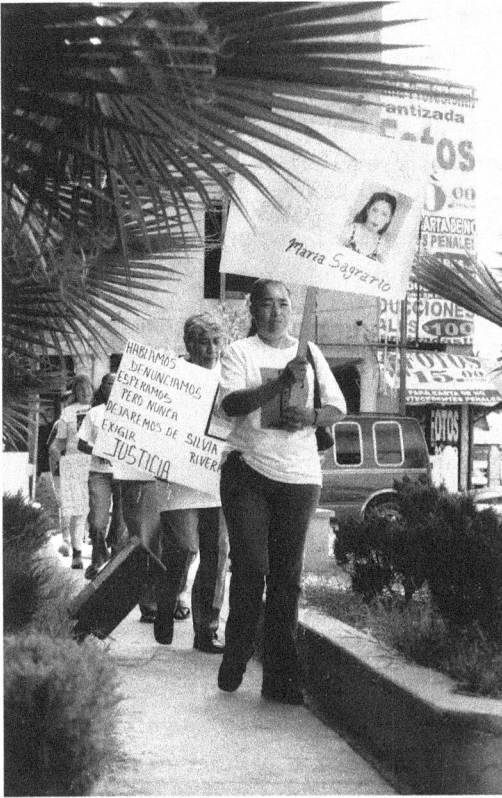

1.1 Led by Paula Flores, activist-mothers march silently for one hour at the office of the special magistrate for homicides against women in Ciudad Juárez. Photo by Angela Fregoso.

trauma, vicarious trauma, or secondary trauma, the trauma of witnessing the suffering of others or placing oneself in their place. Bystander trauma is never equivalent to the primary trauma experienced by the victim or survivor of violence, but it is an unforeseen side effect of being a witness to the witness, of bearing witness to those who suffer.

"The power of the collective," to use Angela Davis's formulation, was on full display on the streets of Ciudad Juárez.[31] In the first years of mass protest, the grassroots modes of organizing relied less on images of female victimhood and more on self-empowerment and collective agency. Their mass mobilization took the form of "poner el cuerpo" (to place the body)—an embodied practice of direct action, with or without the accompaniment of spoken words, that in the militarized border city of Juárez had long been considered a bold and risky endeavor.[32] It was deeply inspiring to witness these activist-mothers putting their bodies on the line, even after being intimidated and subjected to frequent death threats for their outspokenness and obstinacy.

In retrospect, I can now see how participating in mass protests was not just a form of solidarity but became a form of self-care for me. Witnessing so many spirited, brave women and their allies was empowering, and it tempered the deeply distressing feelings that emerged in the course of my research, from listening to horrifying stories of sexually assaulted and tortured victims and holding the hand of a sobbing mother. Whenever I felt anxious and distraught, I garnered strength from the collective movement: the countless times mothers, feminists, and human rights activists commandeered the streets, held silent vigils in public plazas, disrupted traffic on the international bridge between Mexico and the United States, yelled at public officials, and interrupted official events. The power of the collective deeply inspired me.

Beginning in the 1990s, researchers and local feminist activists kept tallies of the feminicide victims in Ciudad Juárez that by 2003 had swelled to nearly four hundred women and girls murdered and close to two thousand disappeared.[33] The actual numbers of victims remain unknown to this day. Scholars and independent organizations like the National Citizens Feminicide Observatory have consistently reported much higher deaths than the official government figures.

While the significance of publicizing these statistics remains indisputable, it's also the case that this form of representation turns the women and girls who have been victimized into a data set and tool for quantitative analysis, objectifying human lives and obscuring their humanity and histories. The activist-mothers group Nuestras Hijas de Regreso a Casa transcended the objectification of human lives by adopting the strategy of "saying her name" or publishing an alphabetically ordered list of names for 286 feminicide victims from 1993 to 2003.[34] The list began with Adriana Martínez Martínez and ended with Zulema Olivia Alvarado Torres.[35] "Saying her name" was a small but significant step toward recognizing the humanity of the victim, which I adopted in my subsequent public talks in modified form.

For the PowerPoint presentation that accompanied my talks, I created seven slides with the names of the 286 feminicide victims. Each slide was timed to change at intervals of one minute and forty-five seconds, roughly the time it took to say or read the names on the slide projected onto the screen. These seven slides appeared during the portion of my talk where I discussed disputes between official statistics on the number of victims and the far greater number tallied by academics and activist organizations. Although reading the names probably distracted audiences from my oral presentation, the significance of the audience saying (or reading) the names outweighed its drawbacks, because it helped honor and restore each woman's identity and recognize her existence. This recitation strategy grew into a common practice at memorials and candlelight vigils for feminicide victims.

International news coverage of the groundswell of contra-feminicide activism in Mexico drew the attention of feminist activists in many other countries. The planetary visibility and impact of the movement multiplied when Amnesty International launched its worldwide "femicide" awareness campaign in 2003 and released a devastating indictment of the Mexican government in a report titled *Mexico: Intolerable Killings: 10 Years of Abductions and Murders of Women in Ciudad Juárez and Chihuahua*. The report was the most comprehensive documentation of feminicide undertaken by a globally prominent human rights organization at the time.

With the support of Amnesty International, the following year, the V-Day movement spotlighted the murders and disappearances of women and girls in Mexico. Founded by author, playwright, and activist Eve Ensler on February 14, 1998, the V-Day events of 2004 held in Ciudad Juárez opened with a march that drew close to eight thousand participants from over twenty countries.

I arrived in El Paso the day before the march and later joined my coauthor, Cynthia, and members of Amigos de las Mujeres de Juárez for the trek across the border. When we arrived in downtown Juárez, hundreds of protestors were already gathered at the Estacionamiento de la Presidencia for the march. We marched to the international bridge and met the V-Day delegation of women's rights activists and prominent celebrities, including Jane Fonda and Sally Field, congresswomen Hilda Solis (CA) and Jan Schakowsky (IL), and V-Day founder Eve Ensler, who all then crossed the border into Mexico.

The ambiance felt simultaneously somber and festive, a gathering of women, children and men, young and old, workers and union members alongside feminist activists. Some carried professionally made signs while others lifted homemade ones. Dozens of protestors held brightly colored dresses hanging on pink crosses and just as many mijongas, the gigantic puppets frequently paraded during Mexican religious festivals and community celebrations.

On the Mexican side of the border, mothers led the march, each holding a poster-size photo of a disappeared or murdered daughter, with the word *Justicia* in bold letters. They were followed by another group of protestors carrying an Amnesty International banner with multicolored hand imprints and names of many victims. We walked alongside Mujeres de Negro, some clutching pink and black balloons while others held a ten-foot banner imprinted with the words "Campaña Ni Una Más." Mexican news media were well represented, and on two separate occasions I saw reporters interviewing family members of Javier García Uribe (el Cerillo) and Gustavo González Meza (la Foca)—both men accused of the Campo Algodonero killings.[36] Human rights and mother-activists, supporting the families' contention that the accused had been scapegoated to protect the actual killers, explains the presence of families of accused murderers in the protest march.[37]

Afterward, several hundred protestors attended the bilingual performance of *The Vagina Monologues* in Juárez, featuring Mexican actresses Laura Flores, Lilia Aragón, Marinitia Escobedo, and Monica Alicia Juárez, along with Jane Fonda, Sally Field, and Christine Lahti.[38] From there, we joined an invitation-only reception hosted by the American consulate in Juárez, in appreciation of the V-Day delegation's support for efforts to raise awareness about feminicide in Ciudad Juárez. The impact of V-Day 2004 was enormous, with over 2,300 local V-Day events taking place around the world, in solidarity with women's rights activists in Mexico. A month later, Chihuahua's state attorney general, Jesus José Solís, resigned.[39]

Yet despite the international campaign to raise awareness and end violence against women in Juárez, the murders and disappearances continued their upward trend through the tenure of President Vicente Fox. Activist-mothers remained defiant and intractable toward local authorities who ignored demands for justice and failed to solve these gender crimes. As I write in chapter 4, activist-mothers continued to stage sit-ins, appropriate the streets, and install memorials on public sites, without securing permits.

I joined one of their monthly vigils in 2007, as they rushed past armed guards into the office of the special prosecutor for crimes against women. It was an impetuous and risky impulse on my part, as my Houston-based attorney sister, Angela, later chastised me. "You could have been shot for trespassing on state property. Or ended up in jail, for who knows how long." But it was exhilarating to chase after the mothers as they hurried up the stairs of the government building, barged into a large meeting room, pounded their fists on the conference table, shouting raucously as they demanded to speak to the special prosecutor, who was supposedly away on state business. The mothers refused to leave until the assistant promised to schedule a meeting for the following week.

The psychological toll of these endless battles against government authorities was immense. The activist-mothers were exhausted, their emotions raw, their nerves in tatters. They were wounded mothers. Mothers in pain. Women who consoled themselves with collective memory rituals.

"We gathered on each of our daughters' birthdays," Eva Arce once told me. "Then we'd march to the place where her body was found or where she disappeared and from there toward the prosecutor's office to demand justice."[40]

The activist-mothers drew strength from their shared vulnerability, as my coauthor, Cynthia Bejarano, reminds us: "Tragedy forced the mothers to come together and forge a shared identity. Despite their diverse personalities, migrant histories, and work backgrounds as housewives, cooks, maquiladora workers, and cleaning women, they bound together as mothers, sharing their grief and collective action against feminicide."[41]

There is no doubt that the critical work activist-mothers undertook helped frame feminicide in Juárez as a prototypical case of gender violence and an issue that shook global consciousness. Yet like all social movements, the mother-led groups had their share of conflicts over money, power, and leadership. Struggles over resources and political strategies underscored what Gayatri Spivak calls the "fragility of collectivities."[42]

Government officials readily exploited this fragility. The attorney general of Chihuahua alleged that the largely middle-class Mujeres de Negro members were "prostituting themselves by benefitting financially and politically from the pain of the mothers." As Melissa Wright explains in her article on Mujeres de Negro, "The allegation also implied that many of the Mujeres de Negro were personally fortifying their own coffers and political futures by peddling the sorrow and pain of families to international organizations, who provided donations, and to sensationalist reporters who made them famous."[43] The government's accusation drove a wedge between the economically poor activist-mothers and their middle-class supporters in women-run organizations affiliated with the Ni Una Más campaign.

An overly optimistic and celebratory assessment of maternal activism plagued my own earlier writing on the subject.[44] But through interviews with members of Voces sin Eco and Nuestras Hijas de Regreso a Casa, and fifteen years of visits to Juárez, I gradually learned about some of the mutually shared suspicions and resentments that undermined the movement. There were times the mothers abandoned collective thinking and the politics of communal bonds and fell into competition over who got to speak on behalf of victims, who got to represent the activist-mothers, and how donations from national and international supporters should be spent. These internal divisions illustrate the "fragility of collectivities" and how women-led groups can internalize the competitive individualism of patriarchal capitalism and the divide-and-conquer mentality of a government elite that still retains its colonial lineage.

The activist-mothers who mobilized to end feminicide in Juárez were not necessarily unified or working together for a progressive feminist agenda. Their primary concern centered on the arrest and punishment of culprits, less so on the culpability of heteropatriarchy, transphobia, or the limitations of state-centered solutions. The emphasis on victimized daughters inadvertently or perhaps even knowingly marginalized other targets of cruel masculinity, including sex workers, queers, and transgender people who were also feminicide victims.[45]

Despite the highs and lows, to outsiders like me, the power of the collective was inspiring. My time in the contra-feminicide movement taught me to appreciate the light and shade of the world we live in. Countless times, we witnessed mothers and sisters consoling each other in their darkest, grief-stricken moments, commiserating and sharing stories about their deceased loved ones, while cursing at police and politicians who continued to ignore their pleas for justice. The mothers endured infighting and truces, defeats and victories, emotional shocks and healings. Their acts of defiance and resistance to unjust authority, their disappointments and aspirations for justice, their determination in the face of so much bitterness, their ability to laugh and dance despite their anguish, taught us to hold the beauty and the horror of existence simultaneously in our hearts. For all these reasons, the activist-mothers left a lasting legacy that continues to inspire subsequent generations of Ni Una Más activists.

Activist-mothers chose to name their group Voces sin Eco to highlight the unheard and disregarded voices of their daughters as they were kidnapped, tortured, or murdered. "Because apparently no one heard their screams," Paula Flores once told me, a pointed and subtle foreshadowing of Rebecca Solnit's words: "In patriarchy, no one can hear you scream."[46] The activist-mothers spoke for their dead, activating their presence, recalling those whose lives had been extinguished with such impunity. Like Paula, these mothers dedicated their lives to giving voice to their daughters, so that they would be recognized, remembered, and heard, so their voices would pierce through the wall of patriarchy. Some activist-mothers and human rights defenders paid with their lives for denouncing the powerful forces behind or enabling the gender violence (see chapters 2 and 5).

V

In November 2010, on my return trip from the American Studies Association conference in San Antonio, Texas, I received an email from Paula Flores announcing that she was leaving Ciudad Juárez and closing the Fundación María Sagrario, the organization she'd established in honor of her slain daughter. As I waited to board my flight, I stared at my screen in disbelief, feeling a ringing in my ears as I responded, "Really? This can't be possible." But it was. The entire family was leaving the city, closing their small neighborhood grocery store and abandoning their life's work.

Housed in a small building down the unpaved street from Paula's in-home grocery store and residence, the Fundación María Sagrario had served as a refuge for children in the poverty-stricken neighborhood, Lomas de Poleo, providing recreation, alternative kindergarten, and after-school learning activities. In the group email she sent to twenty supporters, Paula gave no indication as to why her family was leaving Juárez.

Five days before receiving the fateful email, I'd interviewed Paula over the phone for my review of *La Carta*, a documentary codirected by Rafael Bonilla and Patricia Ravelo. In the review, I reflected on the significance of this work: "Unlike documentary realism, where the stress is on the authenticity of the event or the story told, 'La Carta' accentuates the creativity of social actors like Paula Flores who channel their suffering and outrage into community activism and social justice campaigns to end feminicide. Paula is a social actor who is not just testifying or bearing witness to the feminicide of her daughter Sagrario and the other women and girls . . . but through Paula's creative intervention, including establishing the Fundación María Sagrario, she is transforming their/our social world."

Before we said our goodbyes over the phone, Paula had invited me to the annual posada and toy drive that she organizes every December, insisting that filmmaker Lourdes Portillo accompany me because, Paula hinted, "Este año el programa será diferente" (This year the program will be different).

The annual drive was a blessing for the impoverished community, offering a glimmer of hope and joy to children whose families were economically impoverished, living on the outskirts of the city, lacking the most basic public services and utilities. Community activists from both sides of the border attended the annual festivities, including my coauthor Cynthia, whose organization Amigos de las Mujeres de Juárez organized donations for the toy drive.

1.2 Fundación María Sagrario's kindergarten in Lomas de Poleo, Ciudad Juárez. Photo by Angela Fregoso.

For the past few years, Paula had poured her heart into planning and establishing her organization. She always spent weeks preparing for the December festivities. Given her passionate dedication to this work, I feared something menacing had led to her abrupt decision to shut down everything and leave town.

My suspicions were confirmed a week later when I phoned Paula in El Paso and learned that a group of men (de una pandilla, gang members) had entered her home, beaten her oldest son, Chuy, and issued an extortion demand: money in exchange for allowing the store and Fundación María Sagrario to remain open. Speaking haltingly, Paula seemed to hint that there was more she couldn't say over the phone, that perhaps there had been even more powerful forces behind the threats. Paula confided that she could endure threats against her own life, but she would never place her entire family at risk.

A few months later, Paula defied the threats against her life and resumed her resistance against the injustices in her community. She returned to Ciudad Juárez and to this day continues her campaign to end feminicide.

Eight years after her life was threatened, in 2018, at a human rights forum held after the election of Manuel López Obrador (AMLO) as president of

Mexico, Paula "handed him information about Sagrario's case . . . but no one from AMLO's office ever contacted her to follow up."[47] Although the Fundación María Sagrario did in fact come to an abrupt end, Paula's courage, drive, and determination to fight for social justice—and her displays of resourcefulness—remain exemplary of mother-activists who channel their suffering into what the Zapatistas call "digna rabia," dignified rage against the system, born out of wounded dignity. She is an indelible model for how "people free themselves and others from subordination, imagine how things could be otherwise, and move toward enacting that vision" in the face of so much suffering and adversity.[48]

VI

Known to endure highs and lows, mother love enables the ordinary person to do the impossible. Refusing to give in to physical threats and other intimidations, she remains dauntless, with no concern for her own safety.

TRINH T. MINH-HA, *Lovecidal: Walking with the Disappeared*

Marisela Escobedo Ortiz sits behind a table, knitting Christmas decorations while leafleting in the Plaza Hidalgo on December 16, 2010. Pedestrians, cars, and buses pass by in the heavily trafficked city's center and, as she starts to tidy up, a man approaches her, points a gun at her head, and misfires. Marisela abruptly stands and dashes across the street, running toward the governor's palace, her hands moving frantically in the air while the man chases her, points a gun, and shoots her. She falls and, seemingly unruffled, he walks beside her body to a vehicle waiting at the street corner and drives off.

"I will not leave until they arrest my daughter's assassin," Marisela had declared only days before. Weathering frigid winds from the Chihuahua desert, she staged a hunger strike for nine days, next to the Ni Una Más ten-foot memory cross in the Plaza Hidalgo that faces the governor's palace in Chihuahua City. A few days earlier, on November 25, Marisela had participated in a protest for the International Day for the Elimination of Violence against Women alongside mother-activists from Justicia para Nuestras Hijas, who had nailed, on that same memory cross, the names of over three hundred women murdered in the state of Chihuahua during 2010. Nearly every day of the year a woman or girl was murdered. Nine days later, the protest became her final, solo act.

An acquaintance from Juárez once confided, "In Mexico today, you can pay a sicario [hired assassin] 500 pesos to kill someone." That's the value of life, US$50. His words haunted me when I received the email about her murder from activists in Chihuahua. Grupo Reforma uploaded the gruesome video of Marisela's murder on YouTube shortly thereafter.

I replayed the video on my laptop, tears streaming down my cheeks as I watched, in a hypnotic trance, the final moments of Marisela's life. Shot from a distant bird's-eye view, the soundless video captures her assassination in grainy footage. I kept wondering if her killer had been paid 500 pesos to assassinate her, knowing that the doors of the governor's palace would remain closed? The usually open palace doors, decorated with Christmas lights, had stayed shut, as if to ignore "the desperate cries of a mother asking for help, aware that her life would be terminated like thousands in the State [of Chihuahua]."[49]

My outrage at her murder coalesced with deep sorrow as I replayed the video, showing cars, buses, and pedestrian bystanders who undoubtedly witnessed her assassination. No one responded. No one came to her rescue. Were people in Chihuahua City really that terrified and intimidated?

Ironically, it was the government's security camera that recorded the calamity of her public execution in front of the governor's palatial doors. The recording of Marisela's murder confirmed my fears about the precarity and dangers faced by women who speak out for justice in Mexico.

Like other mothers who denounce gender violence in the region, Marisela had remained dauntless and persistent to the end, despite concerns for her own safety. Her attorney, Lucha Castro, of the Centro de Derechos Humanos de las Mujeres, declared, "Marisela is a woman who went from a victim to a defender of human rights. A mother who never allowed defeat and fought for justice for her daughter Rubí's feminicide, paid with her life."[50]

Marisela's daughter, Rubí Marisol Frayre, was sixteen years old when she disappeared in 2008. A few weeks later, her incinerated remains were found after the family conducted a rastreo (combing) among animal bones and detritus scattered in a pigsty. Marisela pleaded for an official investigation, and after months of her insistence, the authorities in Ciudad Juárez relented, opening an inquiry and pursuing a tip from the suspected perpetrator's stepfather. Police arrested Sergio Barraza, Rubí's abusive boyfriend, who confessed to her murder. They held him for thirty-six hours and then released him with a fine of 2,600 pesos (the equivalent of US$250).

Barraza faced murder charges. During his initial trial, the Oral Tribunal of three judges dismissed charges for lack of evidence, disavowing his confession and pleas to Marisela for forgiveness, as well as the testimonies of witnesses who overheard Barraza bragging openly about the murder. Shortly thereafter, Barraza fled the state. Undeterred, Marisela hired Lucha Castro as her attorney and appealed the case to a second Oral Tribunal. This time, on May 26, 2010, the Oral Tribunal overturned its prior ruling and sentenced Barraza in absentia to fifty years in prison.[51]

Marisela endured these highs and lows with a mother love that enabled her to continue to fight for justice, despite ongoing intimidation and threats of retribution. Like other activist-mothers spearheading public acts of resistance, Marisela's strength and vulnerability were entangled with deep emotional scars. She suffered from depression and uncontrollable rage, barely able to contain her agony and self-blame: "Here I am, destroyed," she stated in an affidavit presented to the Oral Tribunal. "My family is destroyed; there are repudiations of some against others, for the 'what if . . . you would have been more alert'—so many reproaches, and so much rage that we have, which doesn't allow us to live, doesn't allow us to remake our family, only to share the hell in which we live."[52]

Marisela's uncontrollable and dignified rage captured the attention of national audiences. I have vivid memories of news coverage of her performative protest marches for justice on the state highway of Chihuahua, where she walked naked with a poster-size image of Rubí draped over her body, while pushing her granddaughter, Heidi, in a shopping cart.

Marisela's demands for the arrest and incarceration of her daughter's assassin struck me as a punitive justice approach generally shunned by those of us who advocate against carceral solutions to gender violence and on behalf of restorative or transformative justice alternatives to punishment and incarceration (discussed further in chapter 2). It is important to gauge our ambivalence toward an incarceration model against the backdrop of near absolute impunity for violations of women's rights—an impunity that is both an effect and a cause of gender-based murders.

Feminicide would not have ravaged Mexico as fully as it did without institutionalized misogyny, which inclined many Mexicans to ignore violence against women. It is a paradox facing abolition feminists: how to reconcile a commitment to restorative forms of justice and redemption with the state's absolute disregard for any form of justice for women and trans people. There's no easy answer. When women and trans people are not even regarded as human, whenever their lives are not deemed grievable, the demand for their legal rights and their juridical subjectivity is a stepping-stone toward establishing their value, humanity, freedom, and recognition as human beings.

Marisela spoke from the space of dignified rage whenever she confronted government and police authorities, as well as a Mexican civil society that was prone to forget. Remembering and mourning her daughter before the Oral Tribunal, Marisela's plea has had a lasting humanizing impact on those who heard it: "I wish my daughter's death was not in vain, that it becomes the last feminicide in the city."[53]

VII

Ciudad Juárez vivió y vive una masacre continua.
JULIA MONÁRREZ FRAGOSO, "Feminicidio: Muertes Públicas, Comunidades Cerradas y Estado Desarticulado"

Marisela's daughter, Rubí Marisol, was not the last feminicide victim in the city. Not by a long shot. Despite twenty years of mass protests that waxed and waned, worldwide solidarity campaigns, international court rulings and diplomatic pressure, annual reports from international NGOs and the United Nations denouncing the Mexican government's human rights record on women, the creation of special prosecutors at local and national levels, and the world's first-ever legislation that named and targeted feminicidal violence, the murders and disappearances of women continue to plague the war-torn city of Juárez.

In late September 2012, a group of feminists—campus researchers, community activists, and human rights attorneys—gathered in Juárez for the "Borders and Bodies" seminar on gender violence, sponsored by the Colegio de la Frontera Norte (COLEF).[54] It had been a year since my last visit, and the city's deterioration was shocking. Calderón's war on drugs had taken a heavy toll on Juárez, transforming it into a war zone and forcing hundreds of residents to flee. The 100,000 homes recently abandoned throughout the city reminded me of post-Katrina New Orleans, dilapidated houses with boarded-up windows and doors, overgrown vegetation, stray dogs and cats roaming the eerily empty streets and lots. Given the spike in violence, we were transported in a van to the seminar site, which would, under normal circumstances, be a pleasant ten-minute walk from our hotel.

"There have been two generations of feminicides," Susana Báez declared on the first day of the seminar.[55] The exasperation felt among participants was palpable, after all the killings that began under the government of Miguel de la Madrid continued through the tenure of Vicente Fox and now Felipe Calderón. We heard directly from mothers of this second generation of victims, Sylvia Banda and Luz Elena Muñoz, both members of the newly formed Comité de Madres de Juárez y Familiares con Hijas Desaparecidas (Committee of Mothers of Juárez and Relatives of the Disappeared Daughters), who spoke at length about their ordeals.

"They kept my daughter's body for two years before the authorities released her body to the family," said Sylvia Banda, whose daughter Fabiola Janette Valenzuela was assassinated on September 26, 2010, leaving behind a two-year-old son. Luz Muñoz continued to search for her daughter, Nancy Yvette Navarro Muñoz, "who disappeared while looking for work in the city's central district." Their stories were disconcertingly familiar, giving me the feeling of having already experienced this before. This second generation of feminicide victims shared a demographic profile of vulnerability, as well as the pattern of government subterfuge, impunity, indifference, and disregard for women's lives.

Francisca Galván, the attorney for this second generation of activist-mothers, vehemently denounced the government's grossly inadequate response: "Ciudad Juárez has been bleeding for two decades. The crime of feminicide has been normalized. . . . For the past twenty years there has not been a single [government] authority who responds with justice to a mother of a disappeared daughter. . . . The authorities speak of human remains as though they were objects and forget that these young women [had] lives, with hopes and dreams and families." Galván also emphasized the vulnerability of the victims: "These are class-based feminicides. . . . The women are selected because they are poor, from a precarious class, without power or resources to defend themselves."

Feelings of déjà vu sparked memories of a mother speaking years earlier before a public assembly in Juárez: "For the poor, there is no justice. If they had murdered a rich person's daughter, they would kill half the world to find the murderer. But since they have only murdered poor people, they treat us like dirt."[56] Feminicide has, for the most part, affected the most vulnerable lives in Mexico and elsewhere, particularly in Juárez where the young women were selected, murdered, and disappeared precisely because they were both poor and women. To this day, it is poor women, mestizas, Indigenous, Afro-descendant women, and transgender people who are the chief targets of feminicidal violence across the Américas. Given the colonial legacy of a heteropatriarchal, capitalist state like Mexico, these are the human lives less likely to matter or to merit respect, justice, and redress.

Two decades prior to the pandemic of feminicide in northern Mexico, an alliance of Black radical feminists, known as the Combahee River Collective, penned a manifesto denouncing the unsolved murders of a dozen women in the Boston area. In "Why Did They Die?" the Collective wrote, "Our sisters died *because* they were women just as surely as they died *because* they were black."[57] The Collective emphatically and implicitly critiqued the tendency to treat gender and race as mutually exclusive categories, in either/or terms that would render invisible Black women's specific experience embedded in both patriarchal and racial violence. Their treatment of gender and race as both/and rather than in binary either/or terms foreshadowed an intersectional approach to the study of gender violence.

Drawing from "the long tradition of feminist consciousness" (to use Angela Davis's formulation), the Collective debunks the idea of a one-size-fits-all patriarchy.[58] Feminist intersectionality challenges the idea of one-dimensional, universal gender oppression since women are located differently within patriarchy, and their differential social location means that violence impacts them differently. Poor women, Black women, First Nation women, trans women, and immigrant women are at greater risk than elite white women in the United States or Mexico. Why? Because nonwhite women's existence is impacted by multiple vulnerabilities derived from the intersecting structures of power in their lives. For intersectional feminists, the entangled systems of domination affecting the lives of women of color suggest that there is no hierarchy among them. All are interconnected and overlapping: sexism and misogyny inseparable from racism, inseparable from transphobia, inseparable from classism and colorism (see chapter 2).

A few months prior to attending the "Borders and Bodies" seminar in Juárez, I had participated as a member of the Red de Investigadoras por la Vida y la Libertad de las Mujeres (Network of Researchers for the Life and Liberty of Women) in a national seminar on the General Law on feminicide.[59] The seminar took place at the headquarters of the Human Rights Commission in Mexico City, and its main objectives centered on assessing the implementation of the General Law and codifying feminicide as a serious crime in Mexico and Central America. In light of the heavily legalistic focus of the seminar, I chose to present an analysis of the criminal justice approach to gender violence, which formed the basis of my subsequent talk at the "Borders and Bodies" seminar.

In both instances, my talk was based on an intersectional analysis of gender and sexual violence and the critical scholarship of abolition feminists. Since the publication of our edited collection *Terrorizing Women*, I felt increasingly ambivalent about the law-and-order demands made by more institutionally based feminists in Mexico who worked as lawyers, functionaries, academic researchers, and directors of NGOs. Their demands for carceral solutions—criminalizing gender violence, greater enforcement of the law, and arrest, conviction, incarceration, and longer prison sentences for perpetrators—echoed the punitive justice mentality in the United States.

Inspired by the works of abolition feminist activists and scholars who have shaped my thinking about the criminal justice and legal system, my talks centered on the limitation and reach of a punitive justice approach to ending gender/sexual violence.[60] This was a delicate perspective to broach because I didn't want to come across as a colonialist US feminist lecturing my Mexican colleagues about the unforeseen outcomes of their carceral remedies for ending violence against women. I opted for an analogical argument, focusing on the social consequences of the Violence against Women Act (VAWA), signed into US law in 1994.

Laws like VAWA and the General Law are designed to protect the rights of women, yet evidence suggests that VAWA has not reduced the overall rates of gender violence, as Michelle De Casas and others have found.[61] In addressing the effects of VAWA, I zeroed in on the paradox confronting mainstream feminists (also known as carceral feminism). In the struggle for gender justice, mainstream feminist approaches have adopted the carceral logic of the state. The carceral feminist's approach to gender violence, embodied in VAWA, is inseparable from the unprecedented growth and privatizations of the prison industrial complex during the past three decades. Although VAWA is not the sole reason for the rise in mass incarceration, it is part of a neoliberal capitalism's tendency to individualize and criminalize social problems.

In the United States, the criminalization of social problems, such as substance abuse and gender/sexual violence, has had the astonishing and predictable effect of contributing to the mass incarceration of men of color who, along with poor whites, are more likely to be arrested, charged, and imprisoned than elite white males. As I explain in chapter 2, one major drawback of the carceral feminist approach lies in its emphasis on locking up convicted individuals in a prison system that fosters punishment rather than rehabilitation. Punitive justice forecloses demands for justice that transcend the legal system as envisioned in restorative and transformative justice models, which foster repairing and restoring injuries for the crimes committed.

"The remedies for gender-based violence depend on how we define its causes," note Weissman and Weissman.[62] If we attribute violence solely to the criminality and pathology of an individual, then we fail to forge connections between gender violence and other forms of cruelty, nor do we grasp its multifaceted and mutually constituted expression. If feminicide is treated as corporal violence, we fail to take into consideration the social and economic structures that engender violence against women. As feminists, our challenge is "to open up the analytical lens," as Cecilia Menjívar suggests, "to include a wide range of sources of pain and injury that are not found in the actions of individuals, though often they are carried out by individuals, but in the 'social order of things.'"[63]

If we consider violence against women to be structural or systemic, then as feminists our challenge is to fight for the transformation of the structures of racial, neoliberal capitalism and heteropatriarchy that fuel violence. Gendered forms of violence are also structural: disappearing infrastructure; increased economic insecurity; malnourishment; unequal access to education, jobs, and health care; criminalization of abortion; and symbolic and systemic sexism, transphobia, and racism that naturalize gender and racial inequality. Carceral feminism fails to address these modalities of violence and its legal remedies fail to explain how gender is inextricably inscribed in structures of domination.

The days of attributing feminicide and disappearances of women and girls in Juárez to serial killers are long gone, but the tendency to appeal to the very heteropatriarchal system that has been enabling gender and sexual violence remains evident in state-centered remedies like the General Law in Mexico. I use the term *enabling* deliberately because the Mexican government may not be orchestrating or directing feminicidal violence, but it is enabling and allowing the murders and disappearances of women to intensify, proliferate, and propagate.

Given Mexico's colonialist legacy, it is not surprising that its state apparatus would enable feminicidal violence. As decolonial feminist scholar-activist María Lugones noted, "Spain and Portugal introduced an extremely dehumanizing gender system and racial system, marking all colonized people racially, as inferior by nature, and females as inferior by nature to men."[64] The same dichotomous and hierarchical logics, inherent to systemic racism and sexism, continue to inform the Mexican government's neoliberal capitalist views about race, gender, and sexuality to this day.[65]

The culprits behind the murders and disappearances of women and girls range from partners and intimate acquaintances to unknown individuals, from state agents, police, and the military to paramilitary forces, from local gangs to organized criminal networks. Irrespective of the individual or corporate motives, gender and sexual violence remains an expression of control and domination. One thing that countries across the Américas share is the power of the state to enable, neglect, ignore, and fail to exercise due diligence when it comes to violations and assaults against women's humanity, particularly when they are poor, Indigenous, Afro-descendant, or trans people. As former colonies of Spain and Portugal, the modern nation-states of the Américas share a colonial legacy of dehumanizing gender and racial subjects. This intersectional analysis of power informed the formation of radical feminist activists who coalesced under the Ni Una Menos banner.

VIII

The greatest challenge we face as we attempt to forge international solidarities and connections across national borders is an understanding of what feminists often call "intersectionality." Not so much intersectionality of identities, but intersectionality of struggles.

ANGELA DAVIS, *Freedom Is a Constant Struggle*

By the second decade of the twenty-first century, a paradigm shift in antifeminicide activism was well underway. During one of my research trips to Mexico City, I shared a ride to the hotel with a young activist from Mexico's feminist movement. "There are many divisions among Mexican feminists combating gender violence," Marisol told me. "But you can generalize these into two tendencies, feminismo de la igualdad [equality feminism] versus feminismo de la diferencia [difference feminism]."

Her insight echoed my own experience with the US feminist movement: splits between mainstream and revolutionary feminism; equal rights and radical feminists; hegemonic and multicultural feminisms; white feminism and women of color feminism; carceral feminists and abolition feminists; feminists who essentialized gender, and feminists who embraced an intersectional perspective. Often characterized as divisions between waves of feminism, it is important to recognize their complex entanglement, where the so-called first, second, third, and even fourth waves are not discrete and cut off from one another but rather overlap and intersect. The differences between feminists are more ideological and political than generational or temporal. Similar fractures and divisions have also rattled the contra-feminicide movement.

In their fight against feminicidal violence, equality (a.k.a. equal rights) feminists in Mexico have spent the past two decades demanding justice from the legal system. It is important to recognize that without their unwavering pressure, there would be no General Law criminalizing feminicide, no protocols for feminicide investigations, no gender violence alerts in most states, no National Institute for Women, and no legalized abortion in Mexico City, Veracruz, or Oaxaca.[66] But it is also the case that despite these institutional and legal changes, the problem of gender and sexual violence has persisted in large measure because the systemic structures engendering women's nonworth remain in place.

More institutionally affiliated feminists fight for reforming rather than dismantling the neoliberal state, capitalism, and heteropatriarchy. They seek parity or equality between women and men within a system in which inequality is intrinsic to its foundation. They conceptualize violence against women in terms of a gender—female/male—binary, and as a gender battle apart from ethnic or racial, ecological, and in some cases class struggles. This analysis of patriarchy is less oriented toward other forms of subjugation and fails to address differences within the social categories of gender and sexuality. Their objective is to forge a global sisterhood rooted in a universal paradigm of women's rights: an individualist form of feminism based on personal liberty and the rights of the person. Like radical feminists of color in the United States, feminismo de la diferencia opens a pathway for feminist collectives grounded in the commonality of social bonds and circumstances, and the intersectionality of struggles.

The 2012 election of Enrique Peña Nieto as Mexico's fifty-seventh president did not bode well for the Mexican people. A former governor of the state of Mexico—then considered the most dangerous state for women—Peña Nieto came to power promising to curtail the violence that escalated under his predecessor, Felipe Calderón. Instead, Peña Nieto left office with "one of the worst human rights crises in the entire hemisphere as his legacy."[67] Besides his failure to curtail cartel violence, murders, and extortions in the everyday lives of Mexicans, it was during Peña Nieto's tenure that forty-three students from Ayotzinapa were disappeared in September 2014, sparking worldwide protests and a renewed focus on the collusion between Mexican authorities and organized crime (see chapters 2 and 5).

The feminist collective Pan y Rosas Mexico embraced the intersectionality of struggles early in their work to stop feminicide. Originally founded in Argentina and established in Mexico in 2010, Pan y Rosas Mexico joined the campaign for justice for the forty-three disappeared students and protests against impunity and state violence. As freelance journalist Nidia Bautista reported, "The case detonated a grassroots phenomenon in the streets that served to denounce many injustices from feminicide to the criminalization of social protest under the PRI ruling party."[68] Besides participating in events with the mothers of the disappeared Ayotzinapa students, Pan y Rosas Mexico launched El Otro Ayotzinapa (The other Ayotzinapa) initiative in Mexico City "to discuss and publicize feminicide." In an interview with Bautista, Francisca (a member of Pan y Rosas Mexico) explained, "It's important to say that women are the other Ayotzinapa, because we also experience impunity and because there are hundreds of mothers who began to organize and became activists to demand a return of their daughters."[69]

In March 2015, the Ni Una Menos collective of prominent feminist journalists, artists, and lawyers launched an intersectional social media campaign to combat patriarchy and feminicide in Argentina. Three months after #NiUnaMenos went viral, the collective staged its first mass demonstration against gender violence, gathering 300,000 protestors outside of the National Congress in Buenos Aires and in other cities across the country. In the ensuing months, the Ni Una Menos collective used social media to organize and raise awareness about the problem of gender violence in Argentina, which by the end of the year had registered its highest number of feminicides on record, with one woman murdered every thirty hours.[70] By then, #NiUnaMenos had spread across the region, forging international solidarities and connections with Ni Una Más feminist activists in Mexico, Chile, Peru, Brazil, and Uruguay, all of whom participated in the protests the following June, in 2016.

On October 9, 2016, Lucia Pérez, a sixteen-year-old high school student from Mar de Plata, was abducted outside her school, drugged, and gang-raped. Her sadistic murder led to an unprecedented women's strike on October 19. "Inspired by Poland's 'Black Monday,' in which Polish women demonstrated against a total ban on abortion in the European country," Friedman and Tabbush report, "thousands of Argentinian women commandeered the streets, wearing all black and chanting, 'Patriarchy is going to fall.'"[71] They were joined by hundreds of thousands of allies in Chile, Peru, Brazil, Bolivia, Colombia, Ecuador, Paraguay, Uruguay, Honduras, Costa Rica, and Mexico, who demanded an end to feminicide, misogyny, heteropatriarchy, and neoliberal capitalism.

The Ni Una Menos collective "appropriated the strike as a tool for connecting sexist violence with political, economic and social violence," according to sociologist Veronica Gago, one of its founders. The collective's notion of gender and sexual violence beyond its corporeal manifestation grounds violence within its socioeconomic, political, and cultural expressions. "This form of understanding violence as a network of forms of exploitation within contemporary capitalism allowed us to transform feminism into a form of organization, a practice of alliances, and a diffuse language, truly transversal and expansive."[72] Their manifesto, "Nosotras Paramos" (We Strike), reflects an understanding of the intersectionality of struggles, linking feminicidal violence with cruelties of capitalism against trans people, the Indigenous, and the planet.[73]

Unlike contra-feminicide feminists who aim to transform the legal system and appeal to institutions for the protection of women's rights, the Ni Una Menos feminists insist on systemic changes. They seek to refashion a new economic and social order in its place. Having lost their faith in capitalism and the state, the collective's demands for women's social and economic rights suggest a deeper grasp of the inextricable link between corporal violence and structural violence. In their statement for the International Day for the Elimination of Violence against Women (25N), the collective declares: "From crossing languages and borders, as migrant women do, defying the illegalization of our movements, the rebellion emerges against violence, against the feminization of poverty, against racism, against the lack of political representation, against the attempt to confine women and girls in domestic enclosure, against religious dogmas that appropriate our bodies and our lives, against the mandate of maternity and the criminalization of abortion, against the renewed forms of capitalist exploitation and against the precaritization of existence. Against the multiple dispossessions: because neither the Earth nor our bodies are territories of conquest."[74]

The Ni Una Menos collective demands an end to the social domination of women, queers, and trans people and the necropolitical targeting of multiple communities. Their struggle for freedom and equality intersects with struggles to decriminalize abortion, for the right to equal pay, for racial and ethnic justice, and against neoliberal capitalist economies that exacerbate violence against poor and vulnerable communities and ecologies. From the onset, this movement is infused with the consciousness of the structural character of state violence and with an understanding of the intersectionality of struggles.

In reflecting upon the Ni Una Menos collective's feminist imaginary and vision, Veronica Gago writes, "What is this expansive, popular, communitarian, shanty-dweller feminism that has been able to transgress the borders of a language for a few, that has become a common key, and that manages to express the discomfort and desires of many women? A mode of feminism that composes, in a rather novel way, being massive, inclusive and radicalized. And it accomplishes this by departing from an experience that goes through us: the multiple violences, which we've begun to confront in a mode that escapes victimization."[75]

The Ni Una Menos collective recognizes what it means to embody difference under a dehumanizing regime, where difference means "the line between value and devalued, life and death," in Cherrie Moraga's formulation.[76] Their feminism is a vision and a movement that challenges the social, economic, and political worldviews that the neoliberal state promotes.

IX

A couple of years after the publication of our book on feminicide, I took an early morning flight into El Paso for a meeting with activists and researchers in Ciudad Juárez. Riding in a taxi from the airport to the border reminded me of my graduate student days at UC San Diego, when I'd drive from La Jolla to Tijuana and notice the stark differences in physical and social landscapes between two adjacent countries. The lush greenery due to artificial irrigation on the US side disappeared as soon as one crossed the border into Tijuana, where the scenery took on a more natural desertlike, arid feel. The empty streets of California's car culture gave way to street vendors and pedestrians crisscrossing Tijuana's streets in many directions. The taxi driver interrupted my thoughts: "What brings you to the area?"

"I'm here for a seminar about the murders of women in Juárez," I replied. She asked, "You mean the murders of the prostitutes?"

It didn't matter if all the murdered women had been "prostitutes," I responded to the taxi driver, noticeably annoyed that she'd repeated a well-worn narrative meant to devalue the lives of women, to dismiss the significance of their lives and deaths, and, yet again, blame the victim. Some of the women murdered were sex workers; others were not. Even so, being murdered wasn't their fault.

A few weeks later, I received a voice mail on my campus phone from an official with the National Intelligence University. When I returned the call, he invited me to be a keynote speaker on the subject of gender violence at their Geostrategic Intelligence Seminar on Mexico. Participants in the two-week seminar would include "senior federal government leaders" from the Department of Defense, the Department of Homeland Security, the Federal Bureau of Investigation, and the Drug Enforcement Administration, among others.[77]

My first instinct was to decline. The thought of presenting my research on gender violence to a room full of US intelligence officers petrified me. I'd rather share my work and raise awareness with people who are likely to participate in change-making activities like protesting at Mexican consulates and marching for justice, calling their congressional representative, signing petitions, conducting research, and envisioning alternatives to the criminal justice system. But rather than responding to his invitation with a definitive "no," I stalled, saying that I'd check my calendar for February and get back to him.

For days, I weighed the pros and cons. The taxi driver's comments about the killing of "prostitutes" kept resonating in my mind. What if US government officials had internalized this misogynist narrative designed to diminish the value of women's lives? Then maybe my talk could enlighten them about the complexities of feminicide on the border. Perhaps members of the US intelligence community believed the Mexican government's claims that it was actually doing its due diligence to investigate the murders and disappearances of women on the border. If I chose to attend, I could counter their claims with facts about the exponential increase in gender and sexual violence throughout Mexico. Maybe my presentation would prompt the US agents to exert pressure on their Mexican counterparts to take matters of violence against women seriously.

On the con side, my desire to influence our government's response to the unfolding crisis in Mexico felt delusional. I was doubtful that my feminist research on gender/sexual violence would have any impact on US intelligence officers, whom I assumed worked closely with Mexican authorities on the border. I also felt intimidated and even paralyzed at the thought of speaking to an audience of federal agents trained in policing, counterterrorism, surveillance, and drug enforcement.

Before deciding, I consulted with colleagues whose research on public policy often situated them before public officials or antagonistic audiences, and other colleagues who had testified for congressional committees and even before the Supreme Court. Their nearly unanimous encouragement (including that of my husband) convinced me that, however minor, my presentation could potentially make a difference.

A few weeks after I accepted the invitation, the coordinator of the seminar followed up with a more formal letter, stating:

> Your work on Feminicide and your extensive work on creating awareness for the silent and women's rights would be invaluable as your *strategic intelligence insight and knowledge* would be of exceptional value to our participants.
>
> We look forward to hearing your *assessment* of the issues involved in your publication, Terrorizing Women: Feminicides in the Americas as well as defining and *addressing* regional challenges as we believe your observations would be an *excellent launching point for our examination of the challenges of a bilateral response with Mexico*. (emphasis added)

Three weeks later I boarded a flight to San Diego for the seminar held on Coronado Island, where the North Island Naval Air Station is located.

I overprepared for this keynote address, carefully reviewing my arguments, double-checking the factual information, and assembling an evidence-based slide presentation with statistics, graphs, maps, and bullet points that highlighted my *assessment* of the unprecedented rise in gender/sexual violence over the course of almost two decades, as well as the severity of women's rights violations and the killing of women's rights advocates that had accelerated with the launch of the US-funded war on drugs in Mexico. My presentation *addressed* regional challenges such as the persistence of impunity for gender and sexual crimes and its threat to public (not just national) security.

My keynote address (which I drew from the article "Coming to Grips with Feminicide") provided a working definition for *feminicide* that links the violence perpetrated by individuals with state violence. It implicated the institutions that sanction gender/sexual violence, including security forces, the police, the judiciary, and local and federal prosecutors. I addressed the legal and social challenges women's rights advocates face in the implementation of public policy in Mexico. Since my observations promised to be an *excellent launching point for future examination of the challenges of a bilateral response with Mexico*, I prepared a list of recommendations for how the US intelligence community might assist and intervene.

First, our government could provide logistic support and training to Mexican authorities and forensic investigators on how to investigate crimes from a gender perspective. In order to determine whether or not a murder of a woman should be categorized as feminicide, Mexican authorities should document evidence of physical assault of the body of a victim and determine whether or not the victim was physically or sexually assaulted prior to or after the murder, since this provides evidence of a gender hate crime. And they should document the method used for her murder.

Second, our government could help Mexico demilitarize its war on drugs because soldiers deployed on the border are notorious for violating the rights of local residents, given that the Mexican military does not provide basic training in human rights protocols nor in respect for civil rights of citizens. Moreover, soldiers deployed to the border have been accused of kidnapping and raping women.

Third, our government could monitor the growing criminalization of human rights activism, as well as the assault against women's rights defenders, as mandated by congressional funding of the Mérida Initiative.[78]

Finally, our government could counter misogynist narratives meant to devalue women's lives, including sex workers.

The main thrust of my presentation was solutions-based, although I did express my criticism of the Mexican government waging a war of extermination funded in part by the US government through the Mérida Initiative. Our government had sponsored dirty wars in Latin America during the 1970s and 1980s and now seemed to be repeating the same mistakes by funding a new dirty war on drugs and training Mexican security forces while turning a blind eye to their indiscriminate violence.

I anticipated a substantive discussion centered on my recommendations during the Q&A session. I expected us to discuss the relationship between Mexico's war on drugs and the dramatic rise in the murder rates and/or disappearances of women on the border. I expected that there might be some disagreement about my definition of *feminicide*. I thought we'd enter into a real dialogue. But the blank faces that stared back at me during my presentation foreshadowed what was to come.

Their questions were mostly superficial and nitpicky: "You stated that the impunity rate for women's murder is 99 percent. However, for men, it's also in the lower [not upper] nineties, so there's not much difference here. Why does it matter?" A similar question from another officer: "Isn't it the case that most crimes in Mexico remain unsolved?" A feeling of dread and hopelessness overwhelmed me as I stood in front of the room answering

1.3 Olga Alicia's mother holding poster that reads: "Mr. Governor, silence is also complicit with feminicide." Photo by Angela Fregoso.

their questions, confirming my earlier instincts that my research on gender violence would make no difference to US intelligence officers.

The bulk of their questions dealt with the drug cartels and the state-by-state location of their operations, which had little bearing on my presentation. My body felt heavy, but I was determined to press on and tried repeatedly to steer my responses to the issue of violence against women. At one point, I even located the PowerPoint slide with a map of Mexico that displayed a state-by-state breakdown of feminicide cases. But my efforts fell on deaf ears as they resumed their conversation, mostly among themselves, about the drug cartel operations, their turf wars, and fragmentation of major cartels. I wanted to scream, "Can you stop that and pay attention to what I'm saying?"

It was deeply disturbing to me that the violence, criminality, and impunity of feminicide did not move them or offend them. Disheartened and feeling numb but relieved that this waste-of-my-time talk had ended, I packed my notes and laptop while the senior federal government leaders left the small seminar room. Just as I was walking out to the hallway, a young, blonde female intelligence officer, bearing a friendly smile and warm eyes, approached me. I greeted her with an even wider smile, believing she was the one person who'd say something thoughtful about my presentation. Instead, she addressed me in a fervent tone: "Thank you for your talk. . . . I'm a Christian, and the Bible says that a wife should obey her husband. I'm not married, but that's what I believe. Maybe some of these women were not following God's wishes."

"Really?" I responded, shaking. My ears were ringing, my head ached, and my heart was pounding. "Well, I'm Catholic, which is also Christian, and nowhere in the Bible does it say a husband should murder his wife for being disobedient."

I left Coronado Island distraught and enraged, berating myself for accepting the invitation. The invitation from the National Intelligence University had been pure tokenism. These so-called senior federal government leaders were visibly oblivious and unconcerned about the violence against women and the impunity for gender and sexual violence. They didn't seem to care at all about the hundreds of lives that had been lost to gender-based injuries. Their indifference to the murder and disappearance of women showed me what truly matters to our government: the war on drugs, not the war on people. Women's lives didn't matter. Trans people's lives didn't matter. By turning their backs on human rights violations in Mexico, our government is clearly implicated in state violence.

X

Only in the most extreme conditions you see how broken the world is.
AI WEIWEI, *Humanity*

By the time the Ni Una Menos and Ni Una Más collectives joined forces in 2016, life circumstances forced me to shift my energy away from the contrafeminicide movement inward into more domestic spaces, both personally and politically. A diagnosis of Menière's disease in 2013, with its unpredictable onset of consistent symptoms (vertigo, vomiting, and extreme fatigue), limited my frequent research travels to Mexico. A year earlier, after a thirteen-year battle with the autoimmune disease lupus, my adult daughter Xochitl had received a diagnosis of antiphospholipid syndrome, a disorder that produces excessive blood clotting. In her case, it resulted in several strokes that left her paralyzed.

I was extremely fortunate to have excellent health care insurance through the University of California, which allowed me to take medical leave twice, once to stabilize my Menière's flare-ups and a second time to care for my daughter and grandson. Family medical leave freed me up from teaching and research obligations to coordinate my daughter's medical appointments, therapies, household duties, and care for her son, Jasim, who, at thirteen, was already an accomplished musician with a jam-packed schedule of academics, music lessons, and performances. As I shifted my attention to family and self-care, changes in US asylum law were well underway.

Prior to the Obama administration, only those persecuted on the basis of race, religion, nationality, political opinion, or membership in a particular social group could petition for asylum. Survivors of gender-based persecution did not meet the legal criteria to be refugees and thus could not apply.

In 2009, the Department of Homeland Security lent legal support to a Mexican woman's petition for asylum based on gender. In the case of L-R (2009), the Obama administration proposed new legal norms for granting asylum to female survivors of domestic violence. The legal norms were later solidified in a historic ruling issued by the Board of Immigration. In 2014, the board ruled in the matter of A-R-C-G that domestic violence survivors could meet the definition of *refugee* and thus qualify for asylum. As a result of this landmark decision recognizing women's claims for protection under US asylum law, requests for my expertise in gender violence began pouring in.

Until the reversals in asylum law by the former Trump administration (see chapter 6), I served as expert witness in dozens of gender asylum cases from Mexico and the Northern Triangle countries of Guatemala, El Salvador, and Honduras. In the majority of these cases, women had petitioned for asylum and protection under the UN Convention against Torture for gender-based persecution by an intimate partner. Prior to 2012, I had written affidavits for a gender asylum case in Canada and another one in Washington state. Thanks to my colleague Héctor Domínguez-Ruvalcaba, who shared a draft of his country expert report, I learned how to frame my affidavits and testimony on subsequent cases.

My decision to serve as an expert witness in gender asylum cases was both personal and political. The cases were mostly pro bono, led by dedicated and compassionate attorneys representing women from vulnerable groups, with little or no resources. I continued to be ambivalent about working within the legal system, especially in the United States, where to describe a women as victim of domestic violence conjures what Judith Butler refers to as "a protected status subject to a paternalistic set of powers that must safeguard the vulnerable, those presumed to be weak and in need of protection."[79] Gender asylum cases tend to be framed within the human rights discourse of victimhood, where to be a vulnerable subject means to be "fixed in a political position of powerlessness and lack of agency."[80] Yet these were also women whose very condition of vulnerability had empowered them to take action.

At a deep level, I felt a kinship with the women's corporal vulnerability, having been a survivor of domestic violence myself. I knew what it was to live in fear of a controlling and abusive man who could snap at any moment and extinguish me. I understood what it meant to feel the shame and embarrassment of physical injuries and to be blamed for my own injuries.

I understood the women's agency and resistance, however individually it was being framed. These were women who had lost their homes, their families, their friends, their communities, and their self-respect, who had taken their children by the hand and risked everything for an uncertain future in a strange land. Their resistance might not have taken a collective political or social form, but it took enormous courage and agency to come to another country with another language, another way of life, and to start from scratch. These refugees chose aliveness over death.

From my research on feminicide, I had extensive knowledge about the devastating impact of violence on women's lives, families, and communities. Since the early days of feminicide in Ciudad Juárez, researchers and social workers in facilities for battered women had sounded the alarm about growing rates of domestic violence in the state of Chihuahua, with 70 percent of women reporting incidents of domestic violence in 2000. Many women murdered there were killed by their husbands, lovers, or former partners, who sought to control, dominate, and ultimately enact the most extreme form of disappearance and erasure on the women they had once claimed to love.

Despite the enactment of the General Law on Women's Access to a Life Free from Violence in 2007, violence against women continued to be a grave problem throughout Mexico. A patriarchal society with high levels of sexism, transphobia, and misogyny, the country has one of the highest rates of gender-based violence against women, ranking among the world's twenty worst countries, according to United Nations survey data.

Under Peña Nieto's presidency, human rights violations and violence against women grew at a shocking rate. Over 60 percent of Mexican females had been affected by physical, sexual, or psychological violence, compared with 35 percent worldwide in 2016.[81] That same year, a national survey on family dynamics, encompassing 142,363 households, reported that 43.9 percent of women in Mexico have experienced gender-based violence committed by their partners; and 66.1 percent of women age fifteen years and older have been victims of gender-based violence.[82]

Nongovernmental organizations like the National Citizens Feminicide Observatory (OCNF in Spanish)—a coalition of forty organizations from twenty-one states that documents gender crimes in Mexico—have independently collected and analyzed data on female homicides in the country. According to María de la Luz Estrada, coordinator of the OCNF, in 2016 Mexico registered one of the highest rates of female homicides on the continent, with 7.5 homicides daily, an increase of 63 percent from the previous year.[83]

One of my last affidavits (a.k.a. country reports) for a gender asylum petition dealt with the case of YGB from the state of Guerrero. YGB and her children lived with a man who physically, emotionally, and sexually abused her. Not only did YGB's family not defend her, but they further victimized YGB by shaming her into accepting her husband's abusive behavior out of concern that she would bring dishonor to the family. He repeatedly threatened to kill her and, after one particularly vicious incident involving marital rape, YGB contacted authorities to denounce the violence, to no avail. The failure of police to follow due process and their inability to respond to assaults against women is due in large measure to the fact that "many law enforcement officers are involved in partner violence in their lives."[84]

YGB chose to leave and live because women in vulnerable conditions like YGB have little recourse to justice in Mexico. As outlined in her declaration, she sought help from the Centro de Atención a Violencia Interfamiliar (CENAVI, Center for Attention to Interfamilial Violence) without receiving a response. Their inaction confirms what advocates for the protection of women's rights have underscored about the failure of Mexican institutions set up to safeguard the lives of women and children. According to recent OCNF data, "In numerous cases of feminicide, the murders could have been avoided because the victims had previously contacted authorities to denounce the violence the victims had been subjected to; however the authorities did not generate the mechanisms of protection."[85]

YGB chose to leave and live because police indifference and/or inaction clearly demonstrates that violence suffered by women at the hands of intimate partners is compounded by institutional violence perpetrated by state entities. Poor enforcement of local laws is exacerbated by the failure and negligence on the part of federal, state, and municipal governments to guarantee women's rights to live a life free of violence. Of 3,892 female homicides for 2012 and 2013, only 613 were investigated, and of these, only 1.6 percent led to sentencing. The enactment of the General Laws in 2007 has changed little for women of Mexico.

She chose to leave and live because police recommend that women resort to sex and seduction to resolve partner violence. As sociologist Sonia Frías reports, police officers frequently tell victims of domestic violence: "'If you were raped, it is because you looked for it'; 'Madam, he only hit you a little'; 'It's better that you go home and not make him angry again'; and 'How is it possible that you claim you were raped, when you are not even crying?'"[86] In 2017 a dozen police officers were charged with murdering their domestic partners.[87]

She chose to leave and live because violence against women throughout Mexico continues to be a serious social problem. Despite the passage of the federal law against gender violence in 2007 and the fact that Mexico's states began to change their penal codes in 2008, most states have been lax in instituting the recommended protocols for investigating violence against women.

She chose to leave and live because there continues to be a generalized belief that domestic violence is a private matter, impervious to intervention on the part of civil society in general. Acts of aggression in the public sphere are reinforced by customary rules of silencing, not reporting, and blaming the victim. The patriarchal view of women as property by virtue of their position within a domestic relationship discourages others, including family members, from intervening, thereby perpetuating domestic violence against women.[88]

She chose to leave and live because international human rights organizations have repeatedly accused state and municipal governments of establishing and maintaining a legal and institutional framework that permits grave violations of women's human rights. The Mexican government has been accused of direct and indirect participation, by acts or by omission, in perpetrating domestic violence, feminicide, disappearances, and trafficking, which impede women in Mexico from exercising their rights, liberty, and a life with dignity; the government has not prevented the violation of women's human rights, has failed to investigate gender assaults such as domestic violence, and has not held accountable the public authorities who cover up and silence assaults against women, thereby consolidating a general climate of impunity.

She chose to leave and live because feminicides continue unabated and are on the rise. In 2017 there were seven feminicides per day in Mexico. In the year YBG petitioned for asylum (2018), the country registered 2,720 female homicides, or nine per day, and the following year the number of women brutally murdered rose to 3,825—an increase of 7 percent from the previous year. As the pandemic spiked across the country, Maria de la Luz Estrada, the current director of OCNF, reported that as of May 2020, ten women had been killed per day.

YGB chose to leave and live because increased rates of organized crime and violence in Mexico are making the problem worse. In its July 2018 country report on Mexico, prepared by twenty-three experts, the UN's CEDAW (Committee on the Elimination of Discrimination against Women) highlighted "that the persistence of high levels of insecurity, violence and organised crime in [Mexico] as well as the challenges associated with public safety strategies, is negatively affecting the enjoyment of human rights of women and girls." In its conclusion, the committee underscored "the persistent patterns of widespread gender-based violence against women and girls across [Mexico], including physical, psychological, sexual and economic violence, as well as the increase in domestic violence, enforced disappearances, sexual torture and murder, particularly feminicide."[89]

There is no doubt that violence against women is intimately linked to and even rooted in structural violence in Mexico. YGB's very condition of vulnerability empowered her to take action. Her resistance, while not connected to collective social or political movements, is no less part of a movement of people who resist their dehumanization and reclaim their freedom, justice, and humanity. YGB chose life over death.

XI

Toni Morrison encouraged us to tell every story, no matter how excruciating: "A writer's life and work are not a great gift to mankind; they are its necessity."[90] Writing about feminicide is painful, yet this agony pales in comparison to being its victim. Out of necessity these stories must be told: for the young woman who fears she may be the next victim of feminicide, for the memories of trans people, known and unknown, for those whose lives have been upended by its disastrous consequences, for the activists and movements laboring for its end. We write to remember. To denounce the violence that aims to silence and control women and trans people, to render them less than human, to destroy and erase their humanity everywhere. We write because it is not our fault.

Re-memory for the Dead

There is a necessity for remembering the horror—in a manner
in which memory is not destructive.
TONI MORRISON, in Marsha Darling, "In the Realm of Responsibility"

The painting of La Virgen towers over the solemn space. A beaded
Huichol-inspired headdress crowns her veil, a gold star–dotted mantle
drapes over the pink vestment she wears, as its undulating folds add dy-
namism and movement to her pose. On this dimly lit wall, La Virgen's
image is flanked on each side by dozens of small delicate portraits.

Artist Diane Kahlo painted this rendition of La Virgen de Guadalupe for her *Wall of Memories: Las Desaparecidas,* an installation
dedicated to the women who have been murdered and disappeared
in Ciudad Juárez. On this occasion, Kahlo's *Wall of Memories* is part
of the Day of the Dead celebration at the Mission Cultural Arts Center
in San Francisco.[1]

A distant relative of the renowned Mexican painter Frida Kahlo—
Diane's grandfather was a cousin of Frida's father, Wilhelm Kahlo—
Diane Kahlo has dedicated her work to issues that would have
captivated her famous relative. "I believe that Frida would be very
interested in what is happening in Ciudad Juárez and in everything to
do with immigration and politics on the border," Kahlo says.[2]

For the past two decades, Kahlo's work has dealt with topics of violence against women, immigration, worker rights, and issues of racism,
sexism, xenophobia, and poverty. Currently a resident of Lexington,

Kentucky, her interest in border politics dates to the 1960s when she studied art at the University of Southern California and participated in the Chicanx student movement.

Inspired by the Vietnam Memorial Wall and the emotional impact of thousands of soldiers' names on visitors to the memorial, Kahlo decided to "look at another war . . . a war on women . . . and to personalize it more because these girls are for the most part unknown to us, but they are somebody's daughter, they are somebody's sister, somebody's wife," she tells me.[3] Kahlo did more than carve names of the women and girls on her *Wall of Memories*. She created 150 renditions of female faces painted similarly, each with its own purple frame and full name carved beneath the image.

Kahlo prefers to call her exhibition a "wall of memory" rather than a "memorial wall." Trained as a painter in realism and portraiture, Kahlo painted the portraits by hand, drawing from photographs of the women and girls, and using gold leaf as a background to create an iconic image. "I painted the portraits as little icons because I wanted them to become little memories of the way a mother would want to remember her daughter. I didn't want for them to remember the horror of how her daughter might have died. . . . I wanted them to imagine what she looked like the last time she saw her at her quinceañera or high school graduation."

INTER1.1 Diane Kahlo, small portrait of Sylvia Arce Atayde, in *Wall of Memories*. Photo by Juan Gómez.

Projected on the adjacent wall to La Virgen is a photograph of a young woman's almond-shaped eyes, her gaze towering over the sacred ambiance. The gaze is somber and watchful, beholding the sanctum that honors, mourns, and bears witness to lives sundered by violence and destruction. Kahlo's *Wall of Memories* insists on the ontology of worthy lives, women and girls whose loss merits grief and re-memory.

On the adjacent wall, beneath the projected image of the young woman's penetrating gaze, Kahlo installed a full-sized skeleton, bejeweled with sequins and beads. On the opposite side of the room, she placed ornamented skulls, a reference to Mesoamerican peoples' deployment of skulls to symbolize death and rebirth. For Kahlo, "The installation of skulls symbolizes las desconocidas, the unknown girls' shoes and bodies that have not been identified."

Kahlo assembled each of the small calaveras by hand, taking anywhere from twelve to twenty hours per calavera and six months for the full-sized skeleton, her fingers often bleeding while she threaded the sequins and tiny beads onto the styrofoam molds. Her own blood became part of the exhibition: "I wanted my labor to represent the labor, the bleeding hands of the young women working in the maquilas . . . and the farm labor of migrant workers," she explains.

Whereas other installations have stirred controversy for their blunt portrayal of death scenes, Kahlo's approach to imaging feminicide diverges significantly from those of artists who have engaged with the "aesthetics of gruesome deaths," to use Angelique Szymanek's phrase.[4] Other artists have deployed objects (shoes or garments) symbolizing the dead, morbid use of bodily fluids and human remains, or overt portrayals of mutilated bodies, with mixed results.[5]

Kahlo eschews portraying the body (corpus) as "corpus delicti"—"the body of a crime"—or the corpse of a murdered female as medico-juridical evidence of a crime committed.[6] Kahlo's approach to imaging the corpus's truth is in the interest of memory and as a balm for healing: the body (calavera/skeletal remains) as a "site of mourning, remembering, remaking of self and community."[7] Kahlo conjures the body less as a witness to a crime than as a witness to psychic trauma and a social wound.

It is the portrait of La Virgen, Kahlo's rendition of "La Morena, this hybrid of Catholicism and the Indigenous Mother-Goddess looking over her daughters," that embodies the corpus as witness to psychic trauma and social wound—literally. "Her face is a compilation of all the faces of the young women that I painted in the portraits," Kahlo confides. "I took features

INTER1.2 Diane Kahlo, small bejeweled skulls/ calavera, in *Wall of Memories*. Photo by Juan Gómez.

INTER1.3 Diane Kahlo, full-sized skeleton/ calavera, in *Wall of Memories*. Photo by Juan Gómez.

INTER1.4 Diane Kahlo, *La Virgen*, in *Wall of Memories*. Photo by Juan Gómez.

from many of the different young women whose faces I know very well and made up her face."

By painting La Virgen as a composite of the faces of lives lost, Kahlo shifts our attention to witnessing as recognition of the lives and identities of the victims. *Wall of Memories* is a life-size offering, an altar as sanctuary and space for mourning, a sacred homage to desacralized bodies of beloved daughters, sisters, friends, reminding us that their loss matters and their lives are worthy of being grieved. This is how she re-members the memory of horror, by honoring the women's existence and conjuring up the presence of that which has disappeared, with re-memory—the act of remembering a memory, which is not destructive but productive.

2 Mexico's Longest War

At the end of 2009, we were reviewing the page proofs for *Terrorizing Women* when the Centro de Derechos Humanos de las Mujeres sent out an e-blast announcing yet another feminicide victim in Chihuahua: Flor Alicia Gómez. The latest victim was a teacher in the rural town of Tomochi, Chihuahua. Flor Alicia had been accompanying a group of friends to a meeting when they were assaulted and beaten by an armed commando. Flor Alicia's body was found the next day. She had been abducted, sexually assaulted, and killed by a gunshot to the head. The other occupants in the vehicle were released.

Since the completion of our edited book (Fregoso and Bejarano, *Terrorizing Women*), violence against women who defend human rights has grown at an alarming rate. Flor Alicia's is one of many cases of relatives threatened or murdered for the human rights activities of their family members. Several of Flor Alicia's relatives, including her mother, are well-known human rights defenders in Chihuahua. Her aunt, Alma Gómez, is a longtime women's rights advocate, former state senator, and cofounder of Centro de Derechos Humanos de las Mujeres and Justicia para Nuestras Hijas in Chihuahua.[1] Alma Gómez coauthored one of the chapters in our book.

Despite the surge in violence against women in Mexico, government officials continue to characterize the abductions, murders, disappearances, and threats against women as "social violence" and as "collateral damage" in the war between criminal organizations. This

Justicia para Nuestras Hijas A.C.　　　　*Centro de Derechos Humanos de las Mujeres A.C.*

Participamos con profunda indignación
EL FEMINICIDIO de

Flor Alicia Gómez López

23 años de edad.
Maestra de Tomochi, Chih. Secuestrada, torturada y
asesinada el 29 de noviembre del 2009
Sobrina de Alma y Gabino Gómez nuestros queridos
compañer@s en la lucha por los derechos humanos de las
Mujeres
Chihuahua, Chih. México

! NI UNA MAS ¡

2.1 Flyer denouncing Flor Alicia Gómez López's assassination, distributed by Justicia para Nuestra Hijas and Centro de Derechos Humanos de las Mujeres, Chihuahua City, Chihuahua.

foza común (common grave) mentality about gendered and sexual violence diminishes assaults against women and trans people as much as it distorts its distinctive traits. Referring to violence against women and trans people as social or criminal violence depoliticizes their killing and obscures its colonialist, heteropatriarchal, and capitalist foundations.

In Mexico, there is no single cause behind the ceaseless and senseless killing of women and trans people. Females are not killed and disappeared only because they are "women in a women-hating world," to quote Jane Caputi.[2] As in most areas of the world, heteropatriarchal ideology is surely a determining factor. The persistence of the war on women and gender-nonconforming people requires a multicausal explanation, one that accounts for the patriarchal legacy of colonial modernity that philosopher Maria Lugones calls "the coloniality of gender" and Jean Franco terms "cruel modernity," as she explains: "To consider the exercise of cruelty in Latin America moves the debate into a different and complex terrain that links the conquest to feminicide, the war on communism to genocide and neoliberalism to casual violence without limits."[3]

Feminicide in Mexico is rooted in a conjuncture of multiple structures and technologies that solidified what years ago I called an emerging "necropolitical order" on the globalized world of the Mexico-US border—a politics based on death.[4] Contra-feminicide involves bearing witness to the structures behind colonialist heteropatriarchal violence. Mexico is a patriarchal society, designed to protect men and their privilege. Like most countries in the Western Hemisphere, Mexico was methodically built on a legacy of genocide, slavery, and colonialism. It is a racist society designed to protect the rights of the white and lighter-skinned mestizx elite over those of Indigenous, darker mestizxs, and Afro-descendant peoples. Media, security, criminal justice, the police, and the judiciary are all institutions inscribed by heteropatriarchal ideology and the nation's colonialist legacy.

....

Most analysts attribute the upsurge of violence in Mexico to the conjuncture of neoliberal reforms, the militarization of policing and security, and the penetration of drug cartels into an existing corrupt government. In the late twentieth century, as violence against women grew at an alarming rate, the government signed the North American Free Trade Agreement (NAFTA), consolidating the expansion of neoliberal capitalist development that began in the 1960s with the Border Industrialization Program (BIP) and ushering in the growth of the global assembly line.[5] The BIP was part of the global project of developmentalism in the twentieth century: "Under the hegemony of the United States, the goal of developmentalism was to remove opposition to the world system."[6]

Ciudad Juárez was then the largest export-processing zone on the border, with 350 maquiladoras (assembly plants) owned by transnational corporations. Thousands of female workers, mostly migrants from the southern region, were recruited. The young women labored nearly fifty hours per week, soldering electronic boards, sewing surgical gowns, wiring car dashboards, receiving a non–living wage of US$4 per day while working under precarious conditions, with little or no social benefits. Feminists called this new international division of labor under neoliberal capitalism "global gendered apartheid."[7]

Ciudad Juárez was also at the crossroads of the militarization of border security. The integration of military and border policing on the Mexico-US border has been a cornerstone of US policy designed to reduce unauthorized border crossings. Policy initiatives such as Operation Safeguard and Operation Gatekeeper transformed the border into a war zone and created a graveyard for migrants from the global South. The militarization of the borderland was also due in large measure to the so-called war on drugs instituted first under the Nixon administration, continuing through the tenure of six US presidents. In conjunction with the post 9/11 "war on terror" during President George W. Bush's tenure, the war on drugs expanded with the Mérida Initiative (a.k.a. Plan México), a 2007 binational accord that has had devastating consequences for the border region.

In 2008, President Felipe Calderón exacerbated the bloody conflict when he militarized the fight against select drug cartels operating in Mexico. Funded by the United States through the Mérida Initiative, Calderón's Operación Chihuahua involved the deployment of thousands of soldiers and military police to the border region. Violence and criminality reached pandemic proportions, alongside a disturbing trend of human rights violations committed by the very same security forces sent to restore order. As a result, Chihuahua became home to two of the fifty most dangerous cities in the world: Chihuahua City and Ciudad Juárez.[8]

The murder and disappearance of women and girls is thus rooted in the legacy of heteropatriarchal colonial modernity, neoliberal capitalism, and the so-called war on drugs, as well as what Héctor Domínguez and Patricia Ravelo term the war economy in Mexico, "the official one against crime and the war among mafias, in which the government has played a major role, as the most interested in occupying the streets of Juárez. It all demonstrates that the violation of citizens' rights, from security to freedom of movement, to enjoyment and economic activity, are substantial elements of the economy of death."[9]

Feminicide is also a reflection of an "absent" or "failed state," according to María Guadalupe Huacuz, "which impedes the access to justice for those persons whose 'precarious lives' impede their exercise of citizenship within an armed conflict that began with the appearance of murdered and mutilated female bodies, suffering bodies that constitute 'disposable bodies,' in the face of a state that systematically violates the individual rights of the population."[10]

Domínguez and Ravelo cite two reasons for this "absent state." The first pertains to the "agreement or pact" between the government and organized crime, undertaken by the administration of Miguel de la Madrid in 1982 to alleviate Mexico's financial crisis. They state: "Since then, the criminal networks have expanded and operated with a free reign, establishing a monopoly that controls all the drug trafficking routes into the United States, with guarantees that their earnings are totally protected." The second reason involves the intimate connection between politicians and cartels, due to the financing of political campaigns by the organized crime network: "In that sense, organized crime, besides being a threat to security, is an economic force that has become indispensable for a large sector of the economy, difficult to quantify."[11]

It is the confluence of these systemic structures that consolidated a necropolitical order in the country and explains the significance of feminicide as a new epistemic category for naming extreme forms of violence. Feminicide in Mexico makes evident the exercise of power across the social spectrum: the power of the state over civil society; the white elite over racialized people; men over women and trans people. It is a novel kind of Dirty War, one waged by multiple forces over disposable female and feminized bodies.

"It has been called and still is, the drug war, the war on drugs," writes author and critic Cristina Rivera Garza, "but we know other more truthful names: the war against the Mexican people, the war against women."[12] Mexico's so-called war on drugs exacerbated the war against women and transformed the countryside into a land of mass graves.

Feminicide stands as one of the "mass homicides" Cavarero warns is prevalent today: "The kind of war that matured in the twentieth century and looms over the new millennium is not only asymmetric as were and are all colonial wars, but, like them, consists predominantly of the homicide, unilateral and sometimes planned, of the defenseless."[13] The violence that escalated with Felipe Calderón's national war on drugs grew to unprecedented heights under Enrique Peña Nieto's government.

In assessing Peña Nieto's deplorable human rights record, Erika Guevara Rosas, Americas director at Amnesty International, reports on the "multiple incidents of extrajudicial executions carried out by security forces; and the widespread practice of torture, including sexual torture, as a standard procedure in the justice system."[14] Mexico's war against its own people has resulted in over 100,000 deaths and an equal number of people disappeared, most of them since 2006, according to Karla Quintana, director of the country's Comisión Nacional de Búsqueda de Personas (National Search Commission).[15]

From 2006 to June 30, 2021, 87,855 persons were disappeared, compared with 1,633 during the earlier four decades (1964–2005). Women and girls represent 25 percent of the total disappeared, and of these, girls and adolescent women under the age of eighteen make up 55.3 percent, the majority between the ages of ten and seventeen.[16] "It's the worst crisis of the disappeared in Latin America since the Cold War, when military-backed governments kidnapped and secretly killed their leftist opponents—an estimated 45,000 in Guatemala, up to 30,000 in Argentina, as many as 3,400 in Chile. And Mexico's numbers keep rising. Last year saw a record. Mexicans are uncovering two clandestine graves a day, on average."[17]

In Ciudad Juárez alone, from the 137 cases of feminicide between 1993 and 1998, the number of cases grew to 265 in 2003, then to 1,850 by August 2018, the final year of Peña Nieto's presidency. Of the latter figure, 1,043 cases occurred after the beginning of Calderón's disastrous war on drugs. "The extermination of women continues," writes Patricia Ravelo, "and has become more acute with the war on drugs, since violence and death have increased with this senseless war."[18] As sociologist Julia Monárrez adds, "With the war came new forms of violence against the population: enforced disappearance, sexual torture, youthicide [*juvenicidio*] and the recrudescence of feminicide."[19] Of the 1,850 cases of feminicide, Monárrez identifies 154 cases as "victims of systemic sexual feminicide," which she defines as sexual crimes with systematic methods and a high level of impunity.[20]

As the killings and disappearances of women continued into the new millennium, spreading throughout the region and to other parts of Mexico, it became apparent that impunity for the assassinations of women was both a consequence and an incitement for further feminicide and other forms of violence against women and trans people. To this day, Mexico is a state where its deficiencies exacerbate impunity and violence.

Before delving into the genealogy of feminicide in Mexico, it is important that we address the colonialist spectacle of Latino males as inherently violent and degenerate. This colonialist trope haunted my service as an expert witness for gender asylum in the United States. In one particular case, I had to contend with the legal defense team of an undocumented woman petitioning for asylum, specifically the petitioner's attorney, who requested that I frame my expert opinion in terms of inherent machismo in Mexican culture, which I refused to do. The challenge many of us face whenever we investigate or write (or in my case, provide expert testimony) about violence in Latin America is how to avoid reproducing the stereotype of human rights violations as cultural pathologies. This is both a challenge and a burden, given the long-standing colonialist stereotype about the biological predisposition of Latinxs to violence.[21]

The biological determinism behind the notion of gender violence as inherent to Latin culture fuels the notion of Latin America specifically (and other countries of the global South, more generally), as the "face of human rights violations rather than the voice of criticism."[22] Legal scholars underscore the "'cultural arrogance' in those human rights discourses that characterize violations as discrimination (US/here) and persecution (over/there)."[23]

The colonialist stereotype about violence as rooted in cultural traditions of the global South—also known as the "death by culture" metaphor—uses culture "to explain the different forms and shapes violence against women takes," as Uma Narayna so aptly put it.[24] The "death by culture" metaphor promotes the idea that the subordination of women happens in other cultures or that it is intrinsic to societies of the global South. Even the Mexican government invoked this metaphor. During Amnesty International's visit to Ciudad Juárez in 2003, one Mexican government official told Amnesty's representatives that violence against women would be difficult to stop because "machismo" is an "essential element of Mexican culture."[25]

Challenging this cultural explanation is complicated by the enormous historic weight of symbolic and discursive structures that are largely instrumental in entrenching the stereotype of violence as genetically ingrained in some monolithic Latin culture. Chief among these is the linguistic symbolism of the Spanish term *machismo* (pronounced "makismo" in some English-language circles) as the most favored English synonym for exaggerated or toxic masculinity.

The cultural explanation presupposes a static, reified and homogeneous view of culture, one that ignores the vast diversity and heterogeneity throughout the Americas. There is not one monolithic Latin culture, but dynamic, fluid, and pluriversal cultures throughout the region. Rather than an ingrained cultural predisposition, it is the colonialist legacy of socially constructed gender norms of male domination/superiority and female submission/inferiority that are at stake. These gender norms are not natural, cultural, or essential, but rather are sustained by an assemblage of colonialist heteropatriarchal institutions and transphobic and misogynist practices embedded in liberal law, the family, religion, education, media, the criminal justice system, and corporate culture. Even further, this understanding of violence does not render obsolete male victims, since they too are subjected to gendered forms of domination; nor does it absolve women from perpetuating violence.

The cultural assumption about violence as rooted in a machismo inherent to Mexican culture discounts the long historic resistance to violence, particularly the plethora of antiviolence activism in communities throughout the region. Ultimately, the cultural explanation ignores the colonialist/modernist traces of violence against human and nonhuman lives.

....

"A neologism is always a risk, even more so when it is coined at a scholar's desk," feminist philosopher Adriana Cavarero insists. "But linguistic innovation becomes imperative in an epoch in which violence strikes mainly, though not exclusively, the defenseless, and we have no words to say so or only those that misleadingly evoke concepts from the past."[26] In the past three decades, the concept of feminicide has gained traction as a sociolegal concept for describing, categorizing, and codifying gender-based violence as a serious crime in several Latin American countries. The central argument in favor of a new lexicon is based on the invisibility of gender-specific forms of violence in public discourse, academic analysis, international law (i.e., the legal category of genocide), and national penal codes (i.e., the legal category of homicide), insofar as these sociolegal discursive realms fail to account for the overlapping forms of violence that impact female bodies.

It was the feminist anthropologist Marcela Lagarde who in 1994 first referred to the killings of females in the militarized space of Juárez as *feminicidio*, although she was not the first in Latin America to use the term.[27] During the 1980s, feminist activists in the Dominican Republic referenced feminicidio in their anti–gender violence campaign throughout the region.[28]

Also in the 1990s, sociologist Julia Monárrez proposed the term "sexual systemic feminicides" to characterize the murders of women and girls in Ciudad Juárez as sexual crimes with systematic methods and a high level of impunity.[29] Lagarde and Monárrez drew from Diana E. H. Russell's early theoretical and empirical work, published in the collection *Femicide: The Politics of Woman Killing* (1992), where the US-based sociologist defined *femicide* as "the misogynist killing of women by men."[30]

In a subsequent 2001 publication, Russell and Roberta Harmes defined femicide as "the killing of females *because* they are female." This redefinition extended the concept beyond misogyny as a male motivation for the murder of women to encompass "all manifestations of male sexism, not just hatred."[31] As significant as these early feminist efforts to politicize the killing of women have been, the emphasis on the sexual politics of violence relies on patriarchy and gender as a single axis of analysis and does not adequately attend to the intersecting structures of inequality and colonial histories engendering violence. The problem with a singular focus on patriarchy and gender stems in part from an assumed universalism of social relations across historical and cultural contexts.[32]

The travels and translation of global North theory and concepts are vexed issues for feminist theorizing. Universal and ahistorical definitions of social structures (patriarchy, capitalism, modernity, etc.) and social categories (gender, sexuality, race, etc.) ignore the particularity, pluriversality, and heterogeneity of social worlds and more often repeat the epistemic violence of the colonialist project. A significant decolonial gesture is to recognize the pluriversality of structures (for instance, patriarchies rather than patriarchy) and the local (cultural) specificity of categories like gender, race, and so forth.

Objections may be raised for the reliance on social categories "anchored to race and gender" in a specific US context. As Claudia de Lima Costa explains, "race is a category that is 'read' in specific ways in different racial formations, hence the (un)translatability of the U.S. concept 'woman of color' when carried to other topographies."[33] The literal translation of *woman of color* into Spanish as *mujer de color* and Portuguese as *mulher de cor* actually means woman of African ancestry. And while the anchoring of concepts in a specific locality does not preclude their resignification, adaptation, and reappropriation to other social worlds, it is also pertinent that we account for the contextual field in which phenomena occur.

My aim is not to minimize the problems ensuing from the travels and translations of feminist theories. Yet here the concern is less about context, locality, and specificity of theory, and more about the conjuncture of historical and social forces made visible through a critical feminist approach to violence against female bodies. For "gender," as García Del-Moral argues, "is a necessary but not definitive analytical category."[34]

As Bejarano and I wrote in the introduction to *Terrorizing Women*: "Our preference for *feminicide* over *femicide* in this anthology is both political, in that we aim to advance a critical transborder perspective, and theoretical, in that we aspire to center the relevance of theories originating in the global South for the formation of an alternative paradigm (knowledge, logics, subjectivities, traditions). In taking this approach, our desire is to dismantle the colonialist formulation of Latin America as a 'field of study rather than as a place where theory is produced.'"[35] Our introduction did not explicitly focus on the structures of colonial violence, but we did adopt a critical feminist decolonial perspective that aims "to reverse the hierarchies of knowledge and challenge claims about the unidirectional (North-to-South) flows of traveling theory."[36]

Feminist decoloniality further informed our thinking about the colonialist legacy in modern law and rights. Although anticolonial wars for independence during the eighteenth and nineteenth centuries may have ended formal colonization, colonial rule continued to exert its influence and control in a reconfigured form that decolonial thinkers have termed the colonial matrix of power and the colonial/modern gender system. As feminist decolonial thinkers have taught us, colonial heteropatriarchy persists and permeates the legal, judicial, and religious institutions of the modern nation-states in the Western Hemisphere. For this reason, feminist decoloniality seeks to dismantle the persistence of social and political hierarchies founded on the racial and gendered categorization of humans.[37]

In Spanish, *femicidio* translates into "the homicide of women," according to Lagarde, thereby echoing the definition of *femicide* in the first known use of the term in a British publication of the nineteenth century.[38] Given that the gendering of homicide as *femicide* did not accurately account for the phenomenon of woman killing in Mexico, Lagarde advanced the term as *feminicidio*, "to differentiate from *femicidio* and to name the ensemble of violations of human rights which contain the crimes against and disappearances of women."[39]

As a federal legislator (2003–6) and president of the first Special Commission on Feminicide in Mexico, Lagarde drew on international human rights law to frame the killing of women as a violation of women's human rights and to highlight the complicity of the state in gender violence. We might consider feminicide as an "occluded third term," to use Eng and Puar's phrase, that upends the binary of individual versus state violence.[40]

Feminicidio means more than the killing of women based on their social or biological gender and more than the codification of the deliberate killing of women as a serious crime. Lagarde defines *feminicidio* as a "crime against humanity and genocide against women," a State Crime ("Crimen de Estado").[41] For it is the state's lack of decisive action, its failure to prevent and eradicate violence against women that explicitly and implicitly evidence its implication in gender-based violence.

Although there is a linguistic rationale for the use of *feminicidio* in a Spanish-speaking context, Lagarde's, and later Monárrez's, analysis reconceptualizes gender violence in structural and systemic terms. For Monárrez, "sexual systemic feminicides" refers to clear patterns of sexual abuse on the bodies of a third of the feminicide victims that inscribe "domination, terror, social extermination, patriarchal hegemony, social class and impunity."[42] "Sexual systemic feminicides" refers to killings of women rooted in a social context of structural inequalities based on class, race/ethnicity, religion, politics, and sexuality.[43] Here as well, the complicity of the state is expressed in the silences, negligence, omission, or collusion of authorities and institutions.

In implicating the state as a gendered institution complicit in this violence, the feminist analytics behind the use of *feminicide* over *femicide* transcends the victim-perpetrator relation for an account of how systemic and structural conditions enable violence against women. In a study on gender violence in Guatemala, Victoria Sanford considered feminicide as a form of social cleansing that implicates the state as a responsible party to the killings.[44] Also writing about Guatemala, feminist researchers Cecilia Menjívar and Shannon Drysdale Walsh have argued on behalf of the term *feminicide* over *femicide*: "We prefer the term 'feminicide' because embedded in this term is the role the state plays in these killings . . . complicity of the state through its unwillingness or inability to provide [a] prevention and response mechanism."[45]

It took decades of transnational feminist efforts to challenge the depolitical framing of violence against women as a private matter. One of the major epistemological contributions of the category of feminicide in feminist scholarship and activism is the alteration of the historic system of classification that privatized and thereby rendered invisible gendered forms of violence. Implicit in the concept of feminicide is a structural and intersectional analysis of the nature of and conditions behind gendered violence.

We redefined *femicide* and put forth the new lexicon of *feminicide* by integrating theories that connect structural causes with agential ones and emphasize the broader historical and social milieu that enables and exacerbates gender and sexual violence. The new concept of feminicide attends to the structural roots of violence and incorporates an intersectional analysis of gendered violence. As we wrote in the introduction to *Terrorizing Women*, "feminicide is rooted in political, economic, cultural, and social inequalities, including the equally significant power relations based on class, race, sexual and racial hierarchies."[46]

The redefined concept of feminicide applies to not just cisgender women but also trans and nonbinary people imperiled by gender-based violence, for victims and survivors include women and gender-nonconforming people who are exposed to bodily injury, terrorized, disappeared, or killed by virtue of being feminized.

Although we did not explicitly refer to critical race theory as an influence, our research mirrors its focus on the structural (versus individual) foundations of racism, as is evident in our argument for the structural (and systemic) basis of gendered violence. Our understanding of "how the intersecting dynamics of gender, race, class, and sexuality produce a person's experience of violence" draws from the legacy of women of color feminist activists.[47]

To be sure, women of color feminism is a generative origin for a grounded practice of intersectionality and not just to name positions of difference. Intersectionality is a way of connecting embodied forms of resistance, struggle, and refusal: "Radical feminists of color have historically troubled gender essentialism, forging over time a collective political consciousness of gender violence as always also shaped by racism, class bias, transphobia, heterosexism, and so on."[48]

In opting for *feminicide* rather than *femicide*, we proposed an understanding of violence as systemic, linked to power relations based on gender, specific to sexism, racism, classism, and heterosexualism, across multiple sites, private as well as public: the domestic realm of intimate and interpersonal relations as well as in the public sphere of state, law, judicial, and carceral institutions. Our intersectional approach considers gender-based violence in a conjuncture of state power and domination, social inequalities, and misogynistic acts. This framing of feminicidal violence as an assemblage, engendered by both individual acts and "systemic and structural forces, a multiplicity of factors and intersecting logics,"[49] allows for a broader range of possible interventions and remedies.

The contributions of structural and intersectional analytics are also palpable in our call for a departure from the personal injury model of gendered violence. Conventional analyses often consider violence against women as a matter of personal injury or the result of physical, emotional, or psychological acts committed by an individual or individuals in the private sphere—a formulation that ignores the conditions of possibility that engender violence against women. A single-axis framework such as the personal injury model disarticulates or separates out gender-based violence from the structural factors that enable and exacerbate violent acts in the first place: colonialist heteropatriarchal legal systems and institutions, authoritarian regimes, neoliberal capitalism, the militarization of social conflicts, the historic structure of impunity, rigid social norms, and, in a country like Mexico, the collusion of the state with organized crime in the creation of the feminicide machine and the "Criminal State," to use Héctor Domínguez Ruvalcaba's phrase.[50]

In grappling with the intersectional nature of power, one needs to connect the individual and the institutional, the structural and the agential. The issue is not just about physical, emotional, and psychological acts committed by individual and/or multiple actors. For injury to female bodies also ensues from state policies that expose individuals to conditions of precarity: poverty, displacement, and lack of employment, housing, and health care; limited education, social insecurity, and an unsustainable environment. In Mexico, women's experiences are mediated by class, ethnicity/race, and sexuality, and structured by the entanglement of racism, transphobia, heterosexism, colonialism, and class bias that engender feminicidal violence.

I recall that the first time I used a feminist intersectional approach to violence was during a 2001 talk in Las Cruces, New Mexico. As I noted then, "Let's face it, all women are *not* the same. As in other parts of Mexico, in the northern region, certain female bodies are held in higher esteem than others are. Although the women in Juárez were targeted for their gender, perhaps even more significant are the racial and class hierarchies that constitute their identities as women. As one of the mothers recently put it: 'For the poor there's no justice. If they'd murder a rich person's girl, they'd kill half the world to find the murderer. But since they've only murdered poor people, they treat us like dirt.'"[51]

In developing this line of reasoning, I drew from an intersectional critique of the universalizing rhetoric of all women as similarly impacted by domestic violence. "Thus, as Mrs. González reminds us," I continued, "the universalizing social category of 'gender' ignores how women are differentially positioned within overlapping systems of domination—capitalism, patriarchy, racism—and these differences in their social location mean that they/we are differentially impacted by the phenomenon of feminicide. It is their intersectional positioning as specific class, ethnic/racial, and gender subjects which makes women in Mexico particularly vulnerable to feminicide and Narco-State terror. A poor woman, an Indigenous woman, an immigrant woman is at a greater risk for gender violence than elite, white women in Mexico."[52]

The colonial operations of modern law in Mexico are rooted in Napoleonic codes rather than a common law tradition as in the United States. In this context, the intersectional as well as feminist decolonial approaches to feminicide have been useful for critiquing the state as a gendered institution, as well as for unpacking the role of colonial processes in violence (legal and judicial) against subjects whose lives are impacted by multiple structures of inequality. Despite reforms in the Mexican federal and state penal codes on gender crimes (Feminicide Law of 2007), recourse to judicial remedies for poor, Indigenous, trans people, and Afro-Mexican women continues to be limited.

As decolonial feminist scholar-activist María Lugones reminds us, "Spain and Portugal introduced an extremely dehumanizing gender system and racial system, marking all colonized people racially, as inferior by nature, and females as inferior by nature to men."[53] The colonial/modern gender system is premised on a hierarchical distinction between humans (European subjects) and nonhumans (Indigenous subjects) that designated Indigenous females as inferior to Europeans and Indigenous males.

As part of Mexico's colonial legacy, the coloniality of gender has continued to inform Mexican legal and judicial doctrine and is largely responsible for the long-standing imposition of hierarchical gender relations that perpetuates and sanctions feminicidal violence. In other words, law is a tool of the coloniality of gender, as is evident in cases of spousal murder. Until a few years ago, whenever a female spouse was murdered, the fault lessened considerably when the case involved conjugal infidelity. Known as an honor killing, literally referred to as "la razón de honor" or the "honor rationale," a husband's murder of a wife for being unfaithful is rooted in a colonial patriarchal logic of a woman's infidelity as dishonorable to the family (Holy Family/nuclear family).

Another example of the coloniality of gender and its intersectional structures of inequality is notable in the state's treatment of violence against underage female victims. In Chiapas, a state with one of the largest Indigenous populations in Mexico, the crime of kidnapping, as defined in Article 244 of the state's legal code, "to satisfy erotic sexual desire or marriage" had until recently been exempt from prosecution if the kidnapper agreed to marry the victim. In 2014, in response to feminist social and legal activism, Chiapas's legislature reformed Article 244 of the penal code, removing the marriage exemption. Chiapas was also among a handful of Mexican states in which charges for statutory rape are dropped if the perpetrator agrees to marry the victim, irrespective of (and often against) the minor's consent. The marriage exemption for statutory rape was eliminated in 2009.[54]

In her analysis of feminicides of Afro-Mexican women in the states of Guerrero and Oaxaca, sociologist Marisol Escocer makes the case for an intersectional and decolonial approach to feminicide that takes into consideration the ongoing effects of the coloniality of gender.[55] In so doing, Escocer joins a cadre of feminist scholars like García-Del Moral, whose research on feminicide of Indigenous women in Canada deconstructs dichotomous categorical thinking by incorporating intersectional decolonial frameworks to underscore the limits of "an analytic reliance on gender."[56] For Escocer, gender is not the sole condition of violent inequality operative in the murders of women in Guerrero and Oaxaca. In order to grasp the full dimensions of feminicide in Mexico, there needs to be an account of the multiple structures of inequality and colonial histories that render Afro-Mexican and Indigenous women less than human.

Feminicide of women of color is rooted in a colonialist racialized gendered discourse that conflates Afro-Mexican femininity with hypersexuality. Local police and media coverage have often resorted to stereotypes about Afro-Mexican women as sex workers to ignore accusations that they have been victims of violence. The association of Afro-Mexican women's sexuality with immorality, together with claims regarding their ability to endure high levels of pain, serve to mark them as "disposable objects . . . as well as to legitimize multiple violences against them."[57]

Besides showing the social structural and discursive processes engendering racialized gendered violence, Escocer's study points to the symbolic annihilation of Afro-Mexican victims deriving from the erasure of racialized gendered violence in official registers of feminicide cases. She writes, "There is no clarity—qualitative and quantitative—with respect to violence against racialized women, be they Indigenous or Afro-Mexican, that will account for how gender violence intersects with structural violence, historic and contemporary racisms."[58]

Contemporary research on racialized, gendered violence shows the extent to which subjects are rendered visible and invisible. On the one hand, feminicide makes visible those precarious lives, vulnerable bodies, exposed further by the intersection of power axes that structure unequal power relations—colonialist heteropatriarchy and neoliberal capitalism; on the other hand, Escocer's research documents the invisibility of these lives, the erasure of racialized gendered subjects, evident in the lack of statistical information that could provide greater knowledge and understanding about the level of impunity and violence against Indigenous and Afro-Mexican women.

....

In *Terrorizing Women*, we described the import of feminicide to analytic and legal frameworks for locating state accountability for "crimes against women's life and liberty."[59] It is to the legal aspect of feminist frameworks that I now turn.

In response to feminist antiviolence initiatives, at least sixteen Latin American countries have passed laws that criminalize feminicide. As president of the Feminicide Commission in Mexico, Marcela Lagarde spearheaded the adoption of the first feminicide law in the world. The impact of these new laws on curbing gender-based violence has yet to be determined. Even so, antiviolence initiatives that result in legal remedies remain a vexed issue for feminist politics.

My aim here is to underscore the paradoxical strategy inherent in feminist antiviolence initiatives that opt for legal and carceral remedies for gender-based violence. This paradox is nowhere more evident than in a strand of mainstream feminism that embraces a law-and-order agenda.

Sociologist Elizabeth Bernstein suggestively coined the term "carceral feminism" to describe the "commitment of [sex trafficking] abolitionist feminist activists to a law and order agenda and a shift from the welfare state to the carceral state as the enforcement apparatus for feminist goals."[60] In the struggle for gender justice, carceral feminism has adopted the punitive logic of the carceral state, as evident in demands for criminalizing rape and other forms of sexual violence through the codification of these acts into federal and international criminal law. The appeal to the patriarchal state, along with the valorization of criminal law, results in a troubling alliance between feminism and the neoliberal project of the carceral state.

As feminist legal scholars like Nancy Chi Cantalupo have noted, law is a double-edged sword. "In the context of gender, law is both a tool of oppression and of liberation," Cantalupo once explained.[61] As a tool of liberation, laws have the potential to alter entrenched patriarchal gender norms of male superiority and female inferiority through the recognition of women as equal, juridical subjects of law. Mainstream feminists in favor of criminalizing gender violence argue that these laws can potentially serve as a change agent or deterrent against future acts of violence.

The recent feminicide laws in effect treat gender violence as a crime (violation) against a woman's personhood, her physical and personal integrity, rather than as a violation of her honor or that of the family, as framed within the domestic and/or intrafamilial violence models. Specifying the crime of feminicide in this manner represents a major advance for gender justice, for these laws deprivatize or extricate violence against women from its cloister in the private sphere. In so doing, feminicide laws are designed to harmonize national laws with international feminist jurisprudence on gender violence as a human rights violation rather than as a private, family matter. This represents a major breakthrough in the realm of state-centered law insofar as feminicide laws redress patriarchal law's silences and failures to treat women as legal subjects as much as they further legal advocacy in the realm of gender-based violence against women. The principle of international law, *nulla crimen sine lege* (no crime without law), is a chief impetus behind the drive for passing laws that codify feminicide (or femicide, depending on the country involved) as a serious crime. Toward this aim, several contributors to *Terrorizing Women*, especially Marcela Lagarde, Hilda Morales, and Ana Carcedo, have spearheaded the development of these new laws.

In 1994, the Inter-American Commission of Women (CIM) adopted the Inter-American Convention on the Prevention, Punishment, and Eradication of Violence against Women (Convention of Belém do Pará), which led to the drafting of national laws on violence against women throughout Latin America and the Caribbean. Between 1994 and 2000, twenty countries in Latin American adopted laws criminalizing violence against women. However, within domestic legal frameworks, violence against women continued to be treated as intrafamilial or domestic violence and, in most cases, as violence against the honor of the family/woman—similar to the Geneva Convention's framing of sexual violence in the context of war as a violation of "women's honor." Treating gendered violence as a crime against a woman's (or her family's) honor renders violence against women in moral terms, as much as it consigns it to the private sphere, in effect making it invisible.

The recent laws on feminicide/femicide in Mexico and elsewhere alter the domestic legal framework by recodifying violence against women as gender violence, that is, as a crime against women's personhood. The feminicide laws also frame gender violence within a "structure of gender power relations rooted in masculine supremacy as well as in the oppression, discrimination, and social exclusion of women and girls," as Lagarde proposes.[62] In this respect, introducing the crime of feminicide into the penal codes is a major development in feminist jurisprudence, marking a decided shift away from an understanding of violence against women as an issue of morality to one that treats this form of violence as a violation of women's fundamental human rights to life and liberty.

The first feminicide law in the world, La Ley General de Acceso de las Mujeres a Una Vida libre de Violencia (General Law of Women's Access to a Life Free from Violence), approved by Mexico's Congress in 2006, and the 2008 law on femicide in Guatemala are instrumental to this new conceptual framing in Latin America. Just as significant is that the shift from interfamilial violence to gender violence means that women are now the juridical subject of law, rather than its object. At the same time, under capitalist liberal democracies, law and the criminal justice system function as a tool of oppression, expanding the imprisonment, policing, and surveillance power of the state.

In their remarkable critical genealogy of abolition feminism, Angela Y. Davis, Gina Dent, Erica R. Meiners, and Beth E. Richie write, "The existing criminal justice legal system assumes that justice is retributive, or that punishment is the very essence of justice, and naturalizes the assumption that the only way balance can be re-created in the aftermath of harm is by proportional punishment."[63] Even so, mainstream feminist antiviolence initiatives continue to champion carceral solutions to violence against women through the creation and promulgation of federal law like the Violence against Women Act (VAWA) of 1994 and the reforms and reauthorization of VAWA in 2000 and 2005. More recent reforms have incorporated conceptual definitions such as "date rape," protection orders for undocumented immigrants and survivors of human trafficking, and reforms to the penal code, including higher sentencing guidelines and mandatory detention orders for the accused.

As abolition feminists remind us, the development and expansion of antiviolence legislative initiatives have yet to transform the normative structure of violence nor to diminish the escalating violence against women worldwide. "Not only has violence, measured in the number of women killed and abused, continued to increase," feminist thinker Sylvia Federici recently remarked, "it has become more public, more brutal and is taking forms once seen only in times of war."[64]

The punitive response to gendered violence adopted by carceral feminism coincides with the logic of neoliberal biopower and is especially evident in the growing criminalization of social problems in the United States since the 1980s.[65] This carceral logic is a technology of control that finds its major expression in the expansion of the penitentiary system and incarceration of racialized minorities, the poor, and immigrants.

Elena Azaola confirms a similar demographic in Mexico's incarcerated population: "The prisons are not inhabited by the most dangerous criminals but by the most poor."[66] As Julia Sudbury indicates, the neoliberal logic of the prison system is not just US-based but global, representing both a technology of control and a highly lucrative enterprise.[67]

For this reason, it is urgent that we connect the impetus in favor of criminalizing gender violence to the expansion of the prison industrial complex as well as to "prominent mainstream approaches to gender and sexual violence [that] rely precisely on carceral solutions."[68] The expansion of the carceral system in the United States involves not only enormous financial costs but social ones as well, given that the emphasis is on retribution, or carceral solutions, rather than on "creating alternatives to punishment and imprisonment."[69]

The advantages of antiviolence initiatives like VAWA and the feminicide laws in terms of raising public awareness about the prevalence and severity of gendered violence are eclipsed by their shortcomings. As the composition of the prison population demonstrates, poor and especially men of color are more likely to be arrested, charged, and imprisoned for gender crimes than white middle-class or wealthy men.[70] Bernstein notes a similar scenario in the criminalization of sex work.

The strange alliance between mainstream white feminists on the left and white evangelical Christians on the right around the fight against sex trafficking and sex work has resulted in the growing incarceration of men of color. Clients of sex workers who are arrested are overwhelmingly men of color (62 percent African American; 25 percent Latino), "not because white men are not hiring sex workers, but because they are accessing the more upscale unpoliced indoor market to do so."[71] The tough-on-crime emphasis of antiviolence initiatives, including mandatory arrests and higher sentencing for perpetrators of violence, may have other unintended but equally destructive effects on the larger social world in which we live.

Psychologist and death penalty expert Craig Haney's extensive research on the dynamics of prison life offers sobering lessons about the limits of incarceration. In a compelling account of the devastating impact of the carceral experience, Haney argues that prison environments "are important sites for the production of two pernicious social evils that continue to plague our society: 'toxic masculinity' and 'persistent racism.'" The dehumanizing and degrading conditions of prison life foster pathological prison cultures that "destructively transform and psychologically disfigure the persons who are kept inside of them." As Haney adds, prison culture turns "frightened young men" who enter the carceral system into "vitriolic racists" and "raging misogynists."[72] The psychological harms inflicted on inmates by a prison culture of violent masculinity, as Haney's observations suggest, significantly diminish the likelihood of rehabilitating inmates convicted of gender-based violence. Against this backdrop, locking up violent offenders is the least optimal solution for ending feminicidal violence.[73]

Given this scenario, sanctions that derive from the criminal/punitive justice system are the least optimal for remedying social injuries for, as abolition feminists insist, punitive justice leads to greater institutional violence: "The state does not offer the solution to interpersonal violence, and existing forms of state 'protection,' including police, prisons, and social welfare programs, create more violence and harm," write Davis, Dent, Meiners, and Richie.[74]

Questioning the logic behind neoliberal equal rights discourse, María Guadalupe Huacuz notes, "What's worse, the discourse about women's rights and citizenship can be transformed into a conservative slogan that demands from the State more laws, more sentencing, and consequently, 'hard hand' with the aggressors."[75] In her critique of the codification of feminicide as a serious crime in Mexico's penal code, Lucia Nuñez concurs: "The attempts to criminalize, within the punitive code, the social phenomenon of feminicide without questioning the ideological structure of penal law results in the legitimation of an entire state system that is not only sexist and a product of patriarchy, but also classist and racist."[76]

Not all of the recent laws adopt a purely punitive approach to gender violence. For the eleven Latin American countries that have criminalized feminicide, Elena Laporta differentiates those that have adopted a penal from those with a transversal or integral approach to eradicating gender violence. The feminicide/femicide laws of Peru, Chile, Costa Rica, Ecuador, and Honduras represent "purely penal regulation," whereas Mexico, Guatemala, El Salvador,

Nicaragua, Bolivia, and Panama have opted for a more transversal or "integral focus that impacts diverse branches of the law."[77]

According to Laporta, Mexico's General Law exemplifies a more transversal or integral approach due in large measure to its emphasis on "prevention, attention, sanction, reparation and eradication of violence against women in the educational, media, health and statistical realms, as well as the creation of institutions for the eradication of violence."[78] Despite its more integral focus, Mexico adopted a stronger punitive justice approach in April 2012, with the typification of feminicide as a crime at the federal level, modifying the Penal Code and the General Law.[79]

For this reason, it is imperative that we envision and forge alternatives to feminist initiatives that privilege punishment as the fallback position and first line of defense while ignoring its social consequences. A different approach derived from the work of abolition feminists provides a crucial alternative to the punitive justice model favored by carceral feminism.[80] As Davis, Dent, Meiners, and Richie indicate, "Abolitionists today call into question the prevailing assumption that mass incarceration can be effectively addressed without analyzing the root causes of injustice and the impact [of] other systems of oppression, including, in the first place, global capitalism."[81]

We must first reject the neoliberal logic that attributes violent behavior solely to the pathology of an individual, given that the prescription of remedies for gender violence depends on how we define its causes.[82] If we consider the roots of gender-based violence to be solely personal or interpersonal, then the remedies will most likely result in punishment of the individual, including the application of punitive justice measures. On the other hand, if we treat gender violence as rooted in an assemblage of racist and heteropatriarchal structures, then there is a greater opportunity to design and develop more appropriate long-term strategies and transformative social policies.

For abolition feminists, remedies for gender-based violence cannot be found within the punitive justice system, for "turning to punishment agencies and tactics of social control will not protect women and others harmed by gender violence."[83] Abolitionist feminists emphasize the transformation of structures that foment feminicidal violence, including racial capitalism, economic and social inequalities (e.g., under- and unemployment, lack of education, lack of physical and social infrastructure), the militarization of social conflicts, hierarchical gender and race relations, and transphobia.

Abolition feminists aim to develop prevention programs and the reparation of wrongs rooted in the alternative justice models of restorative and transformative justice, as well as raising consciousness aimed at transforming injurious gender norms and fomenting strategies of nonviolence to resolve social conflicts.[84]

Women's rights defenders in many countries of Latin America are rightfully exasperated. Viewed through the prism of the escalating violence in the region, near-absolute impunity, and government indifference, tough-on-crime initiatives against gender violence, as elaborated in feminicide laws, appear at first glance to be an appropriate remedy. Yet we must remain ambivalent about the efficacy of legal remedies divorced from structural changes, a major overhaul of dysfunctional state judicial systems, the purging of widespread corruption, and the abolition of the historic structure of impunity.

In Mexico, women's human rights groups have long held that police have failed to respond to gender crimes because "they feared organized crime was involved, or because they were involved themselves, or both."[85] Police indifference to gender violence is rooted in a system of illegality so interpenetrated in the state structure that it blurs the distinction between state institutions and criminal networks, and between government agents and criminal agents.[86]

The Campo Algodonero massacre is a case in point. According to journalist Diana Washington Valdez, the autopsy of the victims in Campo Algodonero revealed that one victim had been dead for eight months while another had died three weeks before the corpses were found. The bodies of two of the victims had freezer burns, suggesting that they were kept in a refrigerated area. As Washington explains, "Only a highly organized group could carry out crimes at that scale, and with a sequence of crimes such as kidnapping, rape, torture, assassination, as well as the warehousing and transportation of cadavers. This group, apparently including the police, has been able to operate for years without being discovered. . . . It is apparent that a corrupt network of judicial functionaries, politicians, business leaders and drug traffickers have enabled the murder of women to become a sport for certain men."[87] For this very reason, abolition feminists insist that "the movement to end gender and sexual violence . . . can never be isolated from the work to end state violence, including the violence of policing."[88]

As further illustration of the precariousness of women's lives in the borderlands region, I refer readers to the image on the cover of our book *Terrorizing Women*.[89] Taken by my coeditor Cynthia Bejarano, the photograph features a protest march staged on the Mexican side of the Santa Fe International Bridge, on the site where activists placed the Ni Una Más cross memorializing the hundreds of murdered women in Ciudad Juárez.

Initially, we selected the image because it symbolizes women's agency, the resilience of mothers who weep over horrendous loss yet, despite the devaluation of their lives, courageously transform themselves from victims to human rights activists. We felt that the photograph captures their role as political actors and entangled lives as human rights defenders, mothers, sisters, daughters, and friends of the murdered and disappeared women.

The photograph pays homage to these mother-activists at the forefront of the Ni Una Más movement, first launched in 2002 as a campaign, slogan, and chant taken up by an internationalist network to end feminicide and gender/sexual violence. "Ni una más" are three words appearing in various forms on the cover of our book, as in the background, embossed on the large wooden cross that is fastened on a pink placard bearing 268 soldered nails, each representing a woman murdered in Ciudad Juárez between 1993 and 2002. Next to the cross, the slogan "Ni una más" is printed on the poster held by a woman activist. "Ni una más" adorns the pink hats of members of the Mujeres de Negro (Women Dressed in Black) feminist group that spearheaded the contra-feminicide campaign. It is these courageous women, compelled to act by the life-altering trauma of personal loss, whose lives are now threatened by the terror of feminicidal violence. Their courageous struggle to end violence is being threatened by the forces of greater terror.

Since the launch of the "new Dirty War" in Mexico, several human rights activists involved in the Ni Una Más campaign have been assassinated, assaulted, or threatened. As noted in chapter 1, Paula Flores, a prominent mother-activist, shut down her community-based operations in October 2010 after receiving numerous death and extortion threats. Her close collaborator, Eva Arce, mother of Sylvia Arce, has also been repeatedly threatened and attacked. A celebrated poet and antifeminicide activist, Eva Arce's account is featured as the first testimonial in *Terrorizing Women*.

A few weeks later, the Ni Una Más movement was stunned by the brazen murder of a prominent feminist artivist (artist/activist). On January 6, 2011, poet Susana Chávez, author of the slogan "Ni una más," was brutally assassinated by three men who sawed off her hand after strangling and mutilating her. Later that year, Malú García Andrade (featured on the upper left-hand corner of the *Terrorizing Women*'s cover) was forced to flee the city with her children after unidentified men set her house on fire. Cofounder of the activist-mothers' group Nuestras Hijas de Regreso a Casa, García first became a human rights defender after her sister, Lilia Alejandra García Andrade, was abducted, raped, and killed in 2001.

In December 2011, García's mother Norma Andrade (also cofounder of Nuestras Hijas) was shot in the chest and hands by several gunmen and remained hospitalized in serious condition for several weeks. In the militarized space of Chihuahua alone, dozens of teachers like Flor Alicia, as well as medical doctors, social service providers, journalists, and human rights activists have either been threatened or assassinated. Hundreds more have fled the area.

The Peña Nieto government's response and indifference to the disappearance of the forty-three Ayotzinapa students and a series of extrajudicial executions during his tenure exposed "serious human rights violations committed by military forces, almost all with total impunity and often demonstrating collusion between authorities and organized crime."[90] It is an open secret that Mexican armed forces are infamously corrupt and have a repulsive human rights record.[91]

The involvement of Mexican soldiers in widespread torture, disappearance, extrajudicial murders, and kidnappings is a stark reminder of the atrocious legacy of state terror. During Peña Nieto's administration, the human rights community became increasingly alarmed because the so-called war on drugs served as a smoke screen for a new Dirty War aimed, once again, at criminalizing social activism and civil dissent. Similar to the previous era, this new Dirty War is being waged against urban youth and the poor as well as members of the human rights community: labor rights and Indigenous rights activists, associations of debtors and displaced people, environmental and antiviolence groups.[92]

The criminalization of human rights activism is part of the war against women who denounce the structural inequalities resulting from neoliberal capitalism, colonialism, and heteropatriarchy. Menjívar and Walsh have documented a similar scenario in Honduras: "The State also plays a more direct role in violence used to silence women in the political arena. State agents have committed sexualized violence and participated directly in injuring or killing women."[93] The consolidation of authoritarian regimes in El Salvador, Guatemala, Colombia, and Brazil led to renewed collusion between the state and powerful interest groups. State security forces, paramilitary groups, and private security armies helmed by private corporate interests, including cartels and the extractive and trafficking industries, are responsible for a range of structural harms, including social inequalities and brutal assaults against vulnerable populations.

Women defenders of human rights are especially vulnerable. Over a decade ago, a UN report on the status of human rights defenders reiterated a long-standing concern about the "saliency of gender-based violence and other risks faced by women defenders of human rights."[94] Women advocating on behalf of gender-related issues, sexual and reproductive rights, the rights of women workers and Indigenous women, transgender and nonbinary people, and LGBTI+ defenders in the region are often sexually harassed and abused, raped, threatened, and murdered.[95] Although feminist antiviolence initiatives have multiplied alongside laws passed by governments in Latin American countries like Mexico, Guatemala, El Salvador, Peru, Chile, Argentina, and the European countries of Spain, France, and Italy, violence against women continues to escalate in every part of the world. Far from diminishing, in Mexico especially, the colonial legacies of treating women as less than human remain firmly in place.

As feminists and human rights defenders embraced intersectional struggles that refused to relegate women, Indigenous, Afro-descendants, and the poor to disposability by affirming their humanity, livelihood, and existence, the lives of activists became even more precarious. According to Global Witness, 185 women rights defenders were assassinated across the globe in 2015—of these, 122 in Latin America.[96] By June 2016, sixty women human rights defenders had been murdered: twenty-four in Brazil, nineteen in Colombia, seven in Guatemala, and at least six in Honduras.

"Modern terrorism," writes Cavarero, "makes a precise strategic choice, as is often noted, in which the killing of some aims to produce a terrorizing effect on everyone."[97] In this respect, the ongoing murders of women human rights activists expose the persistence of gender violence against women as a tool of terror in Mexico. As Julia Monárrez remarks, "Although the killers target only a few women—the most vulnerable—the message is for all women."[98]

Women's vulnerability in relation to state and corporate power increased as human rights defenders embraced collective forms of resistance and demanded changes in existing social structures. The war against women is nowhere more evident than in the pursuit of those who denounce injustices against the most vulnerable populations. In Mexico, there is now a second generation of feminicide victims along with a new wave of gender violence targeting feminists, human rights defenders, and journalists.[99]

In chapter 1 we learned about human rights activists who confronted power with courage, in light of their own vulnerability. Haunted by state violence and the retaliatory terror of paramilitary forces and organized crime, feminists and human rights defenders continued denouncing and resisting these very powers. The political stances they undertook—speaking publicly, organizing, standing up to power, naming the culpable—and their commitment to struggles for justice, equality, and freedom compounded their vulnerability in the face of the authorities and other repressive forces opposed to social change. For some activists, their courage and vulnerability has meant paying the ultimate price. "The fight for justice became a catalyst for violence," writes sociologist María Patricia Castañeda. "It is clear that any person that talks about, denounces or researches this subject becomes a target."[100] This new Dirty War in Mexico has led to the marked rise of death threats, physical attacks, murders, and attempted murders of women who speak out against violence or the pervasive impunity for human rights violations.

During Felipe Calderón's administration (2006–12), the reign of violence against journalists and human rights defenders increased dramatically, and it continued into the presidency of Enrique Peña Nieto (2012–18). From 2011 to 2017, forty-five female journalists and human rights defenders were assassinated in Mexico alone. Front Line Defenders reports that 41 percent of human rights activists murdered in Latin America during 2015 participated in eco-activism, working for environmental and land rights of Indigenous peoples.[101] For the past two decades, grassroots environmental activists have resisted drug traffickers' expropriation of farmland for the cultivation of marijuana and opium poppy crops, subjecting themselves to violent, and in many cases state-sanctioned, retaliation.

The Mexican states of Guerrero, Chihuahua, Veracruz, Nuevo León, and Tamaulipas have been particularly dangerous for feminist activists who denounce gender violence, state corruption, and organized crime. Several activists were killed for speaking out about government repression, and assaults continue unabated against those who defend rights and speak out against corruption. In Guerrero, human rights defenders have been especially vulnerable, with several women brutally murdered for denouncing violence by the state and the cartels.

In 2011, armed gunmen murdered Isabel Ayala Nava, the widow of guerrilla leader Lucio Cabañas, and her sister Reyna Ayala Nava, as they left church. The sisters were members of the Asamblea Popular de los Pueblos de Guerrero and were active in demanding justice for the disappeared during Mexico's earlier Dirty War of the 1970s. They had requested police protection after receiving multiple death threats. Also in Guerrero, at least thirty assailants murdered environmental activist Juventina Villa Mojica and her son in 2012, despite police protection, after they killed her husband and other farmers in the village of La Laguna. In October 2016, transgender rights activists Alessa Flores and Itzel Durán were murdered in different parts of the country.

In March 2018, María Luisa Ortiz, also from the state of Guerrero, disappeared after attending a friend's birthday gathering. A few days later her body was found dumped along the Iguala-Taxco highway. An activist with the Network of Women against Violence, Ortiz had been tortured and sexually assaulted. She was one of forty feminicides registered in Guerrero in the first three months of 2018.

For years Mexico has registered one of the highest murder rates for journalists worldwide, according to the Committee to Protect Journalists. Since 1994, over sixty journalists have been assassinated, and countless more have disappeared.[102] Norma Alicia Moreno Figueroa was the first female journalist killed, on July 17, 1986, for covering government corruption and collusion with cartels in Matamoros Tamaulipas.

A week before Moreno was assassinated, posters with her photo appeared plastered on walls in downtown Matamoros Tamaulipas, including one in front of her parents' home. According to retired journalist Laura Cavazos, the posters contained the following warning: "Be careful, this woman who calls herself a journalist writes lies and hangs out with women, she's a lesbian."[103]

Moreno must have seen the posters as she walked to work through the city's central district. A poet, columnist, and managing editor with the Matamoros Tamaulipas newspaper *El Popular*, Moreno wrote a column critical of Jesús Roberto Guerra Velasco, the mayor of Matamoros, with familial ties to the Gulf Cartel. Days later, a group of unknown gunmen bearing automatic weapons assassinated Moreno at the entrance of the publishing house where she worked. She was twenty-four years old.

María Elvira Hernández, journalist and editor of a weekly publication dedicated to local politics and social issues, *Nueva Linea*, was assassinated in 2010, along with her journalist husband. Journalists in other regions of the country have suffered a similar fate. Marisol Macias Castañeda of Tamaulipas reported online as La Nena de Laredo. The drug cartel Los Zetas beheaded her in 2011 and displayed her body in public as a warning to others who investigated organized crime. Dolores Guadalupe García Escamilla, anchorwoman and crime reporter for a local radio station also in Nuevo Laredo, was assassinated the following year.

In the Gulf Coast state of Veracruz, Yolanda Ordaz de la Cruz, a crime reporter who had worked three decades for *Notiver* and the newspaper *Imagén*, was viciously assassinated in 2011. The journalist's decapitated body was found two days after armed men kidnapped her. In 2012, Regina Martínez Pérez, a correspondent who wrote about political corruption and organized crime for the magazine *Proceso*, was gunned down in the state of Veracruz. Kidnapped in 2016, Anabel Flores Salazar, a crime reporter for the newspaper *El Sol de Orizaba*, was later found partly naked, hands and feet bound, her head covered with a plastic bag.

Miroslava Breach, a columnist with *El Diario Norte* in Chihuahua and the Mexico City–based newsmagazine *La Jornada*, was a highly respected journalist known for her investigative reporting on the complicity between organized crime and politicians in the state of Chihuahua. On March 23, 2017, Breach was assassinated as she was taking her son to school. At the time of her murder, she had been working on a story about cartel money laundering that was used as part of the illegal perforation of water wells and the deployment of high-tech equipment for irrigation in nine municipalities in the state of Chihuahua.

Since Andrés Manuel López Obrador won a landslide election for president in December 2018, the number of journalists killed for their reporting has remained at an all-time high. From 2010 to 2020, of the 138 homicides of journalists, over forty were murdered after López Obrador took office, according to Alejandro Encinas, Mexico's deputy interior minister for human rights.[104] To this date, "Mexico is the most dangerous country for journalists in the Western Hemisphere, and it has had that status for a long time," declared Jan-Albert Hootsen, Mexico representative for the Committee to Protect Journalists.[105] López Obrador's incessant attacks on the media for what he considers "unfavorable coverage" has made matters worse.

In August 2021, a masked man, who identified himself as Rubén Oseguera Cervantes and claimed to be the head of the Jalisco Nueva Generación Cartel, issued a death threat to the news anchor with Milenio TV, Azucena Uresti, for her "biased coverage" of cartel conflicts. In the video, circulated on social media, the leader of Nueva Generación is surrounded by several masked gunmen as he threatens Azucena directly: "I assure you that wherever you are, I will find you, and I will make you eat your words, even if they accuse me of feminicide."[106]

During his presidential campaign, as a candidate from the center-left party, Movimiento Regeneración Nacional (known by its acronym Morena), López Obrador made women's rights a central tenet of his party's platform, promising a "fourth transformation" in the creation of a more egalitarian nation, similar to the Mexican Revolution of 1910. After winning the presidential election in 2018, he appointed women to half his cabinet and named former Supreme Court justice Olga Sánchez Cordero as secretary of the interior—the first woman appointed to the second most powerful post in the federal government. In spite of these initial overtures to gender equality, López Obrador's record on the expansion of women's rights is abysmal.

As part of his cost-cutting measures, López Obrador closed thousands of government-subsidized childcare centers and one-third of women's shelters, seemingly indifferent to the alarming increase in acts of gender violence and feminicide. According to government data, 3,825 women met violent deaths in 2019, an increase of 7 percent over 2018. He abandoned his promise to eradicate gender-based violence and angered feminist activists for his dismissive and belittling response to the pandemic of patriarchal violence, telling a reporter that 90 percent of calls reporting gender violence in 2020 were false.[107]

"In Mexico it's like we are living in a state of war; we're in a humanitarian crisis because of the quantity of women that have disappeared or been killed," declared María de la Luz Estrada, director of the OCNF.[108] In 2020, roughly ten women were murdered in Mexico daily (compared to one per day in Argentina); thousands more are disappeared each year. According to Alejandro Gertz Manero, Mexico's attorney general, feminicides have "'shot up in a worrisome manner,' increasing 137 percent in the past five years, four times more than the homicide rate, which increased 35 percent during the same time frame."[109]

CONCLUSION

Every woman and girl murdered in Oaxaca has been a victim of feminicidal violence that grows, spreads and devastates our lives. Here we are, from our periphery, claiming and saying that the State failed each one of them.
#OaxacaEstadoFeminicida pic.twitter.com/drBhkMzg9h
WOMEN OF SALT (@mujeresdelasal), June 22, 2020

In this moment of total upheaval, as governments wrestle with the COVID-19 pandemic, the preexisting social pandemic of feminicidal violence continues to escape their attention, all the while ravaging communities alongside the viral pandemic. With lockdowns worldwide, incidents of gender-based violence and feminicide continue to rise, confirming the assertions of feminists who have long denounced and labeled violence against women as a pandemic, a low-intensity war waged against the most vulnerable female and feminized bodies.

The United Nations recently referred to gender-based violence as a "shadow pandemic" (even though it has been out of the shadows for some time), citing the rising rates of violence against women and girls since the outbreak of COVID-19. Calls to domestic violence crisis centers have increased by 30 percent in Cyprus, 33 percent in Singapore, and 40 percent in Argentina, according to a UN report.[110] In Mexico and Colombia, calls to gender violence hotlines grew 60 percent and 90 percent respectively in the weeks after government authorities issued social distancing recommendations.[111] Since lockdown orders, France, Spain, Germany, the United Kingdom, Canada, and the United States have all reported spikes in gender-based violence and feminicides.[112] Even in China—a latecomer to tracking gender violence cases—women's rights activists are reporting dramatic increases in domestic violence across the country in the wake of the coronavirus outbreak.[113]

In a recent interview, Daniela Inojosa, founder of Tinta Violeta and longtime feminist activist who promotes antipatriarchal initiatives in Venezuela, cited an escalation of gender violence since the country's pandemic outbreak, with feminicides increasing by 67 percent. The OCNF in Mexico recently reported that in 2020, there were 2,223 female homicides, yet only 24.6 percent of these had been investigated as feminicides. After the Mexican government issued its "quédate en casa" (stay at home) measures in March 2020, feminicide increased at an alarming rate, with 267 cases reported in April alone, the deadliest month in five years.[114]

Despite the dramatic spike in racialized, gendered violence and feminicide, Mexican authorities continue their politics of denial, indifference, and corruption that historically has fueled horrific violence, impunity, and the war against women. Notwithstanding record-setting levels of feminicide and emergency calls to gender violence hotlines following stay-at-home measures (26,171 calls in March and 21,722 in April 2020), President López Obrador has rejected meeting with women protestors and even erected a three-meter-high wall around the presidential palace to shut out the protestors' chants.[115]

Four decades prior to the COVID-19 pandemic, the Combahee River Collective penned a manifesto denouncing the unsolved murders of a dozen Black women in the Boston, Massachusetts, area. Their manifesto, titled "Why Did They Die?," was reproduced forty thousand times by the end of 1979. Writing for the Collective, Barbara Smith (one of its founding members) explained the reason she cowrote the manifesto: "What I wanted to show was that the whole thing wasn't just a racial thing and that violence against women is a *pandemic* thing."[116]

From the early days of European modernity, violence against women has been a "pandemic thing." The Catholic Inquisition launched an early war against women in the fifteenth century that coincided with the colonialist conquest of the so-called New World, the enslavement of Africans and Amerindians, and paved the way for the formation of capitalism. To this day, "sexual terrorism functions in much the same way as did the witch burnings—to inhibit, circumscribe, reorder, and in some cases, terminate the lives of women."[117]

The earlier pandemic of gender violence consolidated patriarchal dominion in Europe by demonizing women and instituting technologies of control, supremacy, and sexual terrorism—technologies that continue to threaten women through multiple forms of gender violence, including systemic sexual feminicide and serial killings. Without a doubt, impunity, misdirection, and the worldwide escalation of feminicide continue to inspire and ignite feminist organizing against violence aimed at maintaining heteropatriarchal dominion. Following in the footsteps of our First Nation Iroquois sisters who gathered in Seneca in 1590 to demand the cessation of war among nations, we must once again demand an end to the global colonialist patriarchal war against women and trans people.

POSTSCRIPT: SAY HER NAME

I grimaced upon reading the report of Rubén Espinosa's murder in Mexico City on July 31, 2015. Yet another journalist killed execution-style. A photojournalist with the agency CuartoOscuro, Espinosa had fled the state of Veracruz two months earlier, after receiving numerous death threats for, among other things, the publication of his unflattering photo of Javier

Duarte, the notorious governor of Veracruz, with ties to organized crime. Espinosa was the fourteenth journalist assassinated after Governor Duarte took office in 2010.[118]

Espinosa was not the only victim found inside the apartment located in the middle-class Colonia Narvarte. Four women—Nadia Vera, Alejandra Negrete, Yesenia Quiroz, and Mile Virginia Martín (originally from Colombia)—were killed as well, raped, tortured, hands and feet bound and like Espinosa, shot in the head with a nine-millimeter pistol.[119] From reading the headline news, one wouldn't know it was a mass killing, a massacre. Despite the magnitude of the violence against all the victims, the media focused its coverage solely on Espinosa, sparking a social media campaign, #JusticiaParaRúben, and nationwide protests, including a vigil by journalists from Oaxaca who wore masks with his face.

Shortly thereafter, Mónica Villamizar, a reporter for *Vice* news in Mexico told freelance journalist Alice Driver: "There has to be justice for these girls. [The coverage] has been focused on Rubén, but what about the women?"[120] Unfortunately, when the media finally did turn its attention to the women's murders, the coverage dealt with salacious, mostly false, details about their lives,

Police authorities and media outlets seemed bent on damaging the women's reputations: "one woman was divorced and another, a Colombian, was a model or a prostitute" who owned an "expensive Mustang." Media reports alluded to the women's promiscuity, alleging that they were partying with Espinosa—information that was later recanted by Mexican authorities. Some reported that Nadia Vera was the girlfriend of Espinosa, a statement disputed by Vera's family. Fortunately, conscientious journalists countered the misogynist tropes meant to dehumanize female victims of violence in Mexico and responded ethically to Villamizar's query, "What about the other women?"

In Francisco Goldman's article for the *New Yorker*, I learned details about Nadia Vera's political and social life. Thirty-two-year-old Vera was a social anthropologist and an activist who wrote poetry. More recently she had worked as a cultural promoter for arts organizations. While living in Veracruz, Vera joined the University of Veracruz Student Assembly and the #YoSoy132 student movement, formed in 2012 in protest of the PRI's (Partido Revolucionario Institucional) return to power with the election of Enrique Peña Nieto as president. Vera befriended Espinosa in Xalapa, Veracruz, while he was covering social movements and the repression of activists and demanding government accountability for the murder of journalist

Regina Martínez. As Goldman recounted, Vera and Espinosa "were known critics of Governor Duarte," and "each had reported receiving threats and experiencing serious intimidation" in Veracruz, before fleeing separately to Mexico City.[121]

Vera shared an apartment with two of the murdered women. Yesenia Quiroz, age eighteen, worked as a makeup artist, and Mile Virginia Martín, age thirty, was a Colombian hairdresser. The third woman, Alejandra Negrete, cleaned their apartment and regrettably came to work on the day of the massacre.

The lackluster and misleading coverage of the massacre of these four female victims is akin to the erasure of violence against women that plagues patriarchal societies. Mexico is a patriarchal society designed to protect men and their privilege. Until recently, violence against women has been ignored, treated with indifference or as a personal matter to be settled within the family. With the swelling feminist activism about the roots of violence in patriarchy and male privilege, violence against women is no longer as invisible and privatized as before. But far from diminishing, violence against women has escalated, with police authorities and the media bent on disparaging the reputation of female victims.

The disparity and misogyny evident in the case of the Colonia Narvarte massacre is similar to what often hounds victims of feminicidal violence. As freelance journalist Alice Driver reports, "These tactics—implying that women are prostitutes, partiers, or 'bad' women—are the ones traditionally used by the Mexican government and media to blame women for their own deaths."[122] The backlash against women has become more public and more brutal.

Media attention to Espinosa's death is not surprising, given the persecution of journalists in Mexico. The invisibility and disparaging of the female victims' lives is another matter. It underscores the influence and persistence of patriarchal ideology within media institutions—an ideology designed to protect and enhance male supremacy.

3   The Artist and Witness

The truth does not kill the possibility of art—on the contrary, it requires it for its transmission, for its realization in our consciousness as witnesses.
SHOSHANA FELMAN and DORI LAUB, *Testimony*

"The art of film can be used in the service of the unprotected," Lourdes Portillo once wrote in an article on *Señorita Extraviada*. "And documentary can take a stance and inform, activate, promote understanding and compassion."[1] Her highly acclaimed documentary *Señorita Extraviada* is compelled by a poetic politics and ethics aimed at transforming terror. *Señorita Extraviada* is one of the first documentaries to investigate what was once considered Mexico's number one human rights issue: the murder and disappearance of hundreds of women and girls in the violence-torn border city of Ciudad Juárez. The documentary's poetic politics encourages an understanding and compassion for the victims and survivors of human rights violations that can potentially generate relations of solidarity and political action "Our task is to communicate heart to heart, to join our forces that will put an end to violence and brutality perpetuated on those without voice," she stressed.[2]

Although its true effects may be difficult to gauge, *Señorita Extraviada* is above all driven by a desire to change the hearts and minds of its viewers. In the years following its release, Portillo became a crusader for women's human rights, screening the film before international audiences and raising awareness about the persistence of feminicidal violence in Mexico. As Portillo explains in the essay she published shortly after the release of the documentary, "I traveled endlessly, to Italy, Greece, Norway, Canada, Spain and other countries to get the word out, and to gather signatures and letters to both President [Vicente] Fox and President [George H. W.] Bush. I have spoken to influential journalists in many countries, who have taken it upon themselves to carry the banner for justice in Juárez. No foundations were willing to support this human rights crusade, so I refinanced my house in order to take a year off to do this work."[3]

Señorita Extraviada has screened before members of state and intergovernmental bodies like the European Parliament, the US Congress, and the International Criminal Court, and at human rights conferences and forums, including the Ninth World Summit of Nobel Peace Laureates in Paris. At major international and national film festivals, the documentary has garnered over twenty awards, including the Special Jury Prize at Sundance Film Festival; Amnesty International's first-ever Award for an Artist; the Nestor Almendros Award from Human Rights Watch; Grand Coral—First Prize for Best Documentary at the Havana Film Festival; and the FIPRESCI Award at the Thessaloniki Documentary Film Festival. Portillo has toured with the documentary beyond the festival circuit, screening *Señorita Extraviada* before organizing and activist groups in Latin America, the United States, and Europe. This public visibility and recognition have given Portillo a platform for bearing witness to human rights injustices on the border and denouncing the Mexican government for its complicity in terrorizing women. *Señorita Extraviada* informs its viewers about the issue of feminicidal violence in Ciudad Juárez, but it goes beyond the informative level. It incites the imagination and inspires creative participation in social action.

Early on, Portillo chose to frame the documentary's narrative in ways that explicitly echoed the organizing strategies of the mothers and other women's rights activists whose social justice campaign intensified around the time of *Señorita Extraviada*'s release, which coincided with the assassination of human rights lawyer Digna Ochoa in 2001 and the unearthing of the tortured bodies of eight women in the Campo Algodonero (Cotton Field) adjacent to the Maquiladora Association's headquarters in Ciudad Juárez. The documentary makes no pretense to objectivity but rather explicitly assumes the perspective of the activist-mothers in their demands for justice. In an early interview, Portillo discusses the social impact and role of the documentary in activist politics:

So that was really the whole intention of the film . . . to create a kind of consciousness, to incite people to act, and it did that. I think every time that the film showed someplace, people were outraged, which they should be. Everywhere I went, people wanted to know, "What can I do?" So it was at that moment that I said, "Yes, I need to figure out what they can do." And I need to have addresses, and I need to have people for them to connect with and things to do. Everywhere I went, it was always the same, you know. People wanted to do something, everywhere. There was never a screening where people didn't stand up and say, "I'm going to write a letter to the Mexican consulate." It was amazing. I remember in Quito, Ecuador, I showed the film, and an old man who's about eighty stood up and he said, "Well I'm outraged, and I think this is a vergüenza. This is shameful for the Mexican government, and today I'm going to write a letter when I get home to the Mexican ambassador. And who in this audience," he asked about two hundred people, "is going to write a letter like mine?" And they all raised their hands. It was so touching, so beautiful that people felt that kind of compassion for the girls and were willing to do something.[4]

This astounding effect of moving an audience to action is the highest mark of achievement for a political documentarian like Portillo, or, for that matter, for any political arts movement, like Latin America's Tercer Cine/Third Cinema.[5] Portillo has consistently embraced an aesthetics of social justice, illustrated by such documentaries as *Black God, White Devil* (d. Glauber Rocha, 1964), *The Hour of the Furnaces* (d. Fernando Solanas and Octavio Getino, 1968), and *The Battle of Chile* (d. Patricio Guzmán, 1975, 1976, and 1979), whose "common denominator," as one of its exponents, Argentinean filmmaker Fernando Birri, explains, is a "poetics of transformation . . . a creative energy which through cinema aims to modify the reality upon which it is projected."[6]

This chapter highlights the role of the artist as witness and the power of film to incite the imagination and inspire creative participation in social action. *Señorita Extraviada* is a portal for the experience of witnessing trauma, while it inscribes a communality of kinship and care that entails thinking beyond oneself and abandoning the notion of the individual. As witnesses to the witnesses, we (viewers) are all implicated in planetary kinship obligations and duties to something greater than the self.

In a series of conversations that spanned a decade, Portillo and I discussed the making of the documentary and the role of the artist in the politics of social justice and human rights. We explored the discursive and aesthetic strategies behind a poetics of transformation, the responsibility of the artist and the intellectual in bearing witness to state terrorism and on behalf of people suffering persecution and human rights violations. Our conversations date to the period she first decided to make a documentary about the murders and disappearances of women in 1998, the year we both began our research into the subject of feminicide on the border, and which in my case culminated in two coedited collections and numerous essays on feminicide.[7]

In presenting this reading of the film and discussion with Portillo, I too make no pretense to objectivity, nor do I assume the stance of the disinterested or distanced spectator. Not only would it be disingenuous for me to occupy or claim this position, but it is also an impossibility. I know things about the process, history, and making of this documentary due in large measure to my close friendship with its maker. My intimacy, ongoing conversations, and interviews with Portillo for over two decades have given me a unique perspective on the film, but so too has my own ongoing research on the subject and close contact with activist-mothers in Mexico, as well as my political commitment to and solidarity with the contra feminicide movement. I occupy the position of an interested and intimate spectator, and this vantage point colors and I daresay improves my reading of *Señorita Extraviada*. Yet divulging my position as an interested and intimate spectator is not meant to invalidate other possible readings of the film, for mine is simply one specific and historically situated reading of the many possible analyses of the film.

POSSESSED BY THE SUBJECT MATTER

Portillo first heard about the murders of women and girls in Ciudad Juárez from our mutual friend, filmmaker Reneé Tajima-Peña, who referred to an article written by Debbie Nathan for the *Nation* in 1997. As Portillo recalls, "Reneé said 'Look at this, I can't believe what's happening in Mexico.' I couldn't believe that all these murders went unnoticed; almost a hundred girls had been killed at that point. And Renee said to me 'Don't do this project. I know that it's very tempting for you to do, but you shouldn't do it. It's pretty scary.' So when Reneé said that it was kind of scary, I thought to myself, 'Oh this is something that I'd like to do.'"[8]

Portillo's family is from the border state of Chihuahua, and the "harrowing panorama of what might be taking place" in the border region was something that captivated and ensnared her.[9] The notion of being possessed by an idea is one that Portillo has used in another context to describe how a story takes hold of her imagination: "My world was shaken to its core, and the fear experienced by the people of Juárez became part of my own daily life for the next three years."[10]

By the time Portillo first started filming in 1999, women's rights groups had documented the cases of 162 murdered women and hundreds more disappearances. Until then, Ciudad Juárez had Mexico's highest rate of sexually violent crimes. Apart from media sensationalism about serial killers and sexual predators exterminating young women, speculation about the motives behind the killings was just as macabre: some alleged that women were murdered and disappeared by sex traffickers, others by an underground economy of pornography and snuff films, by a satanic cult, by criminal gangs for their bonding rituals, and even by unemployed men envious of women maquiladora workers. But no one knows for sure.

In her funding proposal to the Soros Foundation, Portillo mentions the "ghoulish theories that the women were victims of a crime ring that smuggles human organs into the United States for transplant surgery." Behind all this loud sensationalism, Portillo discovered "a deafening wall of silence: most people were too terrorized to speak out. The authorities, when questioned, gave only cavalier and confused responses."[11] It was "the silences, the elusiveness, the lies, the misrepresentation, the misinformation," the lack of an evidentiary basis for a conclusive story that gave Portillo the impetus for making a different type of film.

THE ART OF WITNESS

Portillo opens the documentary by declaring, "I came to Juárez to track down ghosts and to listen to the mysteries that surround them." What she discovered in the border city was the unseen presences, the unspoken violence, the unrepresentability of terror. She was so haunted by what she witnessed in the course of tracking down ghosts, so horrified by the sexualized nature of the violence and the enormity of the disappearances, by the indifference, subterfuge, and impunity surrounding gender crimes, by so much grief, fear and despair, that she invested *Señorita Extraviada* with her outrage.

"After realizing that I couldn't get to the bottom of it, it became a different thing. It became a human rights cause," she confided to María Cristina Villaseñor.[12] "Now I'm not investigating. I am witnessing and denouncing something that is unacceptable to human beings."[13] In referring to this dual purpose, witnessing and denouncing, Portillo signals the complex discursive construction of the documentary. She couldn't get to the bottom of things, couldn't produce conclusive evidence about the gender crimes, or of the identity of the perpetrators and their motives for murdering and disappearing so many women and girls. The film's ending is inconclusive and open-ended, not just by the force of Portillo's own volition but because feminicide was then (and continues to be) an ongoing phenomenon, its perpetrators and motivations difficult to pin down with categorical certainty:

> It's a never-ending story that you could go on and on with . . . so you have to finish when you know you have no money. Then the question becomes, how do you make it important, and how do you make a film that doesn't neatly tie up into an ending? I mean, that was the real challenge. And I think a lot of people that are not used to this kind of storytelling are a little bit put off by the story. You know, "You didn't solve it." . . . This is a documentary in which you cannot tie the end into a neat bow.[14]

Inability to tie the end into a neat bow freed Portillo from the documentary burden of veracity. Questions of truth and referentiality became less central to *Señorita Extraviada*'s discursive construction than, say, questions of "documentary poetics."[15] Witnessing and denouncing, as Portillo suggests, are key components of its poetics, but the witnessing dynamics inscribed in *Señorita Extraviada* are less about supplying evidentiary proof of the event or the legal act of proving than about the art of witnessing.

Portillo's coupling of witnessing with denouncing reminds me of Shoshana Felman's observations about Claude Lanzmann's *Shoah* regarding film's "capacity for witnessing."[16] The capacity of art and film to witness involves more than just the documentation of an event; it refers to the act of testifying and to art's "responsibility for truth." As Felman and Laub explain, "To testify is thus not merely to narrate but to commit oneself, and to commit the narrative to others: to take responsibility—in speech—for history or for the truth of an occurrence, for something which by definition, goes beyond the personal in having general (nonpersonal) validity and consequences."[17]

In *Señorita Extraviada*, testifying to the truth of an occurrence involves the recognition of both the literal plight of border women who have been murdered and disappeared and the general (symbolic) consequence of feminicide for the social world in which we live. To explain the documentary's

3.1 Lourdes Portillo interviewing Paula Flores. Courtesy of
Lourdes Portillo.

allegorical figuration, Portillo has cited the observations of colleagues like performance artist Guillermo Gómez-Peña, who once told her, "*Señorita Extraviada* is a metaphor for what is happening in the world today," and those of Mexican filmmaker María Novaro, who, upon seeing the documentary at its premiere in San Antonio, Texas, recognized its literal and symbolic truth: "Esta película es una bomba" (This movie is explosive), then insisted that it be screened in Mexico because *Señorita Extraviada* spoke to the truth of the government's complicity, its failure to intervene and act on behalf of its citizens.[18] In this sense, the documentary bears witness to a truth beyond the occurrence of feminicide—"something which, by definition goes beyond the personal, in having general (nonpersonal) validity and consequences."[19]

As many of us who study feminicide in Latin America maintain, the state's failure to exercise due diligence—to investigate, prosecute, and ultimately stop the killings—in effect perpetuates the historic structure of impunity, a hallmark of authoritarian regimes throughout the region. *Señorita Extraviada* does not "bring proof," as Derrida writes about the act of testifying, but rather "promises to say or to manifest something to another . . . a truth, a sense which has been or is in some way present to [her] as a unique and irreplaceable witness."[20] What is this truth or sense that has been present to her?

In the first place, there is the truth of suffering, fear, and horror that exceeds the limits of didactic documentaries, as I discuss shortly. Then there is the truth of what impunity represents. As manifested in *Señorita Extraviada*, the truth or sense that has been revealed to and by Portillo is a case of Georgio Agamben's homo sacer—bare life—of those who can be killed with impunity since, in the eyes of the Mexican state, their lives no longer count. As Portillo adds, "A poor brown woman in Mexico doesn't have a lot of value. They are worthless. They are sex objects. When you kill one woman, then there are twenty to replace her."[21] The sense of Derrida's notion of *sacramentum* or oath gestures to the truth that conjoins the witness and the addressee: "The same oath links the witness and his addressee," he writes, "but this is only an example—in the sense of justice: 'I swear to speak the truth, the whole truth, and nothing but the truth.' This oath (*sacramentum*) is sacred: it marks acceptance of the sacred, acquiescence to entering into a holy or sacred space of the relationship to the other."[22]

Portillo testifies to this reality. In accepting this oath, she commits herself and the narrative to others, and in so doing forges "intersubjective relations that ground the act of bearing witness" in human connections: between survivor/witness (addresser) and filmmaker (witness/addressee); between filmmaker (addresser) and audience (secondary witness/addressee); between survivor and audience.[23] This form of witnessing differs from and even goes against the grain of the "disengaged, guilt-ridden viewing of atrocity-as-spectacle that many forms of spectatorship take," as Anne Cubilié notes.[24] In contextualizing the historic structure of impunity, violence, and trauma, *Señorita Extraviada* calls to us in the present, to be present in the space of the "figurative witness," as witness to the witness of the atrocity of feminicide. Portillo's form of bearing witness "opens to another poetic and semantic space."[25]

This alternative poetic and semantic space involves a third way of testifying, "not in the sense of 'in favor' or 'in the place of,'" as Derrida explains, "but 'for' someone in the sense of 'before' someone. One would then testify for someone who becomes the addressee of the testimony, someone to whose ears or eyes one is testifying."[26] Kelly Oliver calls this third way of testifying "an ethical-political sense of witnessing." As she explains, "This sense of witnessing not only involves testifying to the events, observed historical facts, but also to the meaning of those events, which goes beyond what the eyes can see."[27]

Portillo is keenly aware of the film's power to act and interpret a reality "which goes beyond what the eyes can see," as well as what the ears can hear. And she recognizes the ethical-political response-ability entailed in testifying before someone about the meaning of those events. As she expressed it to me, "I think the truth for me is in the experience, in the purity of the experience. That's where it resides. If we're to understand each other as human beings, you know, we have to look at each other in the most truthful kind of way, and that has to do with our happiness and with our suffering, and with our feelings, todo lo afectivo."[28] Bearing witness in film is an image-based process, but here Portillo's form of witnessing "opens to another poetic and semantic space": lo afectivo, the affective impulse, an unseen presence and energy beyond what the eyes can see.

From the beginning of the film, Portillo insists on this other form of bearing witness—"I came to Juárez to track down ghosts"—a witnessing that demands our engagement and communion with the truth she re-presents for us. The willful infliction of harm and injury devastated an entire community, as she so compassionately puts it: "The suffering, the amount of suffering that people have gone through and which I did not capture in its totality . . . the suffering that the mothers suffered or the husbands or Maria, for example, who was kidnapped when she came back to Juárez. Yes, I'd like to go back to document the suffering of the children, the girls, the families, and how it's destroyed family after family. The destruction. It's not just five hundred girls that have been murdered. It's thousands of people whose soul has been wounded."[29]

TOUCHING VISUALITY

Señorita Extraviada makes a radical intervention into the rhetorics of the documentary. In her long, accomplished career, Portillo has demonstrated a mastery over documentary form by both embracing and rejecting the conventions of documentary realism, and by utilizing its realist aesthetics in provocative and playfully self-conscious ways. Even as she deploys well-established techniques for communicating documentary truth— interviews, actuality footage, and voice-over narration—she often interrogates the criteria for truth and accuracy in documentary, its reliance on visual evidence, as much as she directs our vision to the plurality of truths and constructedness of the image. In her earliest documentaries, the use of voice-over leaned toward the poetic and speculative, often relying on a wide array of multisensory images to conjure an experience beyond the visual and informative realms. Portillo's style is innovative in its embrace of irreverence as a technique for transcending the literal, explanatory mode for apprehending and interpreting reality. Some of her signature techniques involve playing with the narrative's linear forward-moving temporality, as well as the summoning of disqualified sources of knowledge passed on in the form of legends, gossip, canciones rancheras, corridos, myth, and proverbial wisdom.[30]

Señorita Extraviada continues and expands Portillo's distinctive documentary praxis. This time, however, Portillo eschews irreverence and playfulness for a more solemn tone, basing the factual (explanatory) parts of the narrative on journalistic sources (newspaper reports and television news), yet moving beyond the numbers and statistics. Portillo explains this desire for a "new kind of experimental approach": "I realized early on that there was no way that the footage that had been shot by other people could be used in this new approach. In discussing all this with Vivian, my editor, we realized that this film was just not lending itself to that kind of playfulness because it was so serious and so tragic. . . . You couldn't go back and forth and play with time when things were accumulating, deaths were accumulating; the numbers were increasing."[31]

The film demonstrates a unique stance toward evidence, one that sits less in the realm of factual or empirical truth and more in the domain of the truth of emotions. Here Portillo infuses explanatory documentary discourse with a poetic layer, an alternative and evocative mode of framing truth, which has even sparked criticism about *Señorita Extraviada*'s truth discourse. When the documentary was first shown in Ciudad Juárez, local authorities publicly denounced the testimony of María, one of Portillo's main witnesses, as a fabrication. Then a congresswoman in Chihuahua's Chamber of Deputies accused Portillo of "amarillismo" (yellow journalism) for allegedly perpetuating "urban legends" that attributed the murders and disappearances to the collusion of the government and the narcotrafficking industry.

In the design of *Señorita Extraviada*, Portillo envisioned a "documentary approach with visual metaphors, impressionistic B-roll footage, and exegetic sound-track to enhance the film's coherence and force."[32] She gleaned a number of visual techniques from previous documentaries. *Las Madres: The Mothers of Plaza de Mayo*, as Portillo explains, integrated black-and-white footage excerpted from an experimental film to provide a stylized representation of torture. Similar techniques are utilized for visualizing the corporeal consequences of trauma, such as the use of canted framing and elliptical editing to render a stylized representation in the scene of

María's testimonial, a survivor-witness account of the torture of women. Also from *Las Madres*, Portillo draws on photographs of the murdered and disappeared children; from *The Devil Never Sleeps*, she appropriates the inconclusive ending of a murder mystery; from *Corpus: A Home Movie for Selena, Las Madres*, and *The Devil Never Sleeps*, she borrows the requiem style of storytelling.

Making a film about an unfolding traumatic event raises concern about the ethics of trauma imagery, from the perspective of both viewing subjects and the imaged subjects. The experience of personal loss for family members had been (and continues to be) such a life-altering trauma that Portillo considered a more reverential approach to the subject matter as a way of dealing with the ethics of the image, as she adds, "Lurid pictures of the girls' dismembered bodies were published and added to the brutality of their murders. Their deaths remained no more than statistics for the press for many years. But the increasing number of murders without recourse to justice was devastating to the communities."[33]

This preoccupation with the ethics of visualizing the corporeal effects of atrocity is not Portillo's alone. There is a long-standing skepticism toward visual representations of human suffering—torture, rape, dismembered and mutilated bodies, the monstrosities of war, and so forth—in documentary photography and film, partly because, as Guerin and Hallas remind us, "no representation can begin to convey the truth of the traumatic experience."[34] Apart from this skepticism, Portillo faced the paradox of trauma imagery that Susan Sontag wrote about in the 1970s. Images may indeed figure as one of the major forms through which artists bear witness, yet, as Sontag suggests, trauma photography (and by extension trauma documentary) generates a secondary, albeit unintended effect. Writing about photographs of atrocity she encountered at the age of twelve, Sontag tells us, "What good was served by seeing them? They were only photographs—of an event I had scarcely heard of and could do nothing to affect, of suffering I could hardly imagine and could do nothing to relieve. When I looked at those photographs something broke. Some limit had been reached, and not only that of horror; I felt irrevocably grieved, wounded but part of my feelings started to tighten; something went dead; something is still crying."[35]

Sontag hints at the fine line between trauma photography and traumatic photography, a photograph that traumatizes its spectator. Photographed images of atrocity, horror, and abjection demand an ethically responsible viewing, at the same time as the viewing process itself, through repetition, familiarity, and ubiquity of the images, can inure us, produce numbness in the viewer ("something went dead"), as much as they can traumatize us ("something is still crying"). Documentary photography (and film) of atrocities inadvertently spawns indirect or ancillary (secondary) trauma in viewing subjects from the shock at witnessing the suffering of others, and tertiary trauma from our inability to intervene.

In the course of making *Señorita Extraviada*, Portillo and I talked at length about this dreadful paradox of trauma photography and film. We revisited time and time again our skepticism about images that simultaneously demand an ethically responsible viewing and corrupt the viewing process through repetition and familiarity, as Sontag indicates in the following passage: "To suffer is one thing: another thing is living with the photographed images of suffering, which does not necessarily strengthen conscience and the ability to be compassionate. It can also corrupt them. Once one has seen such images, one has started down the road of seeing more and more. Images transfix and images anaesthetize. An event becomes more real than it would have been if one had never seen a photograph. But after repeated exposure to images it also becomes less real."[36]

In our image-saturated world of YouTube and social media, the abundance (and circulation) of images of violence—what Sontag calls "image-glut"—may portend an era of social insouciance. For others, visual portrayals of human suffering are vital to the forging of a politics of solidarity and intervening in the wider political and cultural arena. "The tortured bodies of the victims were necessary," Diana Taylor writes about images of atrocity in Argentina. "They made a difference in that they made difference visible."[37] Images, in this sense, participate in the transformation of the social world.

Yet Sontag's reflection on the paradox of photographs that can both traumatize and anesthetize the viewer raises another concern regarding trauma photography: the exploitation of subjects. In an earlier critique of the work of journalist Charles Bowden, I voiced my skepticism about Bowden's decision to publish an enormously disturbing photograph of the tortured body of a young girl, which even newspapers in Mexico (notorious for publishing pornographic images of sexualized violence) refused to publish because the image was so terrifying.[38] As Bowden confesses, "the lips of the girl pull back, revealing her white teeth. Sounds pour forth from her mouth. She is screaming and screaming and screaming."[39] From my perspective, whatever Bowden's intentions, his decision to publish the image did nothing but double the abjection and victimization of this murdered young woman. Visualizing the violent procedures of torture and human suffering in cases like Bowden's is a form of traumatic pornography that compounds the exploitation and victimization of the victims of feminicide on the borderland.

Making visible the violent procedures of disappearance and torture that authoritarian states refuse to recognize may indeed make a difference insofar as it serves to rally the international human rights community, but imaging tortured bodies also undermines the full humanity of the deceased and the survivors of atrocities. The ancillary (secondary) trauma affecting viewers of atrocity is even more severe and tangible for the relatives and friends of the deceased and disappeared, who must live daily with their personal loss and the repeated experience of compounded trauma from each new announcement, media report, or image of a murdered and disappeared woman.

In the editing phases of the documentary, Portillo grappled with precisely such questions: How to convey a human story about atrocities without further dehumanizing the victims? How to denounce the abjection and desecration of female bodies without compounding the trauma of survivors? How to portray the dead without further desacralizing their image? How to do so in a manner that is respectful of their relatives' grief and honors the memories of the deceased women's existence?

Portillo abstained from visualizing images of mutilated female bodies that had been lasciviously photographed and published, because she did not want to exploit the suffering of the relatives, add to their trauma, or double the victimization of the murdered and disappeared women.[40] This refusal to show the tortured bodies of the deceased opened up a space for an alternative to image-based proof, an aesthetics grounded in embodied sensory knowledge about the impact of dehumanizing violence that did not sacrifice the veracity of the experience. "We aimed for feeling, for something evocative, something that touches you," Portillo told me. "People wanted to feel the presence of the girls and not just hear numbers and see bodies."[41] This evocation, as opposed to imaging, of the presence of the victims led to the design of a distinctive aesthetics, a "touching visuality."[42]

The quest for an alternative to the vision-centered sensory experience of film has been an enduring search for feminist film and video makers. In the early 1970s, feminist avant-garde filmmakers Barbara Hammer and Carole Schneeman first explored the sense of touch in the visual field. Hammer's film *Dyketactics* (1974) probes the erotics of the female body by appealing to a more tactile kind of vision, a style she called "experiential cinema." This emphasis on film as an embodied practice of "touching" over the modernist "privileging of sight" is crucial to a feminist aesthetics, for, as Hammer posits (riffing on John Berger's[43] "The child looks and recognizes before it can speak"), "children know the world through touching before they can ever see."[44] As an embodied practice, experiential films aim to move beyond the modernist segmentation of the senses and appeal to a full range of sensory experiences that capture what Laura Marks calls "the unrepresentable senses such as touch, smell and taste."[45]

Like Hammer, Marks theorized film as an embodied, experiential practice in her illuminating study of haptic visuality in the intercultural cinema of diasporic and exilic filmmakers like Rea Tajiri (*History and Memory*, 1991), Mona Hatoum (*Measures of Distance*, 1988), Trinh T. Minh-ha (*Reassemblage*, 1982), and Julie Dash (*Daughters of the Dust*, 1991), among others. For Marks, haptic visuality refers to films and videos that conjure a fuller range of sensory impressions, beyond optical viewing alone. Intercultural cinema qualifies as haptic because it "calls upon the memories of the senses in order to represent the experiences of people living in the diaspora."[46]

Films and videos that deploy haptic visuality encourage a "more embodied and multisensory relationship to the image" through representations that evoke memories and engage the sensual in vision.[47] The emphasis on the tactile is a sensual one, as Marks explains, "as though one were touching a film with one's eyes."[48] Its sensual effects result from the fusion of images with sound, editing, and camera movement. By gleaning from other modes of sensory experience, haptic visuality encourages corporeal closeness between the viewer and the image, one that surpasses optical viewing on its own. Whereas viewing through the eyes privileges the modernist separation between viewing subject and viewed object, haptic visuality, as Marks observes, "invite[s] the viewer to respond to the images in an intimate, embodied way, and this facilitates the experience of other sensory impressions as well."[49]

Portillo's touching visuality involves the careful design of multisensory mixes in the form of touching imagery that enhances the viewer's contemplation, vulnerability, and bodily relationship to the image. In developing this touching visuality, Portillo aims to represent the unrepresentable experiences of deep sorrow and grief in ways that invite the viewer to feel vulnerable, intimately connected to, and present in the corporeal experience of a mother's (and one father's) mourning and feelings of loss: "That was my intention for the film," she says, "for the viewer to feel rather than to intellectualize and try to figure out what's happening. We wanted it to be an experiential film. I wanted viewers to feel what it's like to be in Juárez; to feel what it's like to lose a beautiful young girl."[50]

The film mourns the loss of countless young women and girls and conveys the experience of grief through the mothers' testimonials. The viewer's sensory impressions are further enhanced by a series of lyrical images accompanied by a soundtrack of solemn Gregorian chants. First is the recurring close-up image of a flowing dress shot in slow motion as a pair of mature female hands arranges it carefully on a bed. The scene is shot in slow motion, with low-key lighting and warm tones serving to conjure the erotics of a mother's love. Throughout the film, a repetitive stream of photographs of young women and girls, with the dates of their disappearance or murder listed underneath, reappears. The movement of the camera across each photo still, to the tempo of reverential music, makes it seem as though our eyes are touching the film. The composition, repetition, and sensory enhancement of these two different types of scenes, followed by a dissolve to a black screen, invites viewers to contemplate the images on-screen. They evoke deep feelings of sorrow and appeal to our sentiments and vulnerability (more about these photographs later).

This, after all, is Portillo's intention, "for the viewer to feel rather than to intellectualize"; to make ourselves vulnerable to the image; to abandon our ocular mastery for (an)other bodily relationship between ourselves (the viewers) and the image.[51] Portillo developed this touching visuality by working closely with her production team, planning the narrative structure and techniques that would stimulate other sensory impressions. During a retrospective of her work in Madrid, Spain, in 1999, Portillo and I visited the Museo del Prado's exhibition of Goya's dark paintings, which later inspired the documentary's somber tone, as she adds: "I thought, these paintings are just astounding. And I showed Kyle [the cinematographer] the book of Goya paintings I had purchased and said, 'Look, these are the paintings. I want them to inspire us.' One of the things about those Goya paintings is the sky, that sense of doom, the sense of gloom, darkness and mystery—it's what we used for the skies in the film. You see the sky go from light to dark and these clouds passing—well, they are inspired by those Goya paintings."[52]

As Portillo explains in another context, "What the documentary does is to give you a sense of fear and claustrophobia. It starts closing in on you."[53] If Portillo had retained this ominous tone as the film's sole register, to convey the darkness of the "vortex of Juárez," as she calls it, then viewers would more likely have felt shattered and disheartened, "irrevocably grieved and wounded," as Sontag felt on seeing her first photographs of atrocity. To mitigate these feelings of distress and offset the sense of fear and claustrophobia inspired by Goya's dark paintings, Portillo resorts to counterpoint, incorporating into the film's narrative structure aesthetic techniques drawn from what I have elsewhere called "the discourse of religiosity."[54]

Portillo employs religious symbolism and iconography subversively. The strategic placement of images of crosses, montages of crucifixes and home altars, the crescendo musical score of Gregorian chants, including the solemn chant for the dead (Kyrie eleison), establish a meditative, hieratic rhythm in the film. Lourdes describes *Señorita Extraviada* as a requiem. She has, in effect, resignified the requiem into an artistic composition for the dead and transformed the solemnity of the chant for the dead into a form of healing, as a salving effect for the soul. Viewers may be subjected to the dark emotions of fear, despair, gloom, and grief but, at the same time, the film refuses to leave us with an unbearable heartache, with feelings of helplessness and distress.

A central component of Portillo's touching visuality is the emotional charge that aesthetic religiosity conjures, stemming from her own deep feelings for the subjects in her film:

> It is a very intense emotional connection between the subject and myself, one that goes beyond words. I really have no words for it. You can call it compassion, you can call it connection, you can call it understanding. There are many words that you can use. It's not even about thinking. Suddenly that moment of intense emotional connection is just happening. . . . Time just stands still, and sometimes things are just very intense and very deep, and it's an emotional connection, an understanding that happens between two people. Like the vortex that you mentioned, time does stand still.[55]

Portillo translated the energy, emotional intensity, and connection—the time standing still—into narrative form, to arrest the film's forward-moving temporality and communicate her emotional investment with the subjects of the film.

One further example of this translation is found in the placement of photographs of deceased and disappeared young women and girls.[56] The insertion of the photographs between interviews, narration, and news stories is a deliberate and calculated use of photo stills to arrest the narrative's forward momentum and mark the rhythmic pace of the documentary. As noted above, the combination of photo stills with hieratic music, camera movement, and montage makes it seem as though we are touching the images. The photographs in this sense are not just about evidence or bringing proof, as in the expository documentary. They are elements in a subjective documentary, marking Portillo's compassion, deep connection, and emotional closeness to the women and girls. In this sense, the photographs are hagiographic because they honor and sanctify the women's existence and in the process serve to calm viewers who may potentially feel traumatized by the horrific drama unfolding.[57]

In mobilizing this hagiographic effect, the photographs embody the dialectics of still life, a visual rendering of the death (absence) and life (presence) of Portillo's subjects. The dialectical tension between negation of life in the present tense of feminicidal violence (violation inscribed on the female body) and the affirmation of life in the past tense (repetitive images of radiant women and girls) punctuates the entire documentary. For Portillo, there is more to this violence and suffering. There is also the future tense of redemption. Although the photographs appear to conjure victimhood (deceased and disappeared women), they simultaneously reclaim subjecthood (the vitality and sensuality of female existence). The photographs capture moments of happiness in the women's lives, and, as such, the dialectical tension between the imaging of victimhood and subjecthood reaffirms female subjectivity more than victimization or abjection. Were it not for the opening and closing scenes, it might have been the other way around.

3.2 Un rastreo: families combing the desert in search of their loved ones. Courtesy of Lourdes Portillo.

As Sergio de la Mora writes about the opening and closing sequences, the ephemeral superimposed shots of young women in the act of witnessing the events unfolding convey women as social actors, "looking at the world as subjects rather than as objects of the gaze."[58] In opening and closing the film with these poetic, ethereal images of women's agency and subjectivity, Portillo redeems and rescues life from its nullifying death force.

THE ETHICS OF DOCUMENTARY POETICS

In our conversations about the effects of her touching visuality, this penetrating movement into the affective realm of truth, Portillo confides, "We're channeling people's feelings and we're capturing them in this great machinery. . . . We are invoking their suffering, and we're portraying it and disseminating it in the art we create. I'm being honest with you. It's our way of disseminating the truth of suffering in a way that will activate people after they see the film. That they will feel a sense of goodness from doing something."[59] In many ways, this ethical insistence for us to stand as witnesses to the dead and survivors seems very akin to the Latin American tradition of testimonios; it aims to compel the viewer to action. As in Alicia Partnoy's *The Little School*, "Distanced spectatorship is not allowed to remain the 'unmarked' default position," Cubilié tells us, "but is marked as the position that refuses the full humanity of the dead and the survivors of atrocity."[60]

Even as trauma and violence in Portillo's film exist outside the frame, *Señorita Extraviada* troubles the space of distanced spectatorship. Portillo's demand is similar to Judith Butler's call for "modes of public seeing and hearing that might well respond to the cry of the human within the sphere of appearance."[61] The film insists on our hearing and recognizing the "cry of the human," on our recognizing the humanity of "women who are being sacrificed" because, as Portillo laments, "they are viewed as worthless women. They're poor, they're brown, everything that is worthless in Mexico they personify."[62] In recognizing the humanity in the "cry of the human," Portillo reappears the disappeared and murdered women from the profoundly hidden space generated by the state's denial and erasure of feminicide. *Señorita Extraviada* recognizes violence as both a witness against life itself and against a particular kind of identity: poor, racialized women.

The documentary is a portal for the experience of witnessing trauma as much as it is grounded in a communality of kinship and care. As witnesses to the witnesses, we (viewers) are all implicated in planetary kinship obligations and duties to something greater than the self. In inscribing this communality, *Señorita Extraviada* transforms viewers into a life force of witnesses who must now bear part of the burden of responding to feminicidal atrocities and demanding justice in the borderlands.

Channeling people's feelings and disseminating the truth of suffering in a way that will activate people after they see the film reflects the long-standing aspirations of the new Latin American cinema, a poetics of transformation that "generates a creative energy which through cinema aims to modify the reality upon which it is projected."[63] This poetics of transformation calls for the overthrow of systems of domination grounded and perpetuated by violence, slavery, conquest, genocide, and feminicide. Portillo shares this understanding that images participate in the transformation of the social world:

> If you are going to talk about human rights, you can't be didactic. You have to be compassionate, you have to be humane, and you have to be emotional. You have to be all the things that make a person act on behalf of another person. How can you protect a child or denounce violence against women? With your heart. You may be saying, "Here are the human rights violations," yet it's all words. But if you show it and you see it and you feel it, then you become a part of it and it becomes a part of you.[64]

Yes, we become part of it, and it becomes part of us. We enter into the "sacred space of the relationship to the other."

Redressing Injustice

ReDressing Injustice is a collaborative arts project designed by artist-educator Irene Simmons. Installed primarily in outdoor public spaces, the dramatic art installation features hundreds of ornamented dresses hanging from pink crosses, each representing a woman or girl who was murdered and disappeared in Ciudad Juárez. An art-based form of activism or artivism, *ReDressing Injustice* originated as part of the demonstrations organized at Arizona State University in Phoenix to protest the visit of former president of Mexico Vicente Fox. Since then, the *ReDressing Injustice* project has partnered with other activist groups organizing marches and rallies, community forums, memorial events, and encuentros (encounters), and even as part of the exhibition on human trafficking at the Museum of World Culture in Sweden.

ReDressing Injustice is an example of "projects grounded in direct action and participatory training that parallel art-based forms of cultural activism."[1] Simmons developed the workshop as a method of production that involved local residents at all levels of the creative process, from donating the dresses to generating ideas for their own design and messages to drawing vivid patterns and decorating the dresses with photographs, flowers, ribbons, and so on. For Simmons, however, the workshop served primarily as a vehicle for learning and cultivating witness practices of intersubjective solidarity: "At Las Cruces [New Mexico], we had women who said that they had been victims of sexual violence. We had a woman who had just gotten out

INTER2.1 *ReDressing Injustice* workshop in Las Cruces, New Mexico. Courtesy of Irene Simmons.

of the hospital; she had been abused by her husband. A number of women said they had been raped. I felt like I had created a way of talking about it [the issue of sexual violence], and they felt they could do it. . . . They were very willing to share."[2]

In addition to women survivors of sexual violence, other workshop participants have included teenage girls held in a detention center in Phoenix, college art students, families, men, and seniors who learned about the project through media coverage. As Simmons explains, the interactions in the workshop capture the redemptive power of the collective experience:

The main objective is to educate people and the community about the issue. To get them to understand that there's this idea of impunity from justice and that it is a tragedy that these victims are being disappeared and basically not much is being done about it. Educating people about it, allowing them to digest it, and then convey what they're feeling about the issue. I don't want it to be an issue of "Is this art or not?" It is a collaborative public issue. The whole idea right from the get-go was that we wanted to get the issue out into the community . . . to draw people in and allow them to get outraged, passionate, and convey how they felt about the issue.

Community participants played a significant role in the creation and experience of the *ReDressing Injustice* project, and nowhere is this more visible than in the social interaction between audiences and the dramatic art installation. At Las Cruces, New Mexico, the installation opened with a candlelight vigil accompanied by the reading of names of the women and girls murdered and disappeared, at that time numbering close to eight hundred. Moving gently in the breeze, the life-size dresses hanging on pink crosses were aligned symmetrically in rows, evoking the presence of the women, as participants strolled and experienced the work in an open-ended manner.

Holding candles, we paced silently, entranced by the rhythmic chanting of their names. "Sylvia Arce, Elizabeth Castro, Cecilia Covarrubias . . ." The smell of paraffin coating the warm air. "Paloma Escobar Ledesma, Lilia Alejandra García Andrade . . ." The women state officials attempted to erase and disappear became apparitions.

"We were hoping it would remind people of the women's spirits," Simmons confides. "And that's what happened. The dresses came to life when they were outside." They evoked the presence of the women, "the ghosts of the body underneath," as hundreds of people walking through were completely immersed in the space created by the event. Through naming and

INTER2.2 *ReDressing Injustice* dresses on pink crosses at the
V-Day march in Ciudad Juárez. Photo by author.

redressing, the women come to be visible again, their names and bodies engraved in our memory. "María Sagrario González, Jessica Martínez Morales, Mireya Hernández . . ."

> I will literally stand out in the installation and talk to people to see how they are affected. They are devastated by it and, in a sad sort of way, that's what I'm looking for. That's a gauge for me, an emotional gauge. How is it moving people? They are not tossing it aside lightly. They are literally living through it or at least thinking about it. But for me, it's been that and the feedback I get after the installation is over. I still have people who walk up to me . . . total strangers, who know me and I don't know them, who say, "I always see those dresses hanging there. And the impact that you had on me with that issue." I think [I'm] trying to raise their consciousness of the violence against women and knock them out of their little safe, secure worlds. I tell people, "You never know whom you're going to touch who can literally stop this." I really do feel like it's a rising tide.

This "rising tide" that Simmons speaks of is animated by an ethics of reciprocity and responsibility whereby every human being is obliged to contemplate and regard compassionately the suffering of the other. Rights in this formulation are not the property of the individual bearer but entail duties and obligations to something greater than the self and beyond the state.[3]

4   The Art of Witness

There are 268 nails encircling the Ni Una Más crucifix.

Two hundred sixty-eight nails in memory of women and girls murdered in Ciudad Juárez.

After crossing the Paso del Norte International Bridge, we spot it immediately, the large wooden memory cross on the Mexican side of the border, facing traffic that passes into El Paso. It is attached to a twelve-foot metal panel and bears a placard etched with the slogan "¡Ni una más! (Not one more!), in remembrance of the women and girls.

I've stood before this memory cross on many occasions. This time, my sister Angela accompanies me, and we are both grief-stricken by its scale, the throng of six-inch spikes that once held tags with the names of the deceased women. It is a haunting sight to behold. Two hundred sixty-eight iron spikes. I try to count as I walk closer, wrap my fingers around one's surface, cold and raspy to the touch, close my eyes and try to conjure up the lives the Ni Una Más crucifix mourns.

I

"Acompañenos," is how Paula Flores phrases her plea, looking at us with those dark, pensive eyes. In May 2007, I am sitting next to my research collaborator, Cynthia Bejarano, at a feminicide conference

4.1 Memory cross at Juárez tollbooth as cars approach Paso del Norte International Bridge to El Paso, Texas. Photo by Angela Fregoso.

sponsored by Stanford University when Paula asks the audience to accompany the mothers of women and girls who were murdered and disappeared in Ciudad Juárez for monthly protests against the government.[1]

I could not refuse. As a mother, I connected deeply with Paula, who has survived a mother's most unfathomable fear: the brutal and unresolved murder of her teenage daughter, Sagrario, in 1998.

Sagrario left home on the morning of April 16 and never returned. She was not accustomed to traveling alone to work at CAPCOM, a maquiladora or assembly plant located twelve miles away from her home on the outskirts of Juárez, but recently her shift had changed from the one she shared with her father and sister, Guillermina. To get to work on time, Sagrario caught the bus at four in the morning.

The morning shift ended at three in the afternoon, and by ten, she had not returned home. Her father and sister first sought help from the municipal police, who hinted she might have eloped with her boyfriend, Andrés. Yet he was still working the late shift at the plant. The special prosecutor's office charged with investigating crimes against women proved equally dismissive, forcing the Gonzalezes to wait seventy-two hours before filing a missing person report.

For days the family searched frantically, visiting area hospitals and clinics, interviewing friends, retracing Sagrario's habitual routes. Joined by friends and neighbors, the family organized rastreos, or combing the desert area, where other female bodies had been found.

Two weeks after Sagrario disappeared, police recovered a young woman's body in the desert area known as Loma Blanca. "I took my son, Chuy, with me to the police station, and we identified the body," says Paula. "It was Sagrario. She was still wearing the company smock with her name embroidered on it." Sagrario had been stabbed five times and strangled. The body was too decomposed to determine evidence of sexual violence.

Despite the pain and anguish inscribed on her face, Paula remains a dauntless activist-mother, survivor of death threats and multiple assaults on her family, extortion attempts, menacing intimidations by incompetent and corrupt police authorities, all aimed at ending her unyielding campaign for justice on behalf of her daughter and hundreds of women who have suffered similar fates in the border city of Ciudad Juárez.

By 2007, over 450 women and girls had been murdered and hundreds disappeared in the border state of Chihuahua alone, and still the gender crimes remain unsolved and largely uninvestigated. As writer Elena Poniatowska declared in her keynote address, "Mexico is the only country where 450 assassinations of women go unpunished. The problem is impunity and misogyny."[2]

This is a story about accompaniment as an ethical force of witnessing. "Social movements grounded in accompaniment often start with a scream of social pain or a shout of solidarity in the streets," write Tomlinson and Lipsitz.[3] We heard Paula's and other mothers' screams of pain.

As news about the monthly protests spread online, in June 2007, activists from the United States heeded Paula's request for accompaniment and convened in El Paso, Texas, for the trek across the border to march along with the mothers and witness for the first of several monthly silent vigils. Inspired by the weekly protest marches undertaken by the Mothers of the Plaza de Mayo in Argentina, the mothers of Juárez pledged to march in front of the state government building that houses the Office of the Special Prosecutor for Homicides against Women until their claims for justice were validated.

The mothers made an informal plea for accompaniment, a request for our physical presence as an expression of solidarity and support. Paula confided that our presence as international witnesses "nos protegen" (will protect us) from violent attacks by state actors.[4]

Writing about the role of international accompaniment within the framework of the human rights regime, Victoria Henderson agrees: protective "physical accompaniment reduces the chances of assassination" of human rights activists.[5]

In human rights discourse, protective accompaniment involves the presence of "foreign volunteers with the dual purpose of protecting civilian activists or organizations from violent, politically motivated attacks and encouraging them to proceed with their democratic activities," Mahoney and Eguren explain.[6] These "unarmed bodyguards," to use Henderson's formulation, "can influence the dynamics of conflict by bearing witness" and supporting local activists.[7]

The paternalism behind the notion of protecting the so-called defenseless or vulnerable population should not go unnoticed, since it reproduces the unequal power dynamics of global North colonialist imaginaries and subjectivities: "International accompaniment 'may not have racism at its core,' writes Henderson, quoting Coy, "but it nevertheless 'engages the preferential dynamics of racism and it flirts with colonialism.'"[8]

4.2 International witnesses providing accompaniment to the activist-mothers in Ciudad Juárez. Photo by Angela Fregoso.

Those of us who heeded Paula's request for accompaniment did not come under the guise of international protective accompaniment. Rather, our form of accompaniment is more in line with Tomlinson and Lipsitz's notion of accompaniment as a "disposition, a sensibility, and a pattern of behavior" that involves "listening rather than speaking prematurely, and encouraging and respecting the leadership of others, rather than always presuming that role for the self."[9]

Our role as accompaniers represents an ethical force of witnessing in solidarity with the struggle of witnesses/survivors of violence and state terror: the activist-mothers. Our physical presence did not make us the main protagonists in the struggle for justice. We came to accompany, to bear witness, to affirm our participation, response-ability, and collective obligation to the contra-feminicide movement.

For over a year, my sister and freelance photographer, Angela, my research collaborator, Cynthia, and I, along with many others, accompanied the mothers and family members during these monthly protest marches in front of government buildings. Along with their demands for justice, they created a community and reclaimed public space by employing vernacular and religious cultural practices like painting crosses, installing altars, designing posters, and elaborately decorating dresses memorializing their daughters and sisters.

Starting with the brushing of crosses on pink backgrounds in 1999, mother-activists launched their initial campaign for justice for Juárez's women. Paula and her eldest daughter, Guillermina, designed the cross campaign when they founded Voces sin Eco, the first alliance of mothers of the deceased and disappeared girls and women. "We named the group Voices without an Echo because apparently no one heard their screams," Paula tells me.[10]

As part of their campaign to raise public awareness, the mothers painted black crosses over pink backgrounds on utility poles throughout the city. "My daughter, Guillermina, came up with the idea of the cross campaign," says Paula. "The first cross was painted on the twentieth of March 1999, and every time an assassinated body of a girl was discovered," Paula adds, "we'd get together to paint a cross in her memory, so that she would not be forgotten."

For Paula, the cross's pink background represents women: "because we live in a machista society and pink is usually associated with girls." Her daughter, Guillermina, shared a more pragmatic reason for their choice of pink: "When I envisioned the cross campaign, we decided to use the left-over pink paint from the painting of our house."

The black crosses on pink backgrounds are ubiquitous in Juárez, visible on many streets throughout the city. "The cross is no longer found solely in Juárez," Paula declares. "It's present worldwide. We named our group Voices without an Echo, but we've had a great echo, because throughout the world that cross represents the impunity on the part of government authorities. It stands for the memory of the girls, for the protests that continue permanently, and for our plea for respect," Paula adds. "And I have stated publicly, once the assassinations of girls and women end, I will personally remove each and every cross that we have painted on electrical poles."[11]

II

When Angela, Cynthia, and I arrive at the meeting place on the US side of the Santa Fe International Bridge, six members of the Christian Peacemakers Team (CPT) are waiting with twelve other international observers, many holding large crosses painted in the iconic pink that has come to represent the campaign for justice for the women of Juárez.

At nine in the morning, the hot air is already drifting in. It takes us longer to reach the protest site than we had anticipated. A multiracial group of eighteen individuals parading down Juárez city central, holding pink crosses—some bearing elaborately adorned dresses that symbolize a murder victim—we are a definitely noticeable presence. I wonder how the locals perceive us: As Christian do-gooders or foreign agitators? As instigators? As witnesses in solidarity with a cause? Or as defacers of the city's reputation, as the local authorities allege?

A few blocks into the city, the local police stop us to ask about the purpose of our trip. Cynthia speaks for the group: "We are here to witness a protest march in front of the special prosecutor's office." To which the officer quips, "Estamos para proveérles vigilancia" (We are here to provide you with vigilance). Just in case, Angela snaps a few photographs.

On the hour-long walk, I talk briefly to B. of the CPT, a soft-spoken, mild-mannered white man from the Midwest. "I'm with a Borderlands delegation, on a fact-finding mission to the US-Mexico border," B. tells me. "We heard about the march from Sally, so we decided to join the protest."

"I know Sally. She's a nurse who works with migrant support groups and one of the founders of Amigos de Juárez," I respond.

Along with Cynthia, Sally established the local support group to help the mothers and their families in their demands for justice. It's not surprising that the CPT would hook up with Sally. She is active in border issues, and the CPT's Borderlands Project partners with local groups working to end violence against migrants. They provide medical assistance, food, and water to border crossers and monitor the activities of the Border Patrol and vigilante groups like the Minutemen. In partnership with locally based organizations like No More Deaths Coalition and Healing Our Borders, the CPT opposes a militarized border, advocating for a comprehensive and humane immigration policy that reunites families and provides a pathway to citizenship.

When we arrive at our destination, the Office of the Special Prosecutor for Homicides against Women, Paula is the first mother to greet us. "We are so grateful you came to support us. Without the international observers here, the news media would probably ignore our demonstration."

The mothers are already installing the altar as homage to their daughters. Each family member wears a memorial T-shirt bearing the image of their loved one, the date of her murder or disappearance, and the name of the

4.3 Activist-mothers installing an altar before their protest march. Photo by Angela Fregoso.

newly formed organization Movimiento de Familias Fortalezidas para Exigir Justicia.

It is the postcards with photographs that first captivate us. Dozens of stand-up postcards bearing images of nearly alike young women: long, dark hair, a smile, a name printed to the right of each photograph: Sylvia Arce, Paloma Angelica, Miriam Cristina, Diana Yazmin—all in boldface letters. "They are meant to be mailed to the governor of Chihuahua," I tell my sister as I grab one. "See, his name and address are printed on the back, and there's a space for a personal message and a postage stamp. They were designed by the activist-mothers from the Centro de Derechos Humanos in Chihuahua City."

The postcards are casually arranged on the granite seating area that surrounds a bronze sculpture where the mothers and family members create vernacular resistance culture. They seem mindful as they collaborate to arrange the objects on their altar installation. One mother hangs her daughter's school uniform next to a white, organza-trimmed dress; another places a framed photograph above the handwritten sign with a message to the governor, demanding justice; others add their own ofrendas (offerings) to deceased loved ones: a favorite stuffed animal, posters conveying heartfelt messages, love notes on decorated hearts, a small photo of a disappeared sister in the center of a butterfly cutout, interspersed flowers, and candles—each item arranged with utmost care.

Vernacular culture as expressed in altar-making practices enables the mother-activists to share their collective grief with witnesses in a public space and create consciousness about the value of female lives in Mexico.

III

"Altar making is a female-centered practice," Laura Pérez writes. This vernacular practice represents "a terrain of female agency for indigenous mestizas . . . a space of some religious and gender freedom, as well as creativity for the socially marginal and oppressed."[12] Crafted within the domestic sphere of the home, this hybrid vernacular cultural tradition conjures up the unseen but felt presences in our lives: deceased loved ones, ancestors, and deities. The home altar is an homage to the dead, a space for meditation and memory and for invoking the spirits. It is also a private vernacular space for mourning and healing one's suffering.

In taking the vernacular tradition into the streets, the mothers of Ciudad Juárez transformed the altar into an insurgent, radical act. "They transformed the private act of suffering of victimized families into a public discourse that makes evident the absence of public standing and civil rights for the economically poor on the borderlands," as Pineda-Madrid explains.[13] In so doing, activist-mothers remade an intimate cultural practice into a communally shared one, at once spiritual and political: an offering and a protest, a space for mourning/healing and for expressing demands for justice. This convergence of the secular and the sacred reminds me of what Chicana artist Amalia Mesa-Bains once called "politicizing spirituality."[14]

Part of a broader tradition of social activism by Mexican American and Mexican communities on the border, politicizing spirituality involves the fusion of Mexican Catholic vernacular culture with public protests. Demonstrations against militarizing the border often incorporate religious practices: carrying the sacred image of the Virgin of Guadalupe, installing crosses, or lighting luminarias in honor of migrants who perish crossing the border. In politicizing spirituality, Latinx protestors draw from a religious-based morality of right and wrong to condemn US immigration and border policies and, in this case, feminicides.

IV

It is almost ten in the morning, and already nearly two hundred protestors have gathered and more are flocking in. A caravan of mothers with Justicia para Nuestras Hijas from Chihuahua City arrived early yesterday. Some bring signs with handwritten messages; others carry placards with photos of a deceased or missing loved one. An elderly couple holds a pink cardboard female silhouette with a black cross painted on its head. A dozen colorful dresses hang on pink crosses placed throughout the plaza. Yesterday, Irene Simmons, with the ReDressing Injustice project, held a workshop with mothers from Ciudad Juárez and Chihuahua City, where they decorated dresses in honor of their daughters.

The dresses on the pink crosses illustrate the transformative power of vernacular culture in activist politics. The cross symbolizes the crucifixion of Jesus Christ, but in this instance, hanging a dress on a cross disrupts its masculine meaning, as Pineda-Madrid suggests: "These practices, by publically linking female humanity to crucifixion, destabilize a male-centered Christian social imaginary."[15]

Interspersed throughout the grounds, the dresses hang on pink wooden crosses. One dress is black, layered with tiny pink crosses, the slogan "Ni una más" centered prominently; another pale pink quinceañera dress bears the name "Ana María" next to the date of her disappearance. One mother carries a schoolgirl's uniform hanging on a pink cross; another holds a black dress adorned with a bouquet of flowers. Sagrario's dress stands beside the entrance to the special prosecutor's office.

I notice Pilar and several women from Casa Amiga, the women's crisis center, lined up on both sides of the heavily traveled boulevard, holding up photo placards at cars that inch by. Drivers honk and wave in support, but one furiously yells, "Se lo merecían por como se vestían" (They deserved it because of how they dressed), to which we holler back, "Ignorante," "Sexista," "Machista."

The man's attitude does not surprise me. Many residents are largely indifferent to crimes affecting the most vulnerable members of the community. "In Ciudad Juárez, it is socially acceptable to verbally abuse a woman in public, especially if she is poor," journalist Isabel Velásquez once confided.[16] Nearly all of the women murdered and disappeared were poor.

Authorities have made it a point to vilify and blame the victims for their murders. "Your daughter led a double life: maquiladora work by day; prostitution by night." Or, as police alleged to Paula, "Your daughter probably left town with another man."[17]

Excitement builds as more protestors flock in. A dozen reporters from local and national media are mingling with the group, taping interviews with the activist-mothers. One radio journalist approaches Paula and asks, "What do you want to accomplish with these protests?"

"I want to arrive at justice. Simply. To where we see that no more girls disappear, that they don't appear dead. That's what I want to accomplish," Paula responds.

At 10:15, the mothers and family members gather at the far side of the plaza and start their hour-long vigil. We stand as witnesses, observing as the families march silently, in a single file, around the perimeter of the plaza. Paula Flores leads the group, followed by thirty other relatives, each bearing a poster with an image of their deceased relative, a handwritten demand for justice, or a dress hanging from a pink cross.

I feel the weight of their anguish and breathe deeply as my eyes begin to dampen, my heart heavy with sorrow. Some onlookers talk among them-

4.4 Prayer circle of activist-mothers after protest march. Photo by Angela Fregoso.

selves; other witnesses stare intently, their gazes appearing as stricken as my own. We are witnesses to something greater than this moment. The cross the mothers bear becomes our own. We are witnesses with a response-ability, an ability to respond to the fathomless cry of their suffering. We are witnesses to the suffering of others whose relationship to ourselves is in the bonds that suture our humanity.

V

As part of my research on gender violence in Mexico, I visited Ciudad Juárez regularly, often pausing before the cross with 268 iron spikes to recite a silent prayer for the women and girls. The Ni Una Más cross is one of the most potent and visible symbols of vernacular resistance culture. It faces oncoming traffic at one of three bridges linking the cities of Juárez and El Paso, where over 100,000 people cross the border daily. Unemployed workers from Aceros de Chihuahua, wanting to contribute to the Ni Una Más cause, assembled the cross from scrap wood ties for railroad tracks, and later a coalition of women's rights activists in Chihuahua City named Mujeres de Negro (Women Wearing Black) gifted the Ni Una Más cross to the mothers of Juárez because it embodied their collective struggles to end intolerable deaths, their sorrow, and their desire for justice and life.

On International Women's Day (March 8) 2002, Mujeres de Negro embarked on a pilgrimage they called Éxodo por la Vida, spanning 223 miles from Chihuahua City to Ciudad Juárez. Mothers, sisters, daughters, elderly and young women, housewives, students, and professionals braved the cold Arctic winds lashing the Sonoran Desert in March. The women wore black capes to mark their outrage and grief, and pink hats for life, and held a determined refusal to forget the daughters murdered in the state of Chihuahua. "An exodus is always for life," writes journalist Victor Quintana. "Its profound biblical content is just that: a departure from the land of death and slavery, the waters of the sea part and open way for the traverse of the desert and arrival to the promised land."[18]

Accompanying the pilgrims on their ten-day traverse of the Sonoran Desert—their departure from "the situation of slavery, submission and death befalling the land of assembly plants"—the cross bears witness to Mujeres de Negro's courageous trek across the desert, to prayers, chants, and songs along the way, like the "Hymn Ni Una Más" composed by longtime human rights activist Lucha Castro:

> *Paso a paso llegarán*
> *Las mujeres caminarán*
> *Rumbo a Juárez llegarán*
> *La justicia llegará.*
>
> ***Ellas gritan "ni una más"***
> ***Ellas gritan "ni una más"***
> ***Ni una más. Ni una más,***
> ***ni una más, ni una más.***
>
> *Ellas buscan dignidad, paz*
> *Justica y libertad*
> *También amor y equidad*
> *Ellas buscan solidaridad*
>
> ***Ellas gritan ni una más . . .***
>
> *Paso a paso sembrarán*
> *La conciencia expandirán*

Sembraran, sembrarán
La conciencia llegará

Ellas gritan ni una más . . .

No se cansan de gritar
Ni tampoco de luchar
Van sembrando dignidad
Y extendiendo ni una más

Not one more, they shout, not one more . . .

Transported on a pickup truck, the cross arrived with Mujeres de Negro at the outskirts of Juárez, where hundreds of supporters joined them, marching through the city streets, chanting, "Ni una más! Ni una más! Ni una más!" When they reached their destination at the Paso del Norte International Bridge, several men lifted the cross off the truck and with power tools fastened it to a large metal panel, where the wooden cross with 268 iron spikes remains to this day, facing thousands of people who cross the border daily into the "promised land."

VI

The crowds dwindled in the subsequent monthly protests. Gone were the throngs of supporters, reporters, and the festive mood of the first march. In August, six international observers accompanied the mother-activists, whose numbers had diminished from thirty to nine.

"Division among the mothers is an open secret," we are told. Turf wars, battles over leadership, tactics, and agendas—the schisms endemic to social movements—plagued Juárez's activist-mothers as well. For unknown reasons, a prominent local feminist warned one group of mothers against participating in the monthly protests.

The core group of activist-mothers remained undeterred. Paula Flores, Eva Arce, and Malú García Andrade greeted us on subsequent protests, even as they seemed disappointed by the small numbers of protestors and observers. "Few but confident," Doña Eva quipped. Paula echoed the bravura: "We may not be many [muchas] but we are machas!" We laughed, feeling heartened by their spirited tenacity.

On one occasion, the presence of federal police with automatic weapons guarded the entrance to the Public Ministry, casting an ominous shadow.

"They weren't here the last time," I whispered to Cynthia. "They're trying to intimidate the mothers," she responded, "which makes the presence of the internationals even more important."

As news spread about the government's offensive against the drug cartels, international observers were reluctant to cross the border into Juárez. A South African journalist who writes on animal rights once joined Angela, Cynthia, Sally, and me; another time, a reporter from Indy Media came along. When the government moved the special prosecutor's office miles away from the city center, only six mothers and their children participated in the silent vigil.

The vernacular practices of resistance remained unchanged: install the altar, fasten dresses on crosses to nearby trees, walk silently in a circle for sixty minutes, hold the signs or photographs in hand. Of all the monthly protests we attended, the one held in early November represented the boldest demonstration against the government's negligence. At the celebration of Days of the Dead, the mothers symbolically reclaimed public space, using vernacular cultural practices that enabled family members to be present but not consumed by their experiences of suffering.[19]

VII

After crossing the border bridge, four international observers, including my sister and me, meet Paula and drive to a designated spot on the outskirts of Ciudad Juárez, where we park on the side of the road, next to a telephone pole branded with the iconic black cross on pink. In this mostly barren spot, a village dog appears, glancing at us as it strolls across the hill behind the telephone pole before disappearing.

Half an hour later, we caravan in the direction of the Pan-American Highway connecting Ciudad Juárez with Chihuahua City—three cars and a dark blue pickup truck transporting a metallic pink cross so large its horizontal beam, with the word *Justicia* painted in black, reclines over the truck's cabin. Three women with Albuquerque's Peace and Justice Center and Amnesty International ride in the car behind us. We stop on the side of the road for Consuelo, who emerges from the colonia on a hillside. Her one-year-old daughter, Veronica, was murdered twelve years ago.

Forty minutes later, Paula announces, "Ya llegamos," pointing to a gigantic modernist sculpture in the shape of an asymetrical portal that stands above the hillside to our left, facing Ciudad Juárez's incoming traffic. Designed

4.5 Families installing the Justicia Cross beside the Umbral de Milenio monument. Photo by Angela Fregoso.

by Pedro Francisco, the Umbral de Milenio sculpture was installed at the turn of the twenty-first century to welcome visitors arriving in Ciudad Juárez. As we drive up the hill into the parking lot, I recognize several members of Familias Fortalezidas.

Amid the scrubby desert flora sits the Umbral de Milenio, anchored on a granite base, light reflectors illuminating the sculpture from below. We behold the scenic, panoramic view of Ciudad Juárez to the north, the Pan-American Highway to the west below us, and the Sierra Madre to the south. The splendor petrifies me when I think of countless female bodies dumped or buried on this torrid landscape.

On this chilly November day, the cool desert breeze tempers the sun's brightness. Close to fifty people are gathered at the Tierra Blanca park, including ten journalists, fifteen witnesses, and over twenty family members wearing memorial T-shirts, while their children's playful laughter fills the air. The mood feels somber and festive on this Día de los Muertos, when mourning the dead intersects so profusely with celebrating life.

As Paula approaches the media, she exclaims, "Today we are here to commemorate the women who were assassinated. This monument is meant as a welcome to the city, and beside it we are going to place *our* cross so that it is known that Ciudad Juárez is also the capital of feminicides." Paula continues, "The Justicia Cross is our protest to the authorities. On this Day of the Dead, we want the world to know that the crimes against women continue."

One of the reporters questions Paula about the governor's recent statement that "feminicides are a myth."

"My daughter was not a myth," Paula responds, visibly irritated. "A myth is something invented. I named her Sagrario, and I didn't invent that. In my case, there is an empty place for Sagrario, which the governor wants to erase."

"Tierra Blanca is a public park," says another reporter. "Did you receive permission to install the cross?"

Paula responds indignantly, "The government didn't ask me for permission to murder my daughter. So why should we ask for their permission?"

Paula's son-in-law, Felipe, drives the truck off the road onto an unpaved area north of the Umbral. After conferring for a few minutes, relatives work in tandem for nearly an hour. Some use shovels and pitchforks to dig a hole deep enough to bury the steel drum that holds the Justicia Cross in place. Once they finish, six women and men haul the steel drum off the truck and, after almost dropping it twice, manage to roll it into the hole, while others are mixing quick-drying cement with sand, gravel, and water in plastic tubs. A few minutes after pouring the cement mixture around the barrel, the newly affixed cross towers over its onlookers at least twenty feet above the ground, gigantic from our perspective, miniscule next to the Umbral de Milenio.

We stand next to the journalists, observing as events unfold. Before Felipe parks the truck beside the cross, a father fastens a floral wreath on it. The father, Guillermina, and Malú then climb onto the truck's flatbed and with black markers start writing on the cross the names of their female kin while Paula recites, "Sagrario González, Sylvia Arce, Veronica Castro, Lilia Alejandra . . ."

Paula's chant reverberates across the desert, drowning out the traffic's hum emanating from the Pan-American Highway below, the tone in her voice becoming more anguished with each additional name. We stand silently, our hearts heavy with sorrow, love, and compassion. When it becomes evident that Guillermina could no longer reach the cross's uppermost section, a six-foot-tall photojournalist with the Mexico City–based newspaper *Reforma* suddenly climbs on the flatbed and, moving his camera aside, grabs a marker to pen the final names on the cross.

We are tear-stricken by his act. Undoubtedly trained to remain detached and objective from events he witnesses, this photojournalist chooses not to remain indifferent, allowing himself to be stirred by compassion, to be impelled by Paula's recitation of the female victims' names echoing in the desert winds.

Our interdependence and response-ability to the suffering of others is profoundly captured in this spontaneous act of solidarity on the part of the photojournalist. This singular, heartfelt act also evidences the transformative power of vernacular cultural practices of resistance. By installing the cross and inscribing on it the names of the women and girls, activist-mothers and their supporters reclaim public space and create an alternative social imaginary in which their sufferings are transformed into communal consciousness.

After the cross installation, family members assemble the Day of the Dead altar below the cross, placing photographs of their deceased loved

4.6 The Days of the Dead altar created by families below the Justicia Cross, in honor of their deceased loved ones, victims of feminicide. Photo by Angela Fregoso.

4.7 The Justicia Cross. Photo by Angela Fregoso.

ones, teddy bears, papel picado, candied skulls, bowls of fruit and nuts, votive candles, and dozens of cempasuchitl or marigold flowers. Two parallel lines are drawn with salt on the ground, "to help in the soul's transition," Guillermina confides, as a mother places her daughter's school uniform in the center, its sleeves extending Christlike on the cross. Once the altar is complete, adults and children form a circle around the Justicia Cross and Day of the Dead altar and chant prayers for the souls of their deceased ones.

"Angela, take a picture of all of us, for our memories," Malú cries out.

Before departing, my sister Angela and I walk over to the Justicia Cross and read the words inscribed on its metallic plaque—"IN MEMORY OF ALL THE WOMEN ASSASSINATED"—followed by details about the cross campaign: "The painting of crosses began on March 20, 1999 by a group of families of the women who were assassinated in Ciudad Juárez. It is a protest against all the authorities, a demand for JUSTICE, PREVENTION AND CONSCIENCE. The pink background represents a woman and the black cross represents mourning for the women who have been assassinated in this city."[20]

As we stand there paying our final respects to the girls and women of Juárez memorialized by the Justicia Cross, I recall the soulful words of Alice Walker: "The world cannot be healed in the abstract. . . . Healing begins where the wound was made."[21]

5 Witnesses to Mexico's "Living Dead"

"Desaparecen como si las hubiera tragado la tierra" (They disappear as if the earth had swallowed them), a mother testifies on the first day of the hearing. She stands behind the podium, tightly gripping its sides, her voice cracking slightly as she recalls the events of that fatal day.[1]

"On the thirty-first of January 2009, my daughter María Guadalupe left home to buy a pair of tennis shoes," Susana Montes continues, "and when she didn't return home that evening, I went to the police station to file a missing person report. 'Wait for thirty-six hours before filing a report,' the authorities tell me. 'Your daughter will return by then. She's probably left with a boyfriend.'"

Ms. Montes pauses to regain her composure, holding back tears, but her sorrow pierces through her words. "She never returned. How can my daughter disappear into thin air?" she exclaims. "We, the families, are the ones who keep investigating. All the information that the authorities have in their files is what we've given them. After receiving an anonymous call, they found human remains, almost intact, in Arroyo Navajo (Navajo Creek). They only gave us the skull, and the DNA was positive. It was my daughter's. But what happened to the rest of her body? Apparently María Guadalupe was tied while receiving the final blow to the head."

The notice about my nomination to serve as judge came in the form of an email from Alma Gómez of the Women's Human Rights

Center in Chihuahua. "We are organizing the Hearing on Feminicide and Gender Violence for the Permanent People's Tribunal [PPT] that will take place in Chihuahua City on the twenty-first, twenty-second, and twenty-third of September. The Coordinating Committee invites you to be a judge for the Hearing."

I was eager to close a circle of fifteen years that began in 1999, when I first started to research the cases of murders and disappearances of women on the border. I accepted the invitation and waited for a month for the final approval from the president of the PPT in Rome.

The PPT is an international opinion court founded in 1979 in Bologna, Italy, to investigate and adjudicate state crimes against humanity around the world. An heir to the International War Crimes Tribunal—also known as the Russell Tribunal for its founder, Bertrand Russell—the PPT is part of the Lelio Basso International Foundation for the Rights and Liberation of Peoples.

Operating independently of state authority, the PPT hears cases related to government violations of human rights and the rights of peoples, especially under circumstances of impunity, when a government fails to apply national and international legislation to defend people's rights. Although the PPT has no legal authority, its judgments are based on international and domestic laws and can establish a legal precedent for future action.

To date, the PPT has held sessions in nearly forty countries around the world, with Mexico as its latest chapter. After years of petitioning by civil society groups, the tribunal agreed to examine cases of systematic violations of fundamental rights under the theme of "Free Trade, Violence, Impunity and Peoples' Rights in Mexico (2011–2014)," and to conduct thematic hearings, including migration rights and forced displacement, violations of labor rights, food sovereignty and genetically modified corn, the environment, the right to information and freedom of expression, the Dirty War, the status of youth, and feminicide and gender violence.[2]

The coordinating committee in Chihuahua invited me to serve as judge for the latter of these thematic hearings, and the ruling we issue will subsequently be incorporated into the final ruling of the broader PPT. In Mexico, the PPT is known as the Tribunal of Consciousness.

Chihuahua City is the capital of Chihuahua, El Estado Grande, the largest state in Mexico. Bordering New Mexico and Texas, this northern state is home to the Rarámuri (also known as Tarahumaras) and two other Indigenous peoples. Philologists have long debated the name Chihuahua's origins. For some, the name derives from the Náhuatl word *xicahua*, "dry and sandy place"; others contend that *Chihuahua* means "place where the waters of the rivers converge."

Flying across the state at an elevation of ten thousand feet, both explanations ring true. Chihuahua's terrain is vastly diverse, flanked by the rocky mountains of the Sierra Madre Occidental to the west, the spectacular rugged canyon of Las Barrancas del Cobre (Copper Canyon) to the south, the omnipresent "dry and sandy" expanse of the Chihuahua Desert, and myriad valleys "where the waters of the rivers converge."

Chihuahua City is nestled in one of these river valleys, dotted with smaller mountainous ridges. As our small commuter jet makes its final approach, storm clouds linger to the east and the sun sets to the west, while I try to locate El Cerro Grande, one of three mountains imprinted on the state's shield. A popular hiking and tourist destination, known for its splendid view of the city and intriguing caves, El Cerro Grande measures 1,900 meters, the highest elevation in the metropolitan area.

The city's topography reminds me of my father's hometown in Jalisco. The earthy tones in various shades of green, yellow, and blue-gray, pastures set against a majestic ridge of mountains and craggy rocks, home to a diverse assortment of fauna and flora, are so familiar. It's not surprising. Nine hundred miles apart, Chihuahua and Jalisco share the Pacific Ocean and the Sierra Madre Occidental mountain range, an extension of the Rocky Mountains.

As a child, I enjoyed family hikes to the Cerro de Tuxpan's shrine to the Virgen María, nestled in the craggy ledge bulging from the center of the mountain. There I'd stand, awe-inspired by the river valley that cradled the town of Tuxpan below. The distant blue-green mountains, so translucent to my child's eyes, looked like Jell-O gelatin salad mix.

My flight to Chihuahua City arrives on time, and Monica, an organizer from the Women's Human Rights Center, drives me from the airport to the hotel. A talkative woman in her forties, she entices me with stories about hiking excursions to El Cerro Grande, Sierra Mapula, and nearby Copper Canyon.

"Have you ever been to the place in the Copper Canyon where there is no sound?" I ask.

Monica looks at me a bit perplexed as she replies, "No."

"According to the writer John Phillip Santos, his grandmother told him it was one of 'the places left unfinished at the time of Creation,'" I add.[3]

The next morning, Monica drives me, along with two of the other judges, to the site where the hearing will take place, the Teatro Cámara

"Fernando Saavedra," in the city's Cultural Complex. Teatro Cámara is a modern building with large heat-reflective windows, painted in an earthy copper tone that meshes well with its surrounding desertscape. As we walk toward the Teatro Cámara, a gigantic palm tree blocks our view of the entrance, but it's the aqua-tinged banner hanging on the left side of the building that most attracts my attention.

In bold black letters, the fifteen-foot banner announces the Tribunal Permanente de los Pueblos. Mexico Chapter. Hearing on Feminicide and Gender Violences. A prominent feature of the banner is the image of a female silhouette in black, her shackled ankle breaking free from a chain. As her body floats gracefully, one hand reaches for a multicolored cluster of butterflies flying upward. A symbol of justice and freedom? How else to interpret this female image paired with somber words announcing a hearing on violence against women but as a gesture toward liberation?[4]

Once inside the Teatro Cámara, we are surprised to find the theater filled to capacity, roughly five hundred people, with dozens more standing in the back, others occupying the aisles. The atmosphere seems festive, with children running up and down the aisles, people mingling and talking. Some approach to greet and welcome us to Chihuahua. I recognize several mothers and relatives of the victims by the memory shirts they wear or the photos they hold bearing the image of a disappeared or murdered daughter, son, or husband.

The theater features state-of-the-art technology: a high-definition projector and sound system, comfortable cushioned seats, floors and walls made of acoustic material. To the right side of the stage is a podium with a microphone where the witnesses will stand to testify. On the opposite side of the stage, facing the podium, is the judge's table with our name plates: Mireille Fanon-Mendes, Cynthia Bejarano, Rosa-Linda Fregoso, Rita Segato, Sylvia Marcos. Hanging in the center above the stage is a large overhead screen projecting the banner for the hearing.

For three days we will sit in that theater space and hear testimonies from victims of feminicide, disappearances and trafficking, structural violence, forced exile, domestic violence, sexual violence, and the persecution of human rights defenders. Twenty-seven cases total.

Once the theater lights dim, we sit for the opening ceremony, as columnist Victor Quintana walks to the podium and dedicates his welcoming remarks to the Tribunal of Consciousness.

Welcome to the land that made feminicide visible to the world. In Chihuahua there are now over two thousand cases of feminicide. Welcome to the land that ranks fourth in domestic violence, to one of the fifteen worst cities to live in. Welcome to the entity that is number one in suicides, that ranks thirty-third in conditions of well-being for Indigenous peoples. Welcome to the land of a predatory mining industry and dispossession of Indigenous land. Welcome to the land where the Dirty War against narcotrafficking converted itself to a war against civil society, in particular against women. . . . There are ten thousand orphans, 230,000 displaced people. Women represent war booty for one or another gang. . . . In Mexico, it is more dangerous to be poor, female, and young. Neoliberalism has created the conditions presented before this tribunal. Under neoliberalist development, women are the most vulnerable of the collective. They have been reduced to disposable humans. . . . Welcome to the most authoritarian state in the nation, the state that ranks last in the development index. Welcome to the nightmare, welcome to a trip into the heart of darkness.

As Victor castigates the government, feelings of distress and anxiety swell up inside me, so I turn my gaze to the large screen projecting the uplifting banner of female liberation, a shackled ankle breaking free from its iron buckle as she pursues the butterflies in their journey toward justice and freedom. The shackles of oppression and subjugation are not indestructible. They have been broken in the past, are broken every day, can be broken tomorrow, I remind myself. It's the only way to endure Quintana's sardonic welcome and dystopic portrait of the state of Chihuahua.

Chihuahua illustrates the crevasse between nature and society, a breathtaking topography at odds with a horrific social reality. Why can't landscape inspire harmony and conviviality among humans? How does a state with such abundant natural beauty become "the nightmare . . . a trip into the heart of darkness"?

My father was fond of quoting Mexican dictator Porfirio Díaz, who once said, "Poor Mexico, so far from God and so close to the United States." This best describes the sad misfortunes of Chihuahua, a border state whose strategic location favors access to the lucrative US market demand for illicit goods. Long under the reign of the Juárez Cartel, for the past two decades other Mexican cartels have been vying for Juárez's monopoly over drug and human trafficking.

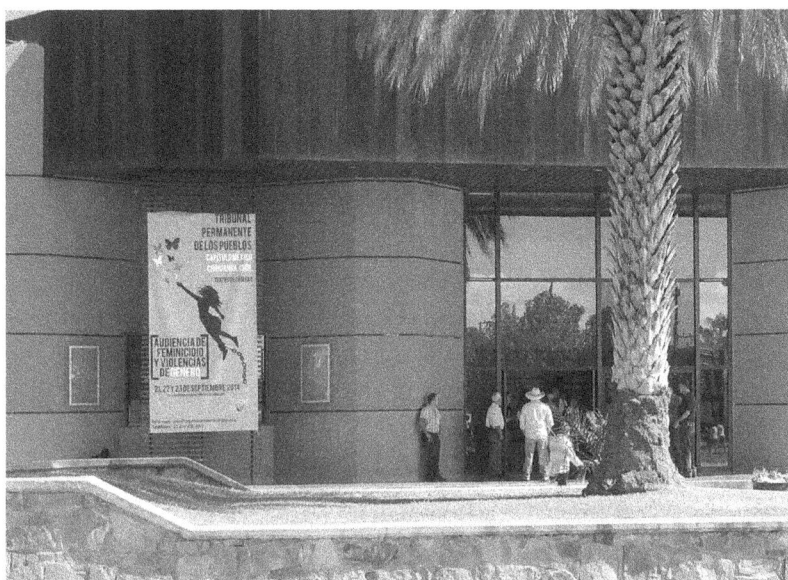

5.1 Poster for the Hearing on Feminicide and Gender Violence, Teatro Cámara "Fernando Saavedra." Photo by author.

In 2008, former Mexican president Felipe Calderón exacerbated the bloody conflict when he militarized the fight against Mexico's drug cartels. Funded by the United States through Plan Mérida, Calderón's Operation Chihuahua involved the deployment of thousands of soldiers and military police to the border region. As a result, violence and criminality reached pandemic proportions, alongside a disturbing trend of human rights violations committed by the very same security forces sent to restore order. Chihuahua is today home to two of the fifty most dangerous cities in the world: Chihuahua City and Ciudad Juárez. With 3 percent of the nation's population, the state was the site of 18 percent of the nation's homicides between 2007 and 2012, one of the highest murder rates in Mexico.[5]

Of the twenty-seven cases presented before the tribunal, most originated in Chihuahua, a state that gained international notoriety in 1993, the year women's rights groups first noticed a spike in female homicides. Violence against women has risen even more dramatically since the militarization of the region.

In 1993, a woman was murdered roughly every twelve days; a year after the launch of Operación Chihuahua in 2009, every 2.74 days; and in 2011, one per day. The state registered a total of 2,178 female murders in twenty years, roughly 108 annually, and hundreds more disappeared. Although the levels of social violence and insecurity have touched the lives of everyone, its impact has been most devastating for women.

The mother walks gingerly to the podium, a nervous tinge seeping through her voice as she begins her testimony. "Good morning, judges. My name is Norma Laguna, mother of Idali Juache Laguna, who disappeared in 2010, the twenty-third of February."

Mrs. Laguna speaks softly into the microphone, words budding from her heart, recounting without notes or prepared remarks a story she knows by heart about the disappearance of her daughter. "I am the mother of eight children. My daughter dreamed of going to college and playing professional futbol. Her dreams were shattered on the day they took her.

"The authorities didn't do their job. When human remains were found at El Navajo [Navajo Creek] in 2011, the authorities did nothing. It was the families who investigated. They said the remains belonged to Idali. I didn't accept their DNA results. Even though we had no money to pay, we asked the Argentinean Forensic Team for a second expert opinion, and on the sixteenth of April 2012, the DNA came back positive. It was Idali."

She pauses, holds back tears, and regains her composure. "They held my daughter captive for two years at the Hotel Verde, drugged her and forced her into prostitution. That's where all the other girls were kept. The municipal police know about it, but they never investigate. They treat us worse than animals. The disappearance of our daughters is a social catastrophe!" Mrs. Laguna cries out.

Her words repeatedly ring inside my head. "The disappearance of our daughters is a social catastrophe!" To maintain the semblance of impartiality, I restrain the surging tears and rage, my urge to scream, "Yes, I agree with you, Señora Laguna. Disappearance is not natural; it's a man-made catastrophe, an atrocity of the highest order against humanity." Remembering pranayama breathing, I inhale deeply until the rage subsides. I turn to my right and notice the judge beside me, tears streaming down her cheeks as she stares intently at the witness.

The tribunal examined the case of Idali Laguna under the category of Enforced Disappearance and Trafficking. In Chihuahua, 2,222 women disappeared in four years from 2008 to 2014, and evidence suggests that many abductions are linked to human trafficking.

It is the families who led the investigation into the Navajo Creek case. They unearthed the sordid facts preceding the killings: the young women were secretly abducted, held in captivity, and forced into prostitution. Two years after the last woman disappeared in 2011, the General Magistrate's Office of the state of Chihuahua announced the arrest of twelve men linked to the human trafficking industry. "The municipal police knew" where the "girls were kept," as Mrs. Laguna testified. They knew, "but they never investigated."

Among the nineteen female remains discovered in the Valley of Juárez, Idali's was one of twelve bodies dumped along El Arroyo Navajo. Seventeen of the nineteen were teenagers between the ages of fifteen and nineteen; two were in their twenties. All disappeared within the span of three years, 2008–11.

Disappearance is a categorical term. Unlike a missing person, whose absence may be willful, the disappeared is a person secretly abducted, taken into custody, or deprived of liberty against her or his will, by agents of the state or by "persons or groups of persons acting with the authorization, support, or acquiescence of the state." The denial of any knowledge about the person's fate and whereabouts hinders his or her recourse to legal remedies, as noted in the Inter-American Convention on Forced Disappearances (1994).[6]

The liminal existence of the disappeared is captured in the words of the head of Argentina's military junta, General Jorge Videla, who once said of persons detained during the military rule of the country (1976–83), "They are neither dead or alive, they are disappeared [desaparecidos]."[7] General Videla's troubling, cynical, and audacious pronouncement helped introduce the term *disappeared* into the human rights lexicon as a term for state-sponsored abductions and killings of civilian participants in movements that challenged the military's rule and authority.

During the Dirty Wars of the 1970s and 1980s, authoritarian regimes throughout the region disappeared political opponents in order to terrorize the general civilian population into submission. Thirty thousand disappeared in Argentina; forty thousand in Guatemala; twenty thousand in Chile; and thousands more in Brazil, Uruguay, Peru, Colombia, and Mexico.

The demise of military regimes in Latin America did not end the practice of disappearing political rivals, nor have their sole targets been groups that challenge the government's political goals and objectives. In the 1990s, other powerful actors linked to organized crime began deploying disappearance as a terror tactic against rivals and private citizens and as part of the lucrative trade in enslaved humans. Sometimes they act alone, other times in collusion with state agents.

Disappearing persons is widespread in Mexico today. In a report presented to the tribunal by the Citizens-led Forensic Project, over thirty thousand persons have disappeared since the government militarized its fight against narcotrafficking in 2006, with over five thousand disappeared in 2014 alone. By some estimates, 80 percent of disappeared persons are men, yet women are by far the "invisible victims."[8]

A large group of mostly women bearing somber expressions file onto the stage, an "I search for you always" placard with an image of their loved one hanging by a black string around their necks. Three women and one man walk to the center of the stage and roll out a banner with the words "PEDIMOS MEMORIA PARA NUESTROS DISAPARECIDOS" (WE DEMAND MEMORY FOR OUR DISAPPEARED) scrolled in capital letters above dozens of photographs of disappeared relatives. From my seat at the hearing, I count 116 photographs and thirty family members onstage.

The witnesses representing Chihuahua's disappeared reside in the municipality of Cuauhtémoc, located in the southern region. With 4.5 percent of the state's population, Cuauhtémoc has 13 percent of its disappeared persons, the highest percentage in the state. The municipality is a gateway to El

5.2 Families representing the disappeared of Cuauhtémoc, Chihuahua. Photo by author.

Triángulo Dorado, the meeting point of the states of Chihuahua, Sinaloa, and Durango. Named after the Golden Triangle of Southeast Asia, Mexico's poppy- and marijuana-producing Golden Triangle is considered a Juárez Cartel stronghold. According to documents presented to the tribunal, organized crime has infiltrated many of the local governments and municipal police.

"Women are the invisible victims," insists Gabino Gómez as he introduces the twenty witnesses who will testify in the Cuauhtémoc case. A prominent community leader and advocate for land, environmental, and women's rights, Gómez looks like he belongs in a Mexican border movie. Short and husky, he wears a big mustache, white sombrero, and black plaid western shirt typically worn by Chihuahua's cattle ranchers.

Flanked by family members on both sides of the podium, Gómez describes how women bear the greatest consequences: "They pay the price for living in this war-torn region. They are psychologically traumatized when masked commandoes abduct their loved ones," he continues. "The mothers take charge of the household and the detective work; they demand justice; they endure threats against their lives; they suffer never-ending trauma from knowing that their loved one is a disappeared person who does not exist legally, 'neither dead nor alive.'"

"Good morning is not for us," is how Olaya Dozal, mother of Alejandra, begins her testimony. "We are victims of the authorities, the greatest liars and dissemblers because they do nothing. I located the culprit, gave the authorities his name, and they did nothing."

Dozal continues, "The authorities have violated our peace, our right to health, because we suffer from different health problems. They have violated us with torture, constant torture, because our loved ones are always on our minds—when we eat, when we sleep, when we bathe. The authorities have violated our right to life, because we don't live; we survive."

Another woman walks to the podium. A placard with seven photographs below the words "I search for them always" hangs from her neck. "My name is Emma Muñoz. My entire family was abducted on the nineteenth of June 2011. Seven of them: my husband, four children—three sons, one daughter—a nephew, and a grandson. We were fighting with the municipal police for failing to protect us, and this is what they did to us. Help us find our loved ones."

Ms. Muñoz sobs quietly as she ends her horrific account. I can hardly take notes or remember what she is wearing. My hand moves automatically, recording words and names. I sit trembling, so distraught by what the women are recounting that my eyes fixate on the witness stand, but I can barely describe what I'm seeing.

"My son Alan and his father, José, disappeared in 2011. They know who the culprits are, and nothing has been done," says a mother who prefers to remain anonymous.

"Chihuahua is a lawless state," says Araceli Cerros, whose son disappeared in December 2013.

"My son, Luis Carlos Hernández, was a student who disappeared four years ago on the twenty-second of May 2010. Armed men took him outside our home. I followed the car until another car blocked my path. Since then I've been fighting for the truth, for justice, for an investigation. Perhaps you will be our voice," Leticia Sánchez pleads.

"It's been one year, nine days, and eight minutes since my twenty-two-year-old daughter disappeared," Sara Patricia Vásquez says hesitantly as her face looks toward us, beseeching, anguished.

Lilia Fragoso recounts the disappearance of her husband, David Fuentes, in February 2013, along with nine others who worked for the Canadian mining company Diabras de México. "The government doesn't listen to us. We ask you to be our voice. To live this way is a struggle—it isn't living." Her fear and desperation are audible in every word.

"My brother disappeared six years ago," says Ana Caridad Ruíz. "We have faith in divine justice. It can't take away my mother's pain. The pain she suffers, I can't take it away. We are muertas en vida [living dead] because we don't know the fate of our loved ones. I ask that this testimony doesn't stay here in the Teatro Cámara. I ask that it goes out into the world."

The litany of accusations and pleas for succor stun the audience into a silence that seems interminable save for the occasional chants of solidarity that pierce our accumulating sorrow: "Vivos los llevaron. Vivos los queremos." (Alive they were taken. Alive we want them.)—chants alleviating pain.

The judges are so overcome with emotion, it's as if we all share one heart, one soul. "What horror!" "Unbelievable!" "So much injustice." "So much bloodshed devastating the country." We whisper among ourselves.

The Chihuahua testimonies are followed by cases from the northern states of Nuevo León and Coahuila.

Sister Consuelo Morales represents the Citizens in Support of Human Rights in Nuevo León, an independent group that tracks disappearances and human trafficking in the state. "We have a humanitarian crisis in Nuevo León," she begins. "Over twelve hundred persons have disappeared, 324 from 2009 to 2014," she tells us. "More than 20 percent are women.

"In this region, women are currency. Women are sexual objects. Women are war booty. And I'm also here to tell you about the institutional violence suffered by women when their loved ones are disappeared. They are revictimized by the authorities who ignore them, call them 'madwomen.' Yes, they are mad. Mad from love, mad from pain and injury."

Modest and unassuming, Sister Consuelo speaks boldly: "Women are terrorized because disappearance is a mechanism of terror, perpetrated by organized crime, the military, and the municipal police."

Rosario Cano next testifies that the municipal police of Torreón Coahuila took her son and his car into custody in July 2013, and to this day they deny knowing his fate and whereabouts. "We have all been tortured psychologically. . . . I thank you for listening, so that our voices will be stronger—the voices of my sisters in pain."

A mother with red hair in a ponytail, wearing a light blue suit, lenses resting on her head, nods to the staff from the Human Rights Center Fray Juan de Larios. "Thanks to the unrelenting warrior women who have supported me," Alma García states. "My son disappeared, and my husband died of sadness. My legal advocates at the center have not let me fall. I am a believer: I believe in God, in the Virgin Mary, I believe in you. Help us find our loved ones," she implores. "Because many of us are muertas en vida [living dead]."

My heart aches and my stomach cramps to hear the mother refer to herself as "living dead." These sisters in pain, these "living dead" mothers, remind me of the "invisible," as the Zapatistas call the poor, the campesinos, the Indigenous peoples, human beings treated as disposable, as though lacking in dignity and rights to their full humanity. "Ay México," I seethe inside, "so much pain and so much suffering, but human dignity and the rights of people are not yours to give and take." For the families of the disappeared, "It's an issue of truth and human dignity," says Ernesto Schwartz of the Citizens-led Forensics Project. The families deserve the right to truth and to mourn their dead, "to go to a grave with a name."

As the second day of testimonies concludes, the systematic violations of human rights and the rights of people are indisputable; the ethical and moral obligations of the PPT, unequivocal. We received the affidavits two days before the hearing, and I completed the reading during the ten-hour trip from Oakland to Chihuahua City. There is a stark difference between reading and listening to the testimonies. The mind can wander from the written text, gloss over graphic descriptions of violent acts, close the text, and return to it later.

Listening to a mother detail the agony she feels over the disappearance of her daughter is far more distressing; mothers who identify as muertas en vida, heartbreaking. The presence of the witness in the flesh is fully sensorial. In her presence, the truth of her pain becomes palpable, as her body heaves, the labored breathing holding back tears to make way for words. Listening, truly listening, and witnessing entails a meeting of hearts, the imagining of oneself in her place.

During the Q&A session, each of the judges takes turns expressing gratitude to family members for their resilience and bravery. We have no qualms about expressing our solidarity. After all, we are the Tribunal of Consciousness, the people's court, and not a judicial tribunal set up by the government; we are here to witness, validate, and respond to civil society's demands for justice.

There is no pretense to objectivity and impartiality among the judges. We took Monsignor Raúl Vera's dispatch to heart: "Listening to these outstanding people is the most important task of the tribunal," the Bishop of Saltillo implored us during the opening ceremony "to be hopeful over helpless, for the proof that there can be a different world is that we are all here."

To be hopeful rather than helpless about the possibility for a different world seems such a distant goal in Mexico, where authorities are so corrupt and indifferent to human suffering that the wrongdoers are not held accountable and continue to commit even more crimes against humanity; and in a country where the border between lawbreakers and law enforcers has become so blurred.

During the Q&A session, I posed this question: "Several of you spoke about knowing the identity of the culprits behind the disappearances. Would you mind sharing their identities here with us, or are you risking your life by doing so?"

One response haunts me to this day, from the mother who spent four years pleading for the arrest of the men who took her daughter: "The majority of the perpetrators are men, young men. They are the same ones: agents of the state by day; sicarios [hired assassins] by night." Her assertion is not so far-fetched.

The prohibition against disappearance is now an established norm under international law. Finalized in 2006, the universal treaty known as the International Convention for the Protection of All Persons from Enforced Disappearance entered into force in 2010. That same year, Mexico signed the treaty. But what good has come of the government's compliance with international law? Ninety percent of the cases of disappearance remain unsolved, and evidence of direct and indirect involvement of state agents keeps mounting.

In its report on disappearances in Mexico, Human Rights Watch distinguishes between two forms of disappearance. Enforced disappearance follows the definition set out in the 2010 UN treaty, which includes the deprivation of liberty against the will of the person; the involvement of state agents, either directly or indirectly through authorization, support, or acquiescence; and the refusal to disclose the fate and whereabouts of the person concerned. For disappearance only, there does not need to be "compelling evidence of the direct or indirect involvement of state agents."[9] But is such a legalistic definition useful in a country where subterfuge is the government's modus operandi?

Human rights groups have for years documented rampant impunity for crimes against civil society, corruption at all levels of government, and the involvement of security forces—the military, federal police, and municipal police—in flagrant human rights violations: torture, arbitrary arrests, and extrajudicial killings. Agents of the state moonlighting as sicarios may seem like a plot in a low-budget movie, but it's the state of affairs in a country that many Mexicans are calling a narco-state.

Three days after the tribunal hearing ended, news broke about the abduction of forty-three students from a rural teachers' college in Ayotzinapa, Guerrero. The mostly Indigenous campesino students traveled to the city of Iguala to commandeer several private buses for their trip to Mexico City, where they would join in the annual march commemorating the Plaza de Tlatelolco massacre of 1968, when the paramilitary force, Batallón Olimpia, gunned down three hundred student protestors and arrested hundreds more. Once in Iguala, municipal police and masked gunmen charged the Ayotzinapa students, killing six people, injuring scores of others, and detaining forty-three students.

The Peña Nieto government's response to the disappearance of the forty-three Ayotzinapa students "exposed its absolute incompetence, the lack of political will to tackle the crisis, and the indifference with which [his] government treated all instances of human rights violations."[10] A year after the disappearance of the students, the Interdisciplinary Group of Independent Experts for the Ayotzinapa Case (GIEI), appointed by the Interamerican Human Rights Commission, issued a 560-page report that contradicted the "verdad histórica" (historic truth) issued by Peña Nieto's attorney general, Jesús Murillo Karam. Detailing numerous failures, omissions, and inconsistencies in the government's official investigation, the GIEI alluded to a collusion between security forces (the military, federal, state, and municipal police) and organized crime.[11] To this day, the bodies of the students have never been found.

While the case of the Ayotzinapa forty-three has sparked global protests and heightened awareness of disappearances in Mexico, the canary in the coal mine appeared in the early 1990s, when women's rights activists first documented an alarming trend of killing and disappearing women and girls in the border city of Juárez. The Ayotzinapa forty-three may be the tipping point for Mexico's human rights crisis, yet the case of disappeared women and girls follows a similar pattern that is "characterized by state secrecy, state links to organized criminal organizations and official cover-up."[12]

During the three days of the tribunal, we heard repeated references to the police and military's long history of violating human rights with impunity, to the complicity of the state authorities with organized crime, to cartel infiltration at all levels of government, to a narco-máquina (narco-machine) currently ruling Mexico. It became exceedingly difficult to determine whether agents of the state or organized crime groups were perpetrating crimes against humanity. Sometimes, agents of the state were just letting massacres happen, as we learned from the Creel Massacre.

Father Javier Ávila and Lluviana Armendáriz testified about the assassination of twelve young men, mostly students, and one baby. On August 16, 2008, the young men walked to a vacant lot on the outskirts of the small town of Creel, after attending a horse race, when a squad of armed men drove up and, without warning, fired high-powered weapons at the group. Several men escaped; however, twelve were killed, including a year-old baby, shot point-blank in the face.

Father Ávila had just ended Mass when the massacre occurred and immediately accompanied the families and other residents to the killing field. "Before being a priest, one is a human being," he confides. "It was a Dante-esque scene . . . bodies torn to pieces. The police didn't come to the scene until four or five hours later. We learned that the municipal police and the CIPOL [the state police] left town shortly before the massacre occurred."

After three days of hearing evidence and accusations from civil society groups, we are sequestered for hours in a conference room of the hotel, drafting the preliminary ruling. We work through dinner until midnight and convene for breakfast, working through lunch. Following the template provided by the PPT, we synthesize the cases, determine the responsible parties, and finalize the preliminary ruling. The fine-tuning of the document is left for a later date.

Our ruling is based on Mexico's failure to defend fundamental human rights as inscribed in domestic and international legislation, conventions, and treaties signed by the Mexican government. Although a legal framework guides our work for the PPT, its legitimacy is people-centered, as its founder, Senator Lelio Basso, once explained. "The needs of public consciousness can become a recognized source of law." The PPT is described as "an innovation in law and politics" because it "emanates directly from popular consciousness" rather than from "institutionalized power." For Basso, "only a truly popular initiative can try to bridge the gap between people and power."[13] In this sense, the Tribunal of Consciousness affirms a moral and ethical obligation to the rights of the people, rather than a purely legalistic one.

Once we finalize our ruling and agree on its basic contour, we board a van to the city center, where we will render our findings in the plaza facing the governor's palace.

Known as the plaza of the Cross with Nails, the plaza is packed with people. Rarámuri women dressed in native attire stand next to mestizo relatives wearing memory T-shirts with photos of their loved ones and next to dozens of media crews and journalists holding notepads, cameras, or digital recorders.

I feel nervous for the first time since participating in this tribunal, unnerved by the thought of condemning the Mexican government before national media. The monumental responsibility hits me, its full meaning catalyzed here, in this moment. It's as if time stands still.

Our table is placed next to the cross with nails, erected in 2003 by local activists to protest the government's negligence and impunity surrounding the violence, murders, and disappearances of women. Here we are, eleven years later, rendering judgment for these very same crimes against women.

The day is cooler than usual but sunny enough to wear our sunglasses. We will read sitting at a small table with a purple tablecloth, a flower arrangement resting on the ground, victims' relatives standing behind us holding large ten-foot crosses. The one with the words *abogados asesinados* (assassinated lawyers) next to another cross for land rights attorney Ernesto Rábago Martínez, with the words "we ga'ra rejoi"—"good man" in Rarámuri—"Defender of Human Rights of the Indigenous People," catches my attention. I sense the power of the people standing behind us—so

5.3 Tribunal judges present their final ruling in front of the governor's palace. Photo courtesy of author.

dignified and solemn. We share a microphone, taking turns reading portions of the ruling:

> The tribunal condemns the Mexican state and its governments . . . agencies, legislative, administrative, and judiciary bodies responsible for the public safety and security of women, for the procurement of justice . . . the prevention, investigation, and prosecution of crimes against women, as well as the authorities obliged to promote, respect, protect, and guarantee the human rights of women, as well as to prevent, investigate, sanction, and repair their violations.
>
> The tribunal condemns state and municipal governments accused in these hearings . . . for establishing and maintaining a legal and institutional framework that permits grave violations of women's human rights, as recognized under different international treaties . . . for its direct and indirect participation, by acts or by omission, in perpetrating feminicide, enforced disappearances, trafficking, and violence, which impede women in Mexico from exercising their rights, liberty, and a life with dignity; for not preventing the violation of women's human rights . . . for failing to investigate gender crimes . . . for not prosecuting

public authorities who cover up and silence crimes against women, thereby consolidating a general climate of impunity . . . for disparaging the value of women and for failing to recognize their work on behalf of human rights, for criminalizing their work as human rights defenders and causing their assassination. . . .

The tribunal condemns the transnational corporations denounced in these hearings and listed in the general accusation, including the mining industry, banking industry, and financial groups for contributing and aggravating a climate of violence against women, and for failing to recognize their fundamental rights. . . .

The tribunal condemns local and national media for violating the right to be informed and to communicate; for minimizing and silencing the crimes and egregious violations perpetrated against women.

After reading our judgment, we place a plaque at the bottom of the cross with nails, with these words engraved: "The Mexican State is guilty of the feminicides and gender violence, for failing to guarantee the life, dignity, work, and liberty of women."

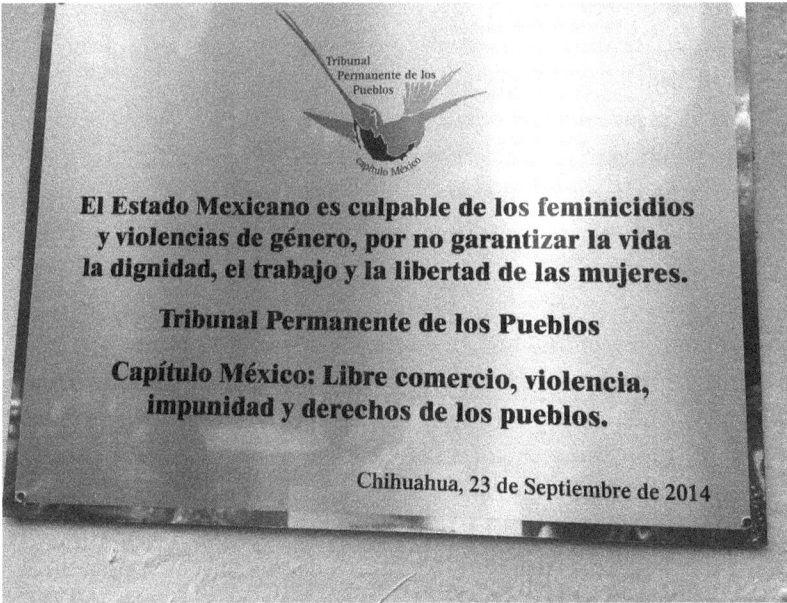

5.4 Plaque with final ruling placed on the cross with nails.
Photo by author.

For my return flight, a young woman who works at a domestic violence shelter drives me to the airport in a van. We talk about the shelter's clients, the challenges facing women who leave violent relationships, the capacity-building services provided by the shelter.

When I arrive at the ticket counter, a friendly young woman in her twenties, wearing a blue company uniform, greets me with a huge smile as I hand her my passport and itinerary. After printing my boarding pass, she instructs me to accompany her to a different security area, where a female security agent waves her wand across my body while another opens and rummages through my luggage and carry-on bag. All the while, the Aeroméxico ticket agent holds onto my documents.

"Is this what happens for criticizing the Mexican government?" I ask.

I hear nervous laughter as she assures me it's only routine.

Once my luggage and I are cleared, she hands me the boarding pass and passport and wishes me "buen viaje. Espero que a la próxima nos visite por placer" (I hope your next visit to Mexico is for pleasure).

I perceive a hint of sarcasm in her voice, or am I imagining it? Is this really just random, or are government authorities trying to harass me? Am I being paranoid? Or is this just a coincidence?

The casual remarks by the ticket-counter agent foreshadow events in Hermosillo. First, the call over the airport loudspeaker, "Rosa-Linda Fregoso, please report to the Aeroméxico boarding gate," sets me on edge. The attendant asks for my exit visa.

As I hand my documents to the agent at the boarding gate, she requests that I follow her to an inspection area, where I'm again asked to open my bags. The Mexican TSA wipes a plastic strip across different parts of my belongings, then inserts the strip into a metal device, repeating the process for several parts of my body.

"Are you checking me for explosives?"

"Yes," she responds. "You are clear and can board the plane."

I have been cleared but rattled. I walk rapidly toward the small commuter jet to LA. My fear of flying in small planes is compounded by a fear of the narco-state. Three days of chilling testimony about the role of Mexico's security apparatus, the military, federal, and municipal police's long history in violating human rights with impunity, have taught me that harassing international human rights experts to teach us a lesson about meddling in Mexico's internal affairs is not so far-fetched.

I sit trembling with fear and anger over this clear instance of harassment. Then I sob uncontrollably, from the impact of the hearing, the heart-wrenching testimonies, from grief for so many disappeared and dead in Mexico, for the living dead mothers, for families who are surviving rather than living. Right before takeoff, I text my husband: "Just remember I love you and my children."

Walking out of the airport, my eyes fixated on Oakland's sunshine and grand hills, I feel unsettled by the stark contrasts. Just a few hundred miles away, thousands of families search for their loved ones. Countless others demand justice for their murdered kin.

I recall the family of Manuelita and Ismael Solís Contreras testifying about the assassination of their parents in October 2012, en route to a meeting for water rights in the municipality of Cuauhtémoc.

Six adult relatives stand stone-faced behind the podium as a photo of Manuelita and Ismael projects onto the gigantic overhead screen. "They look so much like my grandparents," I remember thinking, "elders, in their mid-seventies." Manuelita and Ismael were active members of the community organization El Barzón and staunch opponents of NAFTA (the North American Free Trade Agreement).

"Manuelita and Ismael were human rights and environmental defenders," Siria Solís tells us, "driven by their love for the earth and water. 'Worth more than gold,' Manuelita would say."

5.5 Poster demanding justice for Ismael and Manuelita. Photo by author.

Joaquín Soloria speaks next. "They fought to defend the community's rights to land and a safe environment, especially water. . . . The mining industry consumes large quantities of water, draining the water reserves and jeopardizing our community's access to water for their daily needs. . . . We have information that someone hired sicarios [paid assassins]."

"They tried to topple us." Siria again takes the microphone, speaking with so much dignity and bold spirit: "But here we are, present on behalf of the people. For the authorities, we are worthless, but we will continue defending our heritage."

Manuelita and Ismael Solís Contreras's family are the last witnesses I speak to after the ruling. They are sitting apart from other witnesses when Cynthia and I approach them to say goodbye and express our gratitude for their audacious words. Tears swell in our eyes, as well as in Siria's and Joaquín's eyes as Siria responds, "Gracias a ustedes por ser nuestra voz y por llevar nuestra causa a la comunidad internacional" (Thank you for being our voice and for taking our cause to the international community).[14]

Flor de Arena

"The dead do not like to be forgotten, especially those whose lives had come to a violent end," writes M. Jacqui Alexander.[1] Yes. The relatives of the women who were murdered and disappeared honor those wishes by performing duties and obligations to something greater than the living human.

For indigeneity, what is alive and what is dead are not antithetical but mutually integrated states, and death is not the end point of the human or person: it marks the passing, the transition from one form of being to another. There is no linear current between life and death. "No you without mountains, without sun, without sky," say the Wintu. The human belongs to a community of interrelated beings, to the mountains, to the sun, to the sky, to the plants, the rocks, the animals, and the water. These mostly mestiza mothers of the murdered and disappeared women may not reside within Indigenous communities, yet they incorporate an Indigenous worldview that ruptures the boundary between the spirit and material worlds. "Within this cosmos," as Susan Miller indicates, "the remains of a community's dead are inseparable from the land itself, and their spirits are inseparable from the living community."[2] Verónica Leiton's Flor de Arena sculpture conjures this worldview on the integral nature of Beings.

On the land where the remains of eight women and girls were discovered in 2003 is the Campo Algodonero memorial. Previously an unofficial memorial or gathering site for protests, altar installations, and vigils, Campo Algodonero became Mexico's first state-funded official memorial to the victims of gendered violence after the Inter-American Human Rights Tribunal found the government guilty of negligence in the Ciudad Juárez feminicides.

The last time I visited Campo Algodonero, it was a barren field. The only objects on its grounds were eight crosses painted in the iconic pink, each bearing the name of one of the slain women or girls. The crosses are still standing, although they are now encircled by the walls of the newly configured memorial site, a small urban park bordered on one side by a heavily trafficked boulevard, on the other by two newly built apartment complexes that overlook the park's interior space. In its current state, the Campo Algodonero memorial is clean and unassuming. Three undulating walls mark its perimeters, separating the park from the exterior urbanscape. Its sandstone-colored walls, paths, blue-mosaic waterways, and curving walkway leading to polished marble-topped stone benches appear to be designed as spaces for public and private reflection. The park's architecture draws visitors to four major focal points.

To the right of the entrance, a plaque dedicates the memorial "to the memory of the women and girl victims of gender violence in Ciudad Juárez." At the next stop, the names of the women found at Campo Algodonero—Claudia Yvette González, Laura Berenice Ramos Monárrez, Esmeralda Herrera Monreal, María de los Angeles Acosta Ramírez, Mayra Juliana Reyes Solís, Verónica Martínez Hernández, Merlín Elizabeth Rodríguez Sáenz, María Rocina Galicia—are engraved on a wall, in a marble-encased panel. The adjacent memory wall is partially filled with names of additional women who were murdered in the city. Next, we face the shrine bearing a large cross, painted in the iconic pink, a tribute to and recognition of the mothers' cross campaign for justice. Finally, at the far side of the memorial site is the centerpiece of the national memorial: Flor de Arena.

A large bronze statue, Flor de Arena conjures a worldview of the integral nature of things. Its name and design derive from the region's topography, as Leiton explains, "fossils made of sand and shaped in the form of roses."[3] Several years ago, Leiton came to the region from Chile via Cuba to conduct theater workshops in Ciudad Juárez. Now a member of the arts collective Antigón, Leiton competed with ten other artists for the design of a sculpture for the national monument. The continuity between life and nonlife in a chain of being is figured through the process Leiton calls transmutation. "Conceptually I aimed for something delicate and very dignified, as far as possible from the grotesque. I envisioned an homage to the 1,500

INTER3.1 Verónica Leiton, Flor de Arena sculpture. Photo by author.

women and girls which would convey the idea of transmutation, the sublimation of pain, the bearing of pain with another."

From the texture of the garment suggestive of Mother Earth to the sand's changing into the form of a woman, transmutation permeates every element in Flor de Arena. Shaped in the form of a desert rose, the pedestal converts into a female figure, the powerful, arid texture of the earth transforming into her soft delicate garment. Fifteen roses are strewn across her full-length gown, each rose symbolizing one hundred women; a petal from the desert rose turns into a swirling mantle that bears the recurring given names of 1,500 women and girls—Paloma, María, Rosa, Jessica, Sylvia, Yesenia, Sagrario. . . . The woman's heart becomes a fountain whose water trickles down toward the fifteen roses. "The young woman's image emerges from the center of the sand rose, transmuting the powerful, arid texture of the earth into her soft and delicate garments." Each of the sculpture's roses is "distinctly unique; like the girls and women, each one is different," and the heart at the center of the statue "contains memory," Leiton tells me, "the memory of the women's pain and suffering." In Mesoamerican cosmology, the heart (teyolia) "has all the wisdom, it is the seat of memory and knowledge, 'through it perception takes place.'"[4] For Leiton, the water flowing onto the fifteen roses is meant to soothe and cleanse the women's pain and suffering, while the water fountain symbolizes "the transmutation of women's weeping into a commemorative elegy for the victims of our city."

This figuration of dynamically changing form is what conveys the continuity between life and death in a chain of being. "Death marks the beginning of life in another plane," Leiton confides, "which is why she faces upward, to the sky. The statue represents a strong and young woman, a female image who projects calm and reflection, wearing the gaze of liberation." In all its splendor and radiance underneath the desert sun of Chihuahua, Flor de Arena is a balm to human loss.

6   Stolen Lives and Fugitivity

This chapter grew out of my work as witness to the witness on gender asylum cases. Beginning in 2010, I served as an expert witness on petitions for asylum and stay of removal for survivors of gender violence, primarily from Mexico as well as from Northern Triangle countries. The chapter was written at the height of Trump-era rulings that reversed asylum protections guaranteed by US and international law for refugees fleeing gender and gang violence.

In June 2021, US Attorney General Merrick B. Garland reversed the Trump-era rulings and declared that the Justice Department would follow the earlier precedent of allowing asylum claims over credible fear of gender violence or gang violence. Garland's ruling means that people fleeing gender-based violence could again be considered as persecuted because of membership in a particular social group, a definition that allows them to petition for asylum in the United States.

Shortly after taking office, Joe Biden fulfilled a campaign promise and halted the Trump administration's Migrant Protection Protocols (also known as the Remain in Mexico policy) that have forced thousands of migrants and refugees/asylum seekers to remain in Mexico while they await a decision on their asylum petitions. In August 2021, a federal court in Texas ordered the Biden administration to reinstate its previous reversal of the Remain in Mexico order, and in December, the Department of Homeland Security complied with the court order and relaunched the controversial policy, while simultaneously appealing to terminate the program.

Not only is the Remain in Mexico order illegal, but it shuns the United States' obligation under international and federal law not to return asylum seekers to danger. According to #Save Asylum, the US government's Remain in Mexico policy has further endangered the lives of asylum seekers and migrants: "As of February 19, 2021, there were at least 1,544 publicly reported cases of murder, rape, torture, kidnapping, and other violent assaults against asylum seekers and migrants forced to return to Mexico by the Trump administration under this illegal scheme. Among these reported attacks are 341 cases of children returned to Mexico who were kidnapped or nearly kidnapped."[1]

Despite its claims of adherence to science and evidence-based assessments, the Biden administration has also left in place an inhumane and illegal policy that excludes all asylum seekers entirely based on public health reasons. In October 2021, former Yale Law School dean Harold Hongju Koh, the US State Department's top legal expert, resigned from the department because the Biden administration has yet to rescind Trump's Title 42 expulsion policy that uses bogus and unscientific public health claims about the pandemic to block and expel asylum-seeking people who are already in the United States.

In light of the continuing vulnerability of refugees and asylum seekers, fugitivity remains key to the speculative futurity of the witness/survivor of feminicidal violence.

Look at them leaving in droves, the children of the land, just look at them leaving in droves. Those with nothing are crossing borders. Those with strength are crossing borders, those with ambitions are crossing borders. Those with hopes are crossing borders. Those with loss are crossing borders, those in pain are crossing borders. Moving, running, emigrating, going, deserting, walking, quitting, flying, fleeing—to all over, to other countries near and far, to countries unheard of, to countries whose names they cannot pronounce. They are leaving in droves.

NOVIOLET BULAWAYO, *We Need New Names*

In "Prospects for Survival," Noam Chomsky writes, "The idea is that we destroy them and then we punish them for trying to escape the ruins—calling it a refugee crisis, while thousands drown in the Mediterranean sea, where Europe does have a history. In fact the so called 'refugee crisis' is actually a serious moral-cultural crisis—in the West."[2]

Chomsky's remarks alert us to the entanglement of destruction and punishment, not just in Europe but wherever xenophobic currents are stoking fear and hatred of refugees. How else to disavow the destructive politics of modern states but by inciting a punitive ethno-nationalist hysteria against foreign others? Without a "refugee crisis," there would be no "serious moral-cultural crisis."

The thousands of refugees from Mexico and the three countries that constitute the Northern Triangle—El Salvador, Guatemala, and Honduras—currently crossing borders can be traced to the accumulated devastation resulting from the US drug wars dating to the 1980s, the massive incarceration and deportation of Latinx youth gang members, the trafficking of arms from the United States to the region, and the growing consumption of drugs in the United States. By disingenuously assuming the role of passive victim of a brown invasion from the Southern Hemisphere, government officials disavow the country's complicity in the state of affairs that caused the problem, its active historical participation in the destructive politics of interventions, coups d'état, extractions, and dispossessions that have left thousands of people displaced. As the militarization of the border reminds us, the deployment of US-financed security forces breeds insecurity and precarity, and not stability and protection, for border residents.

We might also entertain how the West's "serious moral-cultural crisis" is related to the "exterminatory logic" adopted by late liberalism that Mark Duffield labels "the death of humanitarianism." In explaining the blowback to the so-called refugee crisis, Duffield affirms, "This violence seems intrinsic to a polarizing world, a world that is pulling apart just as connectivity is spreading. Borders are being entrenched, architectures of containment are spreading while, at the same time, xenophobic currents are mobilizing around the expulsion of difference."[3]

Violence against migrants and refugees is hardly a new occurrence.[4] For decades, the US government has stripped personhood from migrants of color and subjected them to surveillance, regulation, and punishment. Migrants who are criminalized are further "prevented from being law abiding."[5] Placing refugees and migrants outside of the law's protection follows this country's consistent and perverse pattern of violating international human rights standards. The apparatuses of modernity under late liberalism have succumbed to an epidemic of white nationalist anti-immigrant politics and rhetoric swelling across global North countries, especially among members of the interstate system of the United Nations.

Refugees flee precarious conditions in their homeland, wrought by wars, persecution, hunger, or ecological catastrophes and natural disasters. Their right to refuge elsewhere has, for decades, been enshrined in international human rights standards agreed upon by the interstate system. Until today.

In light of nation-states' continual disregard for human rights norms, I question the utility of *refugee* as a discursive category in the realms of epistemology and everyday life. By examining the vulnerable legal status of the refugee and asylum seeker through the anti-immigrant policies of the United States, I argue that labeling those who flee precarious living conditions as refugees has the effect of victimizing them even further.[6] To be a refugee in the current context intensifies their precarity, subjects people to the whims of governments, and robs those fleeing persecution of their capacity to act as agents.

Alexander Weheliye's notion of "racializing assemblages" supplies an analytic tool for situating the deportation machine and mass incarceration of migrants and asylum seekers as "death spaces" within modern Western humanity.[7] Building on discussions related to "political death," "social death," and "muertas en vida" (dead in life/living dead) as used by Mexican mothers of the disappeared (see chapter 5), this chapter explores alternative framings of the category of the refugee that rely less on international human rights discourse and more on other forms of emancipation.[8] What Nathaniel Mackey calls "the resonant history of African American fugitivity" offers one possibility for reclaiming another articulation of freedom from persecution and enslavement.[9]

THE EXPULSION OF DIFFERENCE

What this decision does is yank us all back to the Dark Ages of women's rights and human rights.

KAREN MUSALO, in Katie Benner and Caitlin Dickerson, "Sessions Says"

The morning I was preparing a country report for the gender asylum case of D. T., then attorney general Jeff Sessions rolled out the Trump administration's latest draconian anti-immigration policy. On May 7, 2018, Sessions stood outdoors, near the border city of Tijuana, to announce Trump's "zero-tolerance policy" aimed at "our southwestern border."[10] The administration's Far Right (and white) ethno-nationalist agenda was so transparent in the targeting of brown people—border crossers from Latin America (rather than Canada)—migrants, refugees, and asylum seekers who would now be treated as lawbreakers. Prosecuted rather than protected. This zero-tolerance policy unleashed an unparalleled attack on asylum seekers and refugees.

The Trump administration's false narrative about asylum seekers and refugees as lawbreakers reversed one of the foundational ideals of the nation, enshrined in the Statue of Liberty—often called the "Mother of Exiles"—of providing refuge to vulnerable individuals. Criminalizing people who flee violence and persecution upended years of US asylum law and treaty obligations.

A month after announcing the zero-tolerance policy, Sessions went even further. On June 11, 2018, he overruled a historic decision set during the Obama administration that recognized women's claims for protection under US asylum law. That landmark decision made by the Board of Immigration Appeals (BIA) in 2014, "known as the matter of A-R-C-G . . . ended a long-standing debate by clearly affirming domestic violence survivors can meet the refugee definition and qualify for asylum."[11] Prior to this ruling, victims of gender-based persecution did not meet the criteria of *refugee* and thus could not apply for asylum.

The Matter of A-R-C-G dealt with the case of Amenta Cifuentes, who fled Guatemala after enduring years of assaults by an abusive husband who burned her with acid and punched her in the stomach when she was eight months pregnant, forcing her to deliver a baby with bruises. In its decision, the BIA "built on more than two decades of growing recognition of gender crimes in the United States, consistent with U.S. treaty obligations."[12] Since 1985, federal courts have repeatedly recognized "that gender-related harms can constitute persecution, that a particular social group can be defined in reference to gender, and that claims can be based on persecution by non-State actors when the government fails to protect."[13] In dozens of decisions, US federal courts have ruled that violence such as feminicide, genital cutting, honor killings, trafficking, and forced marriage qualify as persecution on account of "protected group membership" (i.e., gender), thereby establishing gender- and sex-based persecution as a basis for asylum. One of the most significant of these cases was the Matter of R-A, involving

Rody Alvarado, a Guatemalan woman seeking asylum after suffering years of abuse from her husband, a former military officer. As discussed extensively in my book with Cynthia Bejarano, *Terrorizing Women*, in 2009 a federal immigration court granted asylum protection to Rody Alvarado.[14]

Sessions's reversal of the Matter of A-R-C-G and his restrictive interpretation of US asylum law did indeed "yank us all back to the Dark Ages of women's human rights" when he declared, "Generally, claims by aliens pertaining to domestic violence or gang violence perpetrated by nongovernmental actors will not qualify for asylum."[15] His departure from the positions of the UN High Commissioner for Refugees as well as US asylum law was rooted in an outdated notion of domestic violence as an individual act "and would return us to a period when violence against women was viewed as a personal and private matter rather than one having to do with human rights, and appropriate for refugee protection."[16] Although his use of the word *generally* did not absolutely prohibit asylum applications for gender-related persecution, the attorney general did raise the burden of proof for domestic violence claims.

For the past decade, I have served as country expert in dozens of asylum cases for Mexico and the Northern Triangle countries, in which my role has been to provide evidence about the weakness and inadequacy of state protections for survivors of domestic violence, despite the passage of gender violence laws. Petitions for asylum continue to this date, notwithstanding the attorney general's ruling.[17]

In the weeks leading up to the November 2018 elections, the Trump administration worked incessantly to fuel the anti-immigrant flames. Sounding the alarms of an imminent brown invasion of MS-13 gang members, drug traffickers, terrorists, and hordes of disease-infested Central American migrants traveling in caravans, Trump and the coterie of ethno-nationalist Republicans failed to convince the US electorate of their alarmist propaganda. The Democratic Party won an overwhelming majority in the House of Representatives, and, three days after their sweeping victory, the Trump administration signed a new executive order aimed at restricting asylum.

On November 9, 2018, Trump issued the "Presidential Proclamation Addressing Mass Migration through the Southern Border of the United States," barring refugees from applying for asylum unless they enter through designated ports of entry. Refugees who entered the United States elsewhere would be ineligible for asylum.[18] Prior to this executive order, in the summer of 2018, the Trump administration had implemented a metering process limiting the number of people who can be processed through ports of entry on a daily basis. In effect, the metering process forces thousands of refugees to remain on the Mexican side of the border where, to this day, "they face a level of violence akin to what we think of as occurring in war zones."[19] Rather than living in squalid refugee camps on the Mexican side of the border or facing long lines and up to three months waiting to be processed by US border agents, many asylum seekers opt to cross the border at nondesignated points of entry.

The following January, in 2019, the Department of Homeland Security announced its Migrant Protection Protocols, a new policy that forces immigrants seeking asylum to return to Mexico and wait for their court hearings. As of November 2019, the policy (also known as Remain in Mexico and labeled the "Migrant Persecution Protocols" by immigrant rights advocates) has forced sixty thousand people to remain across the border, where they confront violence, kidnapping, extortion, and houselessness.[20]

The American Civil Liberties Union, the Southern Poverty Law Center, and other migrant human rights defenders immediately challenged Trump's executive order of November 9. Filippo Grande, an attorney with the UN High Commissioner for Refugees, testified in federal court that the executive order violates US treaty obligations under international law, which "forbid punishment for irregular entry and require nations to consider asylum claims individually."[21] On December 7, 2018, US District Judge Jon Tigar concurred. Blocking Trump's efforts to restrict asylum to ports of entry, Tigar ruled that federal law indeed "allows migrants to apply for asylum no matter where they entered."[22]

At the time of this writing there were numerous challenges to the Trump administration's erosion of the human rights of migrants as well as refugee protections. A ruling in March 2019 by the US Court of Appeals for the Ninth District halted the administration's efforts to summarily deport asylum seekers who fail an initial screening by an asylum officer without access to an appeals process or review by an immigration judge. Although federal courts had, with few exceptions, ruled on the side of international law, the Trump administration was determined to file appeals to the Supreme Court.[23] The newly appointed attorney general, William Barr, continued to pursue the president's anti-immigrant agenda. In April 2019, Barr reversed two decades of precedent when he overturned the BIA's decision in the Matter of M-S and eliminated bond hearings for asylum seekers who entered between ports of entry, including those who passed the initial "credible fear screenings."

Article 14 of the Universal Declaration of Human Rights states, "Everyone has the right to seek and enjoy in other countries protection from persecution." On November 1, 1968, the United States signed the 1967 Protocol to the UN Convention on the Status of Refugees. Like the UN Convention and Protocol, the United States Refugee Act of 1980, signed into law by President Jimmy Carter, prohibits "returning vulnerable individuals to a place where they are endangered." Despite treaty obligations, the Trump administration continued to sabotage asylum procedures and deny due process to refugees fleeing persecution or extreme violence. This hardline approach to migrants from the global South who seek asylum in the United States (and Europe) suggests that what we witnessed was "the creation and maintenance of racializing assemblages" entangled with a necropolitics—politics of death.[24]

BODIES IN CAPTIVITY

For Weheliye, racializing assemblages constitute "one of the major political, cultural and economic spaces of exception, although not the only one within modern Western humanity."[25] As such, modernity's order of power "construes race not as biological or cultural classification but as a set of sociopolitical processes that discipline humanity into full humans, not-quite humans, and nonhumans."[26] The white nationalist undercurrents of US anti-immigration policies, aimed primarily at brown bodies, support the allegation that refugees and migrants from the global South, especially those from Latin America, have been "rendered disposable by the pernicious logic of racialization and thus exposed to different forms of political violence on a daily basis."[27] The purging of human rights from brown and Black refugees and migrants, save their mere life, amounts to a technology for governing noncitizens, more akin to the political and social death that scholars have identified as the status of human beings living under slavery.[28]

Daniel Kanstroom examines the historical links between slavery and the deportation system. Arguing that fugitive slave laws served as a model for deportation laws, Kanstroom notes, "Slavery and special restrictions of the entry, movement and residence of people of African ancestry were fundamentally related to the post–Civil War deportation system." As systems of "social control largely deployed against people of color," both slavery law and deportation law render Black and brown bodies in captivity as concrete manifestations of racializing assemblages entangled with social death.[29]

Following a carceral logic, the US government treats refugees and un-authorized migrants as "felons to be placed behind bars," despite the fact that crossing the border without papers is a misdemeanor, not a felony, and overstaying a visa is considered a civil, not a criminal, offense.[30] The fabri-cated lawlessness of refugees, their arbitrary criminalization, subjects them to racializing assemblages, insofar as brown migrants and refugees are sys-tematically treated as not quite human. It is not surprising that a president who has repeatedly stoked fear and hatred of refugees and referred to some undocumented migrants as "animals" would create the conditions of pos-sibility for their dehumanization.

In a letter published by Grassroots Leadership, a woman who signed her name "anónimo" describes her ordeal after she was captured on the border and kept for eight days in a chain-link cage that asylum seekers call "la per-rera," or the dog kennel: "Without allowing us to bathe or brush our teeth they treat us horribly as if we were animals. Sometimes they punish us and give us water without food . . . we slept on the floor, and they gave us alumi-num paper to cover ourselves."[31]

Jonathan Inda recently noted, "This deadly disregard for migrant life in migrant detention can be characterized as a necropolitics of uncare."[32] The abjection of refugees and migrants as animals conjures a form of bare life we have witnessed before in the relational necropolitical spaces of "con-centration camps, colonial outposts and slave plantations."[33] Mirroring the treatment of Black families in slave plantations, thousands of children were separated from their parents under the Trump administration's zero-tolerance policy that required the prosecution of migrants crossing the border. After widespread backlash, Trump ended the policy in June 2018. However, hundreds of children were not reunited with their families and, as of February 2019, nearly fifteen thousand children remained incarcerated in one hundred or so migrant prisons across the country.

The deaths of several Guatemalan children in the custody of Customs and Border Protection in detention prisons drew international attention to the treatment of migrants in the United States.[34] Of twenty-six migrants who perished under government custody, twenty-two died during 2016–18, and of these, in eight cases "violation of medical standards played a promi-nent role."[35]

A plantation economy based on slavery may be an aberration of the past, yet the enslavement of human beings persists across the globe, as evidenced by the incident of forty-nine refugees aboard the *Sea Watch 3* who were stranded at sea for nineteen days because Malta denied the ship entry into its ports. Many of those onboard the *Sea Watch 3* were escaping torture by jihadists from Boko Haram; others, slavery in Libya, where "they are called 'abd,' an Arabic word for slave."[36]

Escaping persecution and violence, asylum seekers and migrants find themselves trapped in detention prisons under conditions comparable to enslavement, subjected to extraordinary human suffering, prolonged detention, neglect, torture in the form of solitary confinement, sexual assault, and forced (prison) labor. Although the Obama administration began phasing out the use of private prisons because of widespread abuse and dismal conditions, the Trump administration decided to reverse that decision.

Fueled by what Michelle Alexander calls "our nation's addiction to caging human beings," the incarceration of migrants is a profitable industry in the United States that expanded further after Congress approved in 2019 the Trump administration's $2.8 billion request to increase the caging of migrants to 52,000 beds.[37] Since the incentive is to maximize profits and minimize costs, the living conditions inside these for-profit migrant prisons are substandard. An average of 48,000 people are held in two hundred migrant prisons, two-thirds operated by private companies. Even though the private prison industry incarcerates less than 10 percent of the prison population, roughly 70 percent of migrants are jailed in for-profit facilities.[38]

The private prison industry is notorious for its abysmal abuse of migrants, who are consistently denied access to "functioning toilets, proper medical facilities and served inedible food."[39] Freedom for Migrants (formerly CIVIC), an organization that monitors human rights abuses faced by imprisoned migrants, has documented firsthand accounts of their inhumane treatment. The following letter, written by an HIV-positive woman held in the T. Don Hutto Center in Taylor, Texas, details the conditions of her incarceration, including the lowering of her T-cell count because detention guards refused to administer her medication. After her transfer from "la hielera" to "la perrera," she details her anguish and distress: "Eight days without bathing, without my medication I thought I'd get sick. Then they took us to court and they handcuffed our hands and feet as though we were delinquents, for eight hours without breakfast or lunch. It's unjust the way they treat us as if we were animals."[40]

According to the Southern Poverty Law Center, under the Trump administration, "the detention and deportation machine built by decades of increasingly harsh immigration policy" has grown to unprecedented proportions, ushering in an era of widespread abuse of detention protocols. Under US laws, "migrant detention is civil, not penal in nature," which means that "conditions that punish the confined are prohibited."[41] Yet numerous reports by human rights organizations continue to document the punitive treatment of migrants and asylum seekers under US custody. In a comprehensive study of hatred and discrimination in US migrant prisons, Freedom for Migrants reports the increase of abusive treatment of migrants since Trump became president, included "at least 800 complaints of abuse motivated by hatred or bias in thirty-four migrant detention jails or prisons."[42]

There are currently six lawsuits accusing CCA/CoreCivic and the GEO Group (the two largest companies of the private prison industry) of mandating "prison labor," under a "Voluntary Work Program in which migrants are forced to work for $1 per day and if they refuse they are punished."[43] The Thirteenth Amendment to the US Constitution abolished slavery, indentured servitude, and prison labor "except as punishment for crimes," thereby rendering unconstitutional the forced labor of incarcerated migrants. Despite the Trump administration's concerted efforts to characterize migrants and asylum seekers as criminals, people held in migrant prisons are not charged with committing a crime but are "detained while waiting for asylum or deportation hearings."[44]

The treatment of refugees and migrants as less than human underscores the shared history and relationality of migrant prisons to other necropolitical institutions—concentration camps, colonial outposts, slave plantations, dark sites, and clandestine prisons. Refugees are criminalized by a US asylum system that treats them as felons to be locked behind bars and tortured in solitary confinement, that denies them due process and habeas corpus, and that enslaves them by enforced prison labor. The purging of human rights from refugees and asylum seekers, except for their biological life, conjures up a different form of existence.

The deadly disregard for their lives amounts to what the mothers of the disappeared in Mexico referred to as "muertas en vida" (dead in life). A mother from Honduras incarcerated in a migrant prison anguished about this condition of living: "I am one of the mothers that flees from her country because they threatened to kill us, me and my children. That is why we fled the country but here they killed us in life by taking away our children. Please help me."[45]

STOLEN LIVES: WHAT THE DEAD TEACH US

Right now, the world is full of refugees, human or not, without refuge.
DONNA J. HARAWAY, *Staying with the Trouble*

A life stolen. Twice. Once from home, "because they threatened to kill me and my children." Again. "Here they killed us in life by taking away our children." She is one of the hundreds of mothers from the Northern Triangle "running away from their own countries." Persecuted at home. Away from home, they dwell in the liminal space between the living and the dead, in a world of "humans and nonhuman refugees without refuge."[46]

In chapter 5, I wrote about the mothers of the disappeared in Mexico who, during their testimony before the Permanent Peoples' Tribunal, referred to themselves as "muertas en vida" or "living dead" / "dead in life." Even as this category "dead in life" suggests "bare life" (Agamben) and/or "social death" (Patterson), we should avoid the temptation of characterizing these mothers as an embodiment of "mere biological life."[47] They are more akin to the emotionally numb survivors of Hiroshima whom Robert Jay Lifton wrote about in his book *Death in Life*—survivors who shut down their emotions in order to survive, but whose shutting down emotionally meant an existence of "death in life." Yet is there an alternative form of life beyond this emphasis on social mortality? As María Martínez suggests about women survivors of gender violence, "muerte en vida" (death in life) does not signify biological death but rather refers to "the idea of the annihilation of the subject and subjectivity."[48]

The actions on the part of Mexican mothers who testified before the tribunal, risking their lives by explicitly denouncing, in a public forum, the criminal state and other perpetrators of disappearance and feminicides, together with their activism on behalf of the disappeared and their resistance to the state's exercise of biopower, are affirmations of and claims to alternative forms of living under the most extreme circumstances within communities terrorized by low-intensity warfare. Embodying the category of "dead in life" or "living dead" conjures the possibility of an alternative notion of "the human" and distinct forms of freedom that lie outside of the context of liberal humanism's juridical subjectivity, or in the words of Martínez, "Death in life is thus not death, but life, even if in another form."[49]

In other words, to dwell in the liminal space between the living and the dead suggests transcending the binaries of human/nonhuman and life/death as much as recognizing how life and death are intertwined with other forms of subjectivity. I came to this understanding by thinking with Weheliye's analysis of humanity under conditions of enslavement.

Under liberal humanism, the basic definition of "the human" is of a subject who exercises corporal control and ownership of the self: "the body" as representing "legal personhood qua self-possession."[50] In contrast to personhood as property, Weheliye urges an alternative social imaginary: "What if we begin with slavery, with a subject who does not exercise control over her body, who does not own her body (because it is someone else's property), then we would have a very different version of humanity, of what it means to reclaim the category of 'the human.'"[51] It is his provocation that prompted me to think beyond inherited categories like "the refugee" and consider alternative framings that rely less on the discourse of international human rights and more on a different conceptualization of freedom.

The vulnerable legal status of the refugee is a fundamental feature of the so-called refugee crisis. Changes in US asylum law have transformed refugees into targets of punishment and regulation rather than of sanctuary and protection. "People who are refugees," writes Liisa H. Malkki, "can also find themselves quite quickly rising to a floating world either beyond or above politics, and beyond or above history—a world in which they are simply 'victims.'" To be a refugee in this floating world is to live in a "deeply dehumanizing environment" that robs those fleeing persecution of the capacity to act as subjects or agents.[52]

The abjection of those seeking refuge from state-sanctioned persecution is neither novel nor exceptional. Nearly seven decades ago, Hannah Arendt wrote a penetrating study of totalitarianism, sketching "the political and symbolic logics that had the effect of pathologizing and criminalizing refugees."[53] Arendt's earlier observations about refugees and displaced persons as subjects without rights remain just as relevant today.[54] Throughout the twentieth century, the United States repeatedly engaged in a xenophobic politics of constituting foreignness as criminal and pathological and deporting migrants on a mass scale.

Emboldened by its foundational history of xenophobic nationalism and white supremacy, the US government previously targeted people of color en masse, deporting Mexican noncitizens and citizens indiscriminately during the 1930s and 1950s and incarcerating Japanese during World War II. The more recent mass incarceration of migrants dates to changes in US immigration policy during the 1980s, as a response to the Mariel boatlift when then president Fidel Castro permitted the emigration of hundreds of

Cubans into the United States, including persons released from Cuba's prisons. Bolstered by the US Supreme Court's decision that revoked a previous ruling in the 1958 Supreme Court case *Leng May Ma v. Barber*, the Department of Immigration and Nationalization instituted new regulations on mass detention, which have continued to expand to this day.[55]

In *Leng May Ma v. Barber* (1958), the Supreme Court had framed its ruling to reflect "the human qualities of an enlightened civilization," concluding that "the physical detention of aliens is now the exception not the rule."[56] The reverse is now the case. Fueled by Eurocentric white nationalism (often misnamed populism), the physical detention of migrants and refugees under the Trump administration became the rule, not the exception.

A key to understanding the limits of the category of the refugee in the current context may be found in its historical moment of reconfiguration as an object of knowledge in the legal and institutional realms. In her study of the term *refugee*, Malkki traces its genealogy to the modern state and locates its construction as an object of social scientific knowledge and law in post–World War II Europe. "People have always sought refuge and sanctuary," she writes. "But 'the refugee' as a specific social category and legal problem of global dimensions did not exist in its full modern form before this moment."[57]

For Malkki, the discursive and institutional domains that render the modern social category of the refugee intelligible are the legal apparatus of international law and the bureaucratic humanitarian realm of the United Nations and related international refugee agencies charged with providing and administrating sanctuary or refuge, as well as the academic disciplines of the social sciences. The emergence of the refugee as an object of knowledge (social category) is at the same time its constitution as a global juridical subject (legal category).

The UN Convention Related to the Status of Refugees of 1951, amended by a 1967 protocol that "removed the Eurocentric geographical restrictions and war-linked time restrictions" defines the refugee as "a person who owing to a well-founded fear of being persecuted for reasons of race, religion, nationality, membership of a particular social group or political opinion, is outside the country of his nationality and is *unable* or, owing to such fear, is *unwilling* to avail himself of the protection of that country; or who not having a nationality, and being outside the country of his former habitual residence as a result of such events, is *unable* or, owing to such fear, is *unwilling* to return to it."[58] Two elements of this international definition stand out. First, as this aggregate of print and online definitions reveals, a person who is *unable* is (a) "powerless"; (b) "lacking the skill, means, or ability"; or (c) "impotent, helpless." A person who is *unwilling* is (a) "not ready, eager, or prepared to do something"; (b) "loathe, reluctant"; or (c) "obstinate."[59]

Second, although both aspects enunciate a presumption of terror ("a well-founded fear of persecution"), the United States, along with other states, has derogated treaty obligations of providing refuge to people fleeing dehumanizing circumstances. As recent changes to asylum policy have made evident, the United States has resorted to criminalizing refugees and migrants, thereby increasing their deep sense of vulnerability.[60] "People who occupy legally vulnerable and criminalized statuses" are both "excluded from law's protection" and "not excluded from law's discipline, punishment, and regulation."[61]

By defining the refugee in such terms, the UN convention reinforces a paternalistic logic that labels persons seeking asylum as vulnerable victims lacking full autonomy and agency. As Freedman insists, "there is also the danger that this adoption of the categories of 'vulnerability' will lead to essentialisation and reification of the categories, and to a failure to understand or take into account the agency of those seeking asylum."[62]

The limited utility of the category of the refugee is obvious when we move beyond its genealogy as a juridical subject in international human rights law and trace the term's etymology. *Refugee* derives from the seventeenth-century French word *réfugié*, which in turn is the noun use of the past participle of *refugier*, "to take shelter, protect," and from Old French *refuge*, "hiding place," which in turn derives from Latin *refugium*, "a taking refuge; place to flee back to," from *re-* "back" (see *re-*) + fugere "to flee" + *-ium* "place for."[63] The word was first applied to Huguenots, French Protestants who fled Catholic France to escape religious persecution after the reversal of the Edict of Nantes in 1685. In an English-language dictionary, *refugee* is defined as "one who flees, especially to another country, seeking refuge from war, political oppression, religious persecution, or a natural disaster."[64]

Historically, then, to be a refugee presupposed the possibility of a spatial sanctuary or shelter and of a country open to its provision. Moreover, the inscription of the refugee as a category in the universalist language of human rights and within the modern juridical tradition of the liberal state was meant to guarantee the rights to protection (shelter or sanctuary). Yet what we are witnessing today is quite the opposite: the closing of borders, the denial of sanctuary, and the transformation of places of refuge into necropolitical spaces (prisons, hieleras, perreras, military-style barracks, tent cities in isolated locales). And when migrants organize these spaces of refuge for themselves, as in the case of Calais, France, they are destroyed by the state.

The current situation of the refugee raises two other related problems stemming from its inscription in modern discourse. If being a refugee in the juridical discourse of rights presupposes or depends on a spatial sanctuary or refuge that no longer exists or is reconstituted as a site of repression, then the category of the refugee becomes an empty category. Second, the refugee as a juridical subject forecloses alternative definitions of what it means to be human. This raises the question of an alternative form of life beyond the mortality of the subject, subjectivity, and sociality within the juridical confines of modernity. Not only is the legal universality of human rights unable to alleviate the precarity of refugees, but it fails to imagine various congeries of "what it means to be human in the modern world" as well as to envision the conditions of possibility for distinct imaginaries of freedom and resistance.[65] Sandro Mezzadra's notion of the "right to flight" or escape (derecho de fuga) is useful for rethinking alternatives to the juridical subject of the modern liberal state.

Mezzadra's right to flight is not inscribed within the modern juridical tradition or the universality of human rights. Rather, migrants are central figures who exercise their right to flight through social practices. Mezzadra urges a focus on the individuality of migrant subjects, in particular the richness of their contributions to host countries, rather than on their victimization and misery, and whose right to flight implies "conditions of co-creation along with a search for freedom."[66] Mezzadra continues, "The right to flight is situated in a line of continuity with other movements of secession."[67]

Earlier I noted the significance of fugitive slave laws "as a model and precedent for federal deportation laws."[68] In evoking the entanglement of enslaved subjects and undocumented migrants, Kirsten Silva Gruesz contemplates their shared "conditions of legal vulnerability as noncitizens," adding, "One parallel emerges when the body in question moves into a space where it is not permitted to be: a refugee whose request for asylum has not been approved, a fugitive from the slave regime or from federal immigration authorities."[69] Moving into this unpermitted space of fugitivity is precisely what evokes the possibility for reimagining another articulation of freedom from persecution and enslavement.

I end by conjuring up a poetics summoned from the traditions of the oppressed, as an alternative to the inherited legal category of the refugee. My suggestions here are based on speculation, aimed less at the public policy and legal arenas and more to the realms of epistemology and everyday life. Fugitivity—the condition or quality of being a fugitive—figures as a generative possibility for reclaiming another form of liberation. Like Mezzadra's rethinking of migration and mobility through the prism of the right to flight, fugitivity permits a glimpse into forms of resistance enacted in the present, into fugitive practices of taking flight from persecution and enslavement. In this time of crisis, it is the fugitive spirit that we should evoke.

I first learned about the concept of fugitivity from poet/critic Nathaniel Mackey's 1997 essay "Cante Moro," in which he features the connection between Federico García Lorca's "duende" and African diasporic culture. Writing about African American poet Amiri Baraka's poem, "Lines to García Lorca," Mackey notes the reverberation of García Lorca's poetry and Afro-American spirituals: "Baraka's early work embodies a mercurial non-investment in the status quo. One of those things going on in the 'Lines to Garcia Lorca,' is the implicit connection between that mercuriality, that nomadism, and the line 'Didn't come here to stay,' behind which is a well known, resonant history of African American fugitivity and its well known resonant relationship to enslavement and persecution."[70]

The subject of fugitivity differs from the legal subject of the refugee in that the former is not invested in the normative status quo of modernity and coloniality as embodied in juridical subjectivity, nor does it evoke the stigma of victimhood. Rather, fugitivity is a form of epistemic disobedience incited by the words of Fred Moten: "The ongoing stealing away of and from the maternal body, maternal shore, maternal language. Steal away from home. Born not in bondage but in fugitivity, in stolen breath and stolen life."[71]

Conjuring up fugitivity has less to do with proposing the fugitive as a new social category to supplant that of the refugee than with reclaiming other forms of living and a different vision of humanity. The focus on fugitive practices of refusal and stealing away as a form of epistemic disobedience shifts the lens away from victimization, misery, and abjection. In so doing, fugitivity embraces the enduring qualities and possibility of "Black social life in the face of anti-blackness as a constant struggle against social death."[72]

If racializing assemblages under slavery and the afterlife of slavery positioned Black subjectivity as outside of humanity, fugitivity reclaims what Tina Campt calls the "'lived experience of Blackness' as a constant practice of 'refusal' to accept and to remain within the ostracized position of social death."[73] The universalist discourse of human rights defines the refugee not as a relational category but in individualist terms, as a vulnerable victim lacking full autonomy and agency. Unlike the refugee, whose vulnerability and victimization derive from their inscription within discursive and institutional domains of international law and universalist human rights, the condition or quality of being a fugitive affirms a stealing away from victimhood. As von Gleich notes, "The concept of fugitivity still demises to the fugitive some capacity to act as subject or agent."[74] In other words, fugitivity allows for a conception of persons fleeing persecution as relational and intersubjective: an agency of creativity and resistance rooted in collectivities.

In the refusal of abjection, victimization, and misery, fugitive practices enact an alternative to the location of the refugee, who remains entrapped within governing conceptions of humanity rooted in the juridical subjectivity of modernity. Conjuring up the fugitive spirit means considering reverberating symbolic practices, knowledges, and thought experiments across social and symbolic life for, as von Gleich reminds us, "The fugitive practices of refusal and the 'stealing away' of the socially dead assume a more indeterminate form of agency."[75] Fugitivity and fugitives can thus be seen as actors and vectors in the transformation of capitalism. Like the fugitive from slavery who fled her captivity on the Southern plantation, migrants in flight from violence and persecution in their home country enact an agency, a refusal and defiance against nightmarish lifeworlds. They teach us what death in life may signify: a collective search for "making a life which as of yet has no form, that has not been thought of: to live without referents."[76]

CODA

Imagine the unimaginable: your domestic partner, in a drunken stupor, beats you when you confront him about cheating and then sexually assaults you.

Imagine he locks you inside your home when he leaves for work, without food or access to the outdoor bathroom.

Imagine he hits you with his fists, yanks your hair, and when his family hears your screams, they come to join him in the beating.

Imagine his brother is a police officer in a town where the authorities ignore your pleas for help.

Imagine your parents abandoned you, and you grew up in a household with grandparents who used cables, belts, and branches to discipline you and your siblings. At fifteen, you escaped this abuse and moved in with a boyfriend, only to discover he too was physically abusive. With nowhere to go, you return to your grandparents' home, where an uncle sexually assaults you.

Imagine you're attending beauty school when you meet the man of your dreams and marry him. Soon afterward he prohibits you from working or finishing your studies. When you protest, he beats you with his hands and a broom, bangs you against the wall, and locks you in the house each day when he leaves for work.

Imagine the first time he threatens to kill you if you report his abusive behavior.

Imagine your husband turns even more abusive when he learns you're pregnant. He kicks you in the stomach, causing bleeding. After two similar incidents, the attending doctor no longer believes your stories about falling down the stairs and threatens to report your husband to the authorities. Your husband stops kicking your stomach but continues slapping you and pulling your hair.

Imagine you're married, with three children, and work part-time as a teacher in a private school. When you receive a promotion to full-time teaching, your husband becomes controlling and jealous, verbally and physically abusive, calling you a "whore" and accusing you of infidelity. He rapes you repeatedly and threatens to kill you. He keeps many guns in the home, and his family has strong ties to the police.

Imagine your husband witnessing his father's murder by cartel members, who then search for your husband. In your home state of Michoacán, the Knights Templar traffic in drugs and humans, and you hear rumors that they snatch children to harvest their organs and kidnap women for the sex trade.

Imagine your dreams of freedom—freedom from violence, freedom from this horrific nightmare of existence. A freedom only possible if you flee and become a fugitive from persecution. Your only hope is a pilgrimage across the border, into the land of the Mother of Exiles.

You choose to leave and live.[77]

Postlude

My daughter and I arrived at suppertime. Cecilia greeted us at the door and walked us down the hallway into a brightly lit meeting hall behind the Presbyterian church. The fluorescent lights in the ceiling reminded me of the bingo hall at Our Lady of Guadalupe Church, back home in Corpus Christi.

The only items I packed were our own pajamas, two days' worth of clothes, toothbrushes, deodorant, and face creams. I forgot the toothpaste and the bar of Ivory soap. The straw beach bag was so full I could hardly clasp it shut.

Cecilia led us to the two twin beds with headboards separated by a small table with a forest-green lamp. There I placed the beach bag and sat down. "I'll explain the rules and daily routine after supper," Cecilia said in a calming voice. Her warm deep brown eyes and cropped hair reminded me of my beloved Tia Fina.

It was a humid summer day in 1977. I wore a short light-blue jean skirt, a peasant blouse, and sandals. Still, I was sweating profusely, my palms sticky, the sharp odor of perspiration scenting the air around me. I turned my focus to the smell of chili and corn bread coming from the kitchen.

I cracked my knuckles, as I often did whenever I felt anxious and fearful, a constant tightness knotting my stomach. "I hope he doesn't see our blue Toyota in the parking lot," I thought. The car my mother had cosigned for.

The room smelled of Pine Sol. "Clean," I told my daughter. "The sheets were washed with Tide, like at home," I added.

"Mom, I don't like it here. I wanna go home," my daughter sobbed.

I held my daughter's hand tightly and stroked her head.

"It's gonna be okay, sweetie. Don't worry. Plus, we're having chili con carne with corn bread for supper. Your favorite!"

"I like chili dogs better," my daughter responded, pouting.

I heard the garbled sounds of women talking and walked into the multipurpose room. The TV in the background broadcast the theme song of *Bewitched*—a show my daughter and I had often watched together. The laughter of kids filled the air as they ran around the meeting room. A baby cried while his mother changed his diaper. Another was being breastfed.

I looked around the room and noticed all the windows had roll-down shades and thick cream-colored curtains. There were twelve sleeping stations, twin beds arranged by twos in parallel formation. Eleven other women, each with one or two kids. Thirty or so survivors, sharing a night in one of eighty-nine recently opened shelters for battered women seeking sanctuary from abusive partners in the United States.

For the first time ever, I met other women who had also left violent lives, determined as I was to forge new paths. I recognized my daughter's pained expression on the faces of other children. Yet despite our mutual despair, we shared a collective desire for a promising future. For the first time ever, I could sense the possibility of a life free from violence. I could envision freedom.

Notes

PRELUDE

1. Butler, *The Force of Nonviolence*, 9.

2. Fregoso, "For a Pluriversal Declaration."

3. Ashuri and Pinchevski, "Witnessing as a Field," 136.

4. Felman and Laub, *Testimony*, 207.

5. See Ashuri and Pinchevski, "Witnessing as a Field"; Oliver, *Witnessing*, 85.

6. Derrida, "A Self-Unsealing Poetic Text," 190.

7. Felman and Laub, *Testimony*, 62.

8. Oliver, "Witnessing and Testimony," 84–85.

9. Oliver, "Witnessing and Testimony," 81; Oliver, *Witnessing*, 16.

10. Felman and Laub, *Testimony*, 75–78.

11. Felman and Laub, *Testimony*, 71.

12. Muñoz, *Dis-identifications*.

13. Oliver, "Witnessing and Testimony," 84; Oliver, *Witnessing*, 7.

14. Oliver, *Witnessing*, 98.

15. Sergio González Rodríguez (*The Feminicide Machine*) refers to the assemblage of structural and agential factors that coalesce in the murder and disappearance of women in Chihuahua as the "feminicide machine."

16. For more about the theory of pluriversality, see Esteva and Prakash, *Grassroots Postmodernism*; and Mignolo, *The Darker Side*. In an earlier essay, I explored ideas regarding pluriversality, witnessing, and interbeing understandings of the

"human." See my essay, "For a Pluriversal Declaration of Human Rights" (2014).

17. Mani, *The Integral Nature*, 116.

18. Butler, *The Force of Nonviolence*, 45. I borrow the concept of interbeing from the Buddhist thinker Thich Nhat Hanh; see also Lata Mani's use of the concept in her *Myriad Intimacies*.

19. For a critique of the masculinist use of the concept by Chicano cultural nationalists, see Fregoso, *The Bronze Screen*; for a feminist reading of In'Laketch, see Pérez, *Chicana Art*.

20. See Connolly, *A World of Becoming*.

21. Holder and Corntassel, "Indigenous Peoples," 147.

22. Paredes, *Hilando Fino*, 30–31.

23. Marcos, "The Borders Within," 93.

24. Rivera Garza, *The Restless Dead*, 52.

25. Borrowing from the practices of the Haudenosaunee, or Iroquois federation, John Brown Childs (*Transcommunality*) develops the concept of "transcommunality" as a way of thinking about communities as coalitions.

26. Rivera Garza, *The Restless Dead*, 47.

27. Rivera Garza, *The Restless Dead*, 47–50.

28. Miller, "Native America Writes Back," 10.

29. Quoted by Oliver, who discusses Maurice Merleau-Ponty's "vision-touch system" in *Witnessing*, 201.

30. Felman and Laub, *Testimony*, 80–82.

31. Cavareno, *Horrorism*, 34.

32. Richardson, *Bearing Witness*, 197.

33. Richardson, *Bearing Witness*, 180.

34. Tomlinson and Lipsitz, *Insubordinate Spaces*, 23.

35. Tomlinson and Lipsitz, *Insubordinate Spaces*, 26.

36. Butler, "Introduction," 9.

37. Mahoney and Eguren, *Unarmed Bodyguards*.

38. Felman and Laub, *Testimony*, 231, 237.

39. Butler, "Introduction," 22.

40. Laub uses the term "witness to oneself" and "witness to himself," which I've adapted here; see Felman and Laub, *Testimony*, 75–85.

41. Felman and Laub, *Testimony*, 67.

42. Felman and Laub, *Testimony*, 85.

43. Oliver, *Witnessing*, 98.

44. Rivera Garza, *The Restless Dead*, 50.

45. Founder of the Zen Peacemaker Order, Glassman makes this statement in the context of the horrorism at Auschwitz in *Bearing Witness*, 33.

46. Butler, "Rethinking Vulnerability," 16.

CHAPTER 1: CHRONICLES OF WITNESS

This chapter benefited from the insightful comments of fellow writers and participants in Laura Davis's writing retreats at the Tassajara Zen Mountain Center and Santa Cruz, California, as well as her ongoing feedback workshop. Special thanks to Johanna Poethig and Lisbeth Haas who provided additional feedback on the final draft.

1. "Esmeralda Garza" is a pseudonym. For safety reasons, this and other names throughout this book have been changed.

2. See Fregoso, "Voices without an Echo."

3. Nathan, "Death Comes to the Maquilas."

4. The 8 de Marzo organization was formed in the 1990s to advocate for domestic violence legislation and to support reproductive rights for women in Mexico. Casa Amiga, under the direction of Esther Chávez Cano (also founder of the Grupo Feminista 8 de Marzo, was the first organization to document the feminicides. See Ravelo Blancas, *Miradas Etnológicas*; Wright, "Necropolitics."

5. "Clara Vega" is a pseudonym.

6. Jorge Ramos is a Mexican journalist with Spanish-language media. Quoted in Ramos, *Stranger*, 167.

7. Monárrez Fragoso, "La cultura de feminicidio," 97.

8. Bejarano, "Las Super Madres," 135.

9. My translation of "Muchas de las mujeres asesinadas trabajaban entre semana de obrearas y los fines de semana como prostitutas para hacerce mayores recursos"; "Visitaba un centro en el que se dan cita homosexuales y lesbianas"; "Le gustaba salir con diferentes hombres y era asidua asistente de salones de baile." Quoted in Benítez et al., *El Silencio que la Voz*, 36.

10. My translation of "¡NO SON PROSTITUTAS; NO SON ESTADISTICAS; PERO SI TIENEN HISTORIAS!" See Fregoso, "Voices without an Echo," 148.

11. See chapter "Toward a Planetary Civil Society," in Fregoso, *MeXicana Encounters*.

12. In 2005, Congresswoman Hilda Solis and Senator Jeff Bingaman of New Mexico introduced a Senate Concurrent Resolution that urged "the President and Secretary of State to incorporate the investigative and preventative efforts of the Mexican Government in the bilateral agenda between the Governments of Mexico and the United States and to continue to express concern over these abductions and murders to the Government of Mexico." https://www.govinfo.gov/content/pkg/BILLS-109sconres16is/html/BILLS -109sconres16is.htm.

13. Fregoso and Bejarano, *Terrorizing Women*. Cynthia and I began working on the book in 2003, and it was published in 2010 by Duke University Press.

14. Quote is borrowed from Tomlinson and Lipsitz, *Insubordinate Spaces*, 181. See chapter 1 in Fregoso, *meXicana Encounters*.

15. See Fregoso, "Voices without an Echo," 137–38.

16. The report is titled "The Case of Assassinated Women in Ciudad Juárez and the Lack of Collaboration of the Offices of the Attorney General of Chihuahua, (1998)," cited in Fregoso, "Voices without an Echo," 138.

17. See Washington Valdez, *Cosecha de Mujeres*.

18. During their research in Ciudad Juárez in 2001, Hector Domínguez and Patricia Ravelo compiled a list of thirty-two hypotheses that aimed to explain the extermination of women in Juárez. See Ravelo Blancas, *Miradas Etnológicas*, 54. Also see Fregoso, "'We Want Them Alive!,'" 109–38.

19. Quoted in Rivera Garza, *Grieving*, 89.

20. Monárrez Fragoso, "La cultura del feminicidio," 94.

21. Arendt, *The Origins of Totalitarianism*.

22. Fregoso, "Voices without an Echo," 143–44.

23. I borrow this phrase from Solnit, "The Longest War," although the Reconquista in the Iberian Peninsula is considered to be the longest war between nations.

24. See Fregoso, *meXicana Encounters*; Bejarano, "Memory of Struggle," 197. Izaguirre was granted asylum and currently lives in the United States.

25. See Fregoso, "'We Want Them Alive!'"

26. Mujeres de Negro translates as Women Dressed in Black. The organization is not officially affiliated with Women in Black, an antiwar movement founded in Israel, although, according to Melissa Wright, it is inspired by "women around the world who have used the black clothing of mourning, domesticity, and female modesty to express their identities as social justice and human rights activists." See Wright, "Mujeres de Negro," 316.

27. Fregoso, *meXicana Encounters*, 23.

28. Wright, "Mujeres de Negro," 320.

29. As Wright adds in her chapter on Mujeres de Negro, "Some participants in Mujeres de Negro do not like each other. . . . For instance, one Mujer de Negro activist explained 'We are not friends. Some of us fight politically with each other. Serious fights. I mean "hasta la muerte (to the death)." But we come together when it is important. And this is important,'" 320.

30. "Luz María Álvarez" is a pseudonym.

31. Davis, *Freedom Is a Constant Struggle*, 1.

32. *Poner el cuerpo* is a term used by Barbara Sutton to refer to the activism of the mothers of the Plaza de Mayo in Argentina. See Sutton, *Bodies in Crisis*, 176–77.

33. Monárrez Fragoso, *Trama de una injusticia*.

34. I borrow the expression "say her name" from the African American Policy Forum that in partnership with the Center for Intersectionality and Social Policy Studies launched the #SayHerName campaign in December 2014 "to bring awareness to the names and stories of Black women and girls who have been victimized by racist police violence, and to provide support to their families." For more information, visit the AAPF website: https://www.aapf.org/.

35. The list was originally published in Comisión Nacional de Derechos Humanos en México, "Informe Especial sobre el tema de los homicidios," in 2003.

36. García Uribe was convicted and sentenced to fifty years in prison in October 2004. His sentenced was overturned in July 2005, and he was released for lack of evidence. González died in jail awaiting trial.

37. Some mother-activist organizations refused to participate in the V-Day protests because they objected to sexualized terms and the festivities. See Aikin Araluce, *Activismo Social Trasnacional*, 209; Tabuenco Córdova, "Día V-Permanente," 21A; and Rojas Blanco, "The V-Day March," 217–27.

38. See V-Day, "2004 Spotlight," https://www.vday.org/2004-spotlight-women-in-juarez.

39. Although human rights activists denounced Solís for mishandling the feminicide cases, there were also widespread allegations about his ties and efforts to protect the Cartel Juárez.

40. Personal conversation with Eva Arce on May 11, 2011.

41. Bejarano, "Memory of Struggle," 197. Ravelo Blancas also writes, "Violence has changed the world of these mothers and their families' lives, provoking in them feelings of strength, justice, resistance, and they've become political subjects, capable of thinking, questioning, acting, and changing.

These sentiments . . . form part of a common emotional structure, due to the pain that unites them." *Miradas Etnológicas*, 38 (my translation).

42. Spivak, *Death of a Discipline*, 47.

43. Wright, "Mujeres de Negro," 323.

44. See Fregoso, "Voices without an Echo"; Fregoso, *meXicana Encounters*, "Towards a Planetary Civil Society"; Fregoso, "'We Want Them Alive!'"

45. To counter the government's official narrative of blaming the victim, the mothers framed their victimized daughters as innocent and virginal.

46. Paula Flores, interview with the author, August 5, 2007; Solnit, "In Patriarchy."

47. Paterson, "The Border's COVID-19."

48. Tomlinson and Lipsitz, *Insubordinate Spaces*, 12.

49. My translation of "los gritos desesperados de una madre que pedía auxilio sabiendo que su vida estaba a punto de ser terminada como la de miles en el Estado." Quoted in Document for the Tribunal 2016, 26, an unpublished dossier provided for the judges of the Permanent People's Tribunal (see chapter 5).

50. My translation of "Marisela es una mujer que pasó de víctima defensora de derechos humanos. La madre que jamás se dejó vencer y que luchó por la justicia en el feminicidio de su hija, Rubí, lo que le costó la vida." Lucha Castro is a contributor to our collection, Fregoso and Bejarano, *Terrorizing Women*.

51. Information from CEDEM, "El Feminicidio de Marisela Escobedo," internal document, February 2011; and Document for the Tribunal 2016, an unpublished dossier provided for the judges of the Permanent People's Tribunal (see chapter 5), 26.

52. My translation of "Estoy aquí destrozada. Mi familia está destrozada, hay repudios de unos a otros, por el hubiera aunque sabemos que el hubiera no existe, repudio de unos contra otros, o si tú o si yo, si tu hubieras estado más pendientes, tanto reproches, corajes que hacemos, que no nos dejan vivir, no nos dejan volver hacer una familia, solo compartir el infierno que vivimos." Quoted in CEDEM, "El Feminicidio de Marisela Escobedo," 11.

53. CEDEM, "El Feminicidio de Marisela Escobedo," 2.

54. The international seminar was titled "Cuerpos y fronteras: Transformando la violencia y rescatando la justicia," sponsored by COLEF in Ciudad Juárez, September 20–21, 2012.

55. My translation of Susana Báez's words, "Se están dando dos generaciones de feminicidio," a statement made at the seminar "Cuerpos y fronteras."

56. Fregoso, "Señorita Extraviada: The Fate of 200 Women," keynote address, Women's History Month, New Mexico State University, Las Cruces, March 2001.

57. Combahee River Collective, "Why Did They Die?"

58. Davis, *Women, Race and Class*, 165.

59. My talk was originally titled, "La violencia de género y los límites del sistema estadounidense." Second international seminar, "Empoderamiento de la Ley General de Acceso de las Mujeres a una Vida Libre de Violencia," Comisión Nacional de Derechos Humanos, Mexico City, February 10–11, 2011.

60. See chapter 2 for a more in-depth discussion of abolition feminism and its influence on my thinking about the limits of feminicide laws in Latin America.

61. De Casas, "Protecting Hispanic Women." I confirm De Casas's analysis of the limited impact of VAWA on overall rates of gender violence in Fregoso, "Violencia de género."

62. Weissman and Weissman, "The Moral Politics of Social Control," 345–46.

63. Menjívar, *Enduring Violence*, 9.

64. María Lugones, "Reading the Coloniality of Gender," a conference talk at the annual meeting of the American Studies Association, 2012. This is also the case with other colonial powers, including England, France, and the Netherlands.

65. See Lugones, "Toward a Decolonial Feminism," 42.

66. In September 2021, Mexico's Supreme Court voted to decriminalize abortion.

67. Guevara Rosas, "Surveying the Damage: Enrique Peña Nieto."

68. Bautista, "'The Other Ayotzinapa.'"

69. Bautista, "'The Other Ayotzinapa.'"

70. Centenera, "Feminicidios."

71. Friedman and Tabbush, "#NiUnaMenos."

72. Gago, "La Tierra Tiembla," 178–79.

73. Ni Una Menos, "Nosotros Paramos," 184–88.

74. My translation of "Cruzando lenguas y fronteras, como hacemos las mujeres migrantes, desafiando la ilegalización de nuestros movimientos, emerge la rebelión contra la violencia, contra la feminización de la pobreza, contra el racismo, contra la falta de representación política, contra el intento de confinamiento de las mujeres y las niñas al encierro doméstico, contra las dogmas religiosas que se apropian de nuestro cuerpos y nuestras vidas, contra la maternidad como mandato y la criminalización del aborto, contra la renovadas formas de

explotación capitalista y contra la precarización de la existencia. Contra los despojos multiples: porque ni la tierra ni nuestros cuerpos son territorios de conquista." See Ni Una Menos, "Nosotros Paramos," 188.

75. Gago, "La Tierra Tiembla," 182.

76. Hong and Ferguson, *Strange Affinities,* 12.

77. The invitation stated, "Our 2-week seminar is conducted in support of educating senior federal government leaders (grade equivalency of GS-14/15) from federal executive departments/agencies such as the Department of Defense, Department of Homeland Security, Federal Bureau of Investigation, Drug Enforcement Administration, Defense Intelligence Agency, and combatant command such as North American Aerospace Defense–U.S. Northern Command and U.S. Special Operations Command."

78. Authorized by the US Congress in 2007, and funded through the State Department and USAID, the Mérida Initiative (also called Plan Mexico) is a security cooperation agreement aimed at combating transnational drug trafficking, organized crime, and money laundering. Initially funded for three years, the assistance includes training, military equipment, and intelligence, and is contingent on the Mexican government's human rights record.

79. Butler, "Rethinking Vulnerability," 22.

80. Butler, "Rethinking Vulnerability," 25.

81. World Health Organization, "Violence against Women." See also Observatorio Ciudadano Nacional del Feminicidio, "La violencia feminicida en México."

82. Encuesta Nacional sobre la Dinámica de las Relaciones en los Hogares (ENDIREH 2016), Instituto Nacional de Estadística, Geografía e Informática,

https://www.inegi.org.mx/programas/endireh/2016/.

See also Amnesty International, Mexico 2017/2018, available at Amnesty International Report 2017/2018, https://www.amnesty.org/en/wp-content/uploads/2021/05/POL1067002018ENGLISH.pdf.

83. Observatorio Ciudadano Nacional del Feminicidio, "La violencia feminicida en México."

84. Frías, "Strategies and Help Seeking Behavior," 17.

85. Observatorio Ciudadano Nacional de Feminicidio, "Informe Implementación del Tipo Penal en México," 217.

86. Frías, "Between Agency and Structure," 542–51.

87. See Arlene Valero, "Policías se vuelven feminicidas." econsulta.com Veracruz, January 11, 2018, https://www.e-veracruz.mx/nota/2018–01–11/nacion/feminicidios-los-policias-que-asesinaron-sus-parejas.

88. Frías, "Strategies and Help Seeking Behavior," 1–26.

89. Committee on the Elimination of Discrimination against Women, "Concluding Observations."

90. Morrison, *Burn This Book*, 4.

INTERLUDE 1: RE-MEMORY FOR THE DEAD

1. I visited the exhibition during the Day of the Dead, November 1–2, 2013.

2. This quote is taken from "Meet Diane Kahlo, Artist and Relative of Frida Kahlo," *Latino Daily News*, February 12, 2013. The article is no longer available online.

3. Diane Kahlo, telephone interview with the author, May 13, 2014. This and subsequent quotes are from my interview with Kahlo.

4. Szymanek, "Elina Chalet"; see also Gómez-Barris, *Beyond the Pink Tide*.

5. Szymanek, "Elina Chalet."

6. Laqueur, "The Dead Body," 75.

7. Laqueur, "The Dead Body," 92.

CHAPTER 2: MEXICO'S LONGEST WAR

1. Both are community-based organizations that provide legal and social support to the families of murdered and disappeared women.

2. Caputi, *The Age of Sex Crime*, 117.

3. Lugones, "Reading the Coloniality of Gender"; Lugones, "Toward a Decolonial Feminism," 42; Franco, *Cruel Modernity*, 5.

4. I'm indebted to Mbembe's canonical essay, "Necropolitics," 11–40; see Fregoso, "'We Want Them Alive!'" and "¡Las queremos vivas!"; also, Wright discussed the necropolitical order on the globalized border world of US/ Mexico in "Necropolitics."

5. In the global assembly line, products are assembled in poorer countries, primarily using women's labor and sometimes children's, whereas research and development take place in rich countries.

6. Franco, *Cruel Modernity*, 6.

7. Fregoso, "Voices without an Echo," 140.

8. With 3 percent of the nation's population, the state has been the site of 18 percent of the nation's homicides between 2007 and 2012, one of the highest murder rates in Mexico.

9. My translation of "En todo caso, tendremos que hablar de la economía de guerra (de la oficial contra el crimen y de la que se da entre mafias), donde el gobierno ha tomado parte, como el mayor interés que atraviesa las calles de Juárez. Todo parece mostrar que la violación de los derechos de la ciudadanía, desde la seguridad y el libre tránsito, hasta el goce y la actividad económica, es parte sustancial de la economía de la muerte" (Domínguez Ruvalcaba and Ravelo Blancas, *Desmantelamiento*, 21).

10. My translation of "Como lo muestra esta parte, los feminicidios son un reflejo de la ausencia de Estado o de un Estado fallido, lo que impide el acceso a las justicia para aquellas personas cuyas 'vidas precarias' las imposibilita para ejercer ciudadanía en el marco actual de un conflicto bélico que tuvo inicio el aparecer de cuerpos de mujeres mutiladas y asesinadas, cuerpos dolientes que constituyen 'cuerpos de desperdicio' frente a un Estado que sistemáticamente viola las garantías individuales de la población" (Huacuz Elías, "Introducción," 24).

11. My translation of "La primera se refiere a que desde 1982, el gobierno de Miguel de la Madrid estableció tácitamente un Pacto de Estado con la delincuencia organizada, para allegarse de recursos que liberaran la crisis. Desde entonces, estas redes criminales han logrado expandirse y operar libremente, hasta llegar a conformarse en un monopolio que controla prácticamente todas las rutas de tráfico de drogas hacia Estados Unidos, y que garantiza que las ganancias ilícitas estén plenamente protegidas. . . . En este sentido, el crimen organizado, además de ser una amenaza a la seguridad, es una fuerza económica que se ha hecho indispensable para una amplia porción de la economía difícil de cuantificar" (Domínguez Ruvalcaba and Ravelo Blancas, *Desmantelamiento*, 134).

12. Rivera Garza, *Grieving*, 3.

13. Cavarero, *Horrorism*, 62.

14. Guevara Rosas, "Surveying the Damage."

15. See "Comisión Nacional de Búsqueda," https://www.gob.mx/cnb.

16. Secretaría de Gobernación, "Búsqueda e Identificación de Personas Desaparecidas."

17. Quoted in Sheridan, "The Search for Mexico's Disappeared."

18. My translation of "El exterminio de mujeres continúa y se ha agudizado a partir de la guerra contra el narcotráfico, pues la violencia y muerte se potencian en esta guerra sin razones" (Ravelo Blancas, *Miradas Etnológicas*, 255).

19. Monárrez Fragoso, "Feminicidio Sexual Sistémico," 97.

20. Monárrez Fragoso, "Feminicidio Sexual Sistémico," 93.

21. See Fregoso, *meXicana Encounters*.

22. Ackerley, *Universal Human Rights*, 289.

23. Bettinger-Lopez et al., "Redefining Human Rights Lawyering."

24. Quoted in Kapur, *Erotic Justice*, 181.

25. See Fregoso, *meXicana Encounters*.

26. Cavarero, *Horrorism*, 3.

27. Lagarde de los Rios is also a former federal legislator/member of the Chamber of Deputies and president of the Feminicide Commission in Mexico, who authored the first feminicide law in the world.

28. Fregoso and Bejarano, *Terrorizing Women*, 5; see also Pola, *Femi(ni)cidio en República Dominicana*.

29. Monárrez Fragoso, "Feminicidio Sexual Sistémico," 95–96. In their report to the Special Rapporteur, Monárrez and Cervera define systemic sexual feminicide as "the assassination of women who are kidnapped, tortured and raped. Their nude or seminude corpses are left in the desert, in empty lots, in sewer pipes, in garbage dumps, and on train tracks. Through these cruel acts, the assassins strengthen the unequal gender relations that distinguish the sexes by emphasizing otherness, difference, and inequality." Monárrez Fragoso and Cervera Gómez, "Spatial and Temporal Behavior," 7–8.

30. See Russell, "Preface," xi.

31. Russell, "Femicide," 26. See also Russell and Harmes, *Feminicide in a Global Perspective*.

32. See García-Del Moral, "The Murders of Indigenous Women," 929–54.

33. De Lima Costa, "Introduction to Debates," 21.

34. García-Del Moral, "The Murders of Indigenous Women," 949.

35. Fregoso and Bejarano, *Terrorizing Women*, 4.

36. Fregoso and Bejarano, *Terrorizing Women*, 4–5.

37. Lugones, "Toward a Decolonial Feminism"; Rivera Cusicanqui, "The Notion of Rights," 29–54; Marcos, "The Borders Within," 81–110; Pérez, "Enrique Dussel's *Etica*," 121–46.

38. Lagarde de los Rios, "Preface," xi–xxv ; for the genealogy of the terms, see Russell, "Femicide," 27.

39. Lagarde de los Rios, "Preface," xi–xxv.

40. See Eng and Puar, "Introduction," 12.

41. Lagarde de los Rios, "Preface," xi–xxv.

42. Monárrez Fragoso, "Serial Sexual Feminicide," 154.

43. Monárrez Fragoso, "Feminicidio Sexual Sistémico," 93.

44. Sanford, *Guatemala*; Sanford, "From Genocide to Feminicide," 104–22.

45. Menjívar and Walsh, "The Architecture of Feminicide," 222. In terms of research on gender violence in Guatemala, Sanford was the first researcher to deploy the term *feminicide* because it implicates the state.

46. Fregoso and Bejarano, *Terrorizing Women*, 12.

47. García-Del Moral, "The Murders of Indigenous Women," 939.

48. Davis et al., *Abolition*, 95. For an overview of intersectionality in Chicana feminist thought, see Hurtado, *Intersectional Chicana Feminisms*.

49. Fregoso and Bejarano, *Terrorizing Women*, 12.

50. Domínguez Ruvalcaba, *Nación Criminal*.

51. This public talk was subsequently revised and published in Fregoso, *meXicana Encounters*, 22.

52. Fregoso, *meXicana Encounters*, 22.

53. Lugones, "Reading the Coloniality of Gender."

54. My thanks to Marisol Alcocer Perulero for this updated information. See "Legislación Vigente," http://congresochiapas.gob.mx/legislaturalxvi/trabajo-legislativo/legislacion-vigente.

55. Escocer Perulero, ""Assassinatos de mulheres negras no México."

56. García-Del Moral, "The Murders of Indigenous Women," 944.

57. Escocer, ""Assassinatos de mulheres negras no México," 11, my translation.

58. Escocer, ""Assassinatos de mulheres negras no México," 6.

59. See Fregoso and Bejarano, *Terrorizing Women*, 10.

60. Bernstein, "The Sexual Politics of the 'New Abolitionism,'"143; Bernstein, "Militarized Humanitarianism," 45–71; Bernstein, "Carceral Politics as Gender Justice?," 233–59; Bumiller, *In an Abusive State*; and Weissman, "The Personal Is Political," 387–450.

61. Cantalupo, "Using Law and Education," 200.

62. Lagarde's comments at the forum "Red de Investigadoras sobre la Vida y Libertad de las Mujeres," Comisión de Derechos Humanos, Mexico City, 2011.

63. Davis et al., *Abolition*, 58.

64. Federici, *Witches, Witch-Hunting, and Women*.

65. See Foucault, *"Society Must Be Defended"*; and Taylor, *Foucault, Feminism, and Sex Crimes*.

66. My translation of "En los penales no habitan en general los delincuentes más peligrosos sino los más pobres" (Azaola, *Crimen, castigo y violencias*, 126).

67. Sudbury, "Introduction," xi–xxviii.

68. Davis et al., *Abolition*, 72. See also Davis, *Are Prisons Obsolete?*; Gilmore, *Golden Gulag*; Ritchie, *Arrested Justice*.

69. Davis et al., *Abolition*, 61.

70. Two-thirds of the prison population are men of color, primarily African American and Latino. See Lauren E. Glaze, "Correctional Populations in the United States, 2009 (NCJ 231681)," Bureau of Justice Statistics, U.S. Department of Justice, https://bjs.ojp.gov/content/pub/pdf/cpus09.pdf.

71. Bernstein, "Carceral Politics as Gender Justice?," 253; quoted in Taylor, *Foucault, Feminism, and Sex Crimes*, 93.

72. Haney, "The Perversions of Prison," 138.

73. Inmates in Mexican prisons fare no better. See, for example, Peláez Ferrusca, "Derechos Humanos y Prisión." Also see *Guardian*, "Twenty Die in Mexican Prison Fight."

74. Davis et al., *Abolition*, 129.

75. My translation of "Peor aún, que el discurso sobre derechos y ciudadanía de las mujeres se puede convertir en un eslogan conservador que demanda al Estado más leyes, más penas y, por supuesto, 'mano dura' con los agresores" (Huacuz Elías, "Introducción," 17).

76. My translation of "Intentar llevar al código punitivo el fenómeno social del feminicidio, sin preguntarse sobre la estructura ideológica básica de la ley penal, conlleva a la legitimación de todo un sistema estatal que no solo es sexista en tanto producto del patriarcado, sino incluso clasista y racista" (Nuñez Rebolledo, "Contribución a la Crítica," 201).

77. My translation of Laporta, "El feminicidio como categoría jurídica." Since the publication of her article, the following countries have adopted feminicide/femicide laws: Venezuela (2014), Brazil (2015), Colombia (2015), Paraguay (2016), and Uruguay (2017).

78. Laporta, "El feminicidio como categoría jurídica."

79. Laporta, "El feminicidio como categoría jurídica."

80. Feminist legal scholar Christina Iturralde argues for an application of Rama Mani's framework of the three dimensions of justice as an alternative approach. See Iturralde, "Searching for Accountability," 243–62.

81. Davis et al., *Abolition*, 68.

82. Weissman and Weissman, "The Moral Politics of Social Control," 345–46.

83. Davis et al., *Abolition*, 119.

84. See Alexander, *The New Jim Crow*; Richie, *Arrested Justice*; Iturralde, "Searching for Accountability."

85. See Paterson, "The Silencing of Women's Voices."

86. The complicity of state authorities with drug cartels is the subject of the French documentary *La ville qui tue les femmes* [*The City That Murders Women*]. Directors J. F. Boyer, Marc Fernandez and Jean Christophe Rampal document how both governors of the state of Chihuahua, Francisco Barrios (PAN) and Patricio Martinez (PRI), prevented investigations linking feminicide to narcotraffickers. In the weeks before he was assassinated, attorney Sergio Dante Almaraz told reporters, "Creo que las muertes de las jóvenes obedecen a una razón fundamental, es el daño collateral de la presencia del narcotráfico en Ciudad Juárez." (I believe that the deaths of young women obey a fundamental logic: they are the collateral damage of the presence of narcotrafficking in Ciudad Juárez.)

87. My translation of "Solo un grupo altamente organizado podría llevar acabo crimes a tal escala, y con una secuencia de delitos como el secuestro, violación, tortura, asesinato, así como almacenamiento y traslado de cadáveres. Este grupo, que en apariencia incluye a la policía, ha logrado operar sin ser descubierto por años. . . . Fue aparente que una red corrupta de funcionarios judiciales, políticos, líderes empresariales y narcotraficantes, hicieron possible que el asesinato de mujeres en Juárez se convirtiera en deporte para ciertos hombres" (Washington Valdez, *Cosecha de Mujeres*, 70–71).

88. Davis et al., *Abolition*, 19.

89. See image at https://www.dukeupress.edu/terrorizing-women.

90. Guevara Rosas, "Surveying the Damage."

91. Statement by Jeremy Kuzmanov, quoted in Paterson, "The Silencing of Women's Voices."

92. See González Rodríguez, *The Femicide Machine*; Paterson, "Mexico's New Dirty War"; Meyer, "Abuso y miedo en Ciudad Juárez"; and Archibold, "Rights Groups Contend."

93. Menjívar and Walsh, "The Architecture of Feminicide," 222.

94. Sekkgya, *Report of the Special Rapporteur.*

95. Sekkgya, *Report of the Special Rapporteur*, 9–12.

96. Ferreyra, *The Risks of Defending Human Rights.*

97. Cavarero, *Horrorism*, 73.

98. Monárrez Fragoso, "Serial Sexual Feminicide," 162.

99. Flores Contreras, "Asesina a activista contra la violencia"; Ballinas and Becerril, "Violencia contra mujeres"; Camacho Servín, "Chihuahua." See also Observatorio Ciudadano Nacional de Feminicidio, *Informe Implementación del Tipo Penal.*

100. Castañeda Salgado, "Feminicide in Mexico," 1059.

101. Front Line Defenders, *Annual Report on Human Rights Defenders.*

102. López, "President of Mexico Speaks Up."

103. López Medellín, *Tamaulipas.*

104. López, "Number of Journalists Killed." During the first month of 2022, four journalists were assassinated, according to the Committee to Protect Journalists, https://cpj.org/2022/02/roberto-toledo-is-fourth-mexican -journalist-killed-in-less-than-four-weeks/. See also https://cpj.org/americas /mexico/.

105. López, "President of Mexico Speaks Up."

106. López Obrador condemned the threats against Azucena Aresti and expressed "his solidarity" with her, in what was characterized as an "unusual defense of a journalist." See López, "President of Mexico Speaks Up."

107. Gallón, "Women Are Being Killed."

108. Orsi, "Mexico."

109. Méndez and Jiménez, "Gertz."

110. UN Women, "COVID-19 and Ending Violence."

111. Fumega, "Tracking Latin America's Other Pandemic."

112. UN Women, "COVID-19 and Ending Violence"; *Euronews,* "Domestic Violence Cases Jump 30%."

113. Allen-Ebrahimian, "China's Domestic Violence Epidemic."

114. UDGTV.com, "Presentó Informe 2020."

115. Gallón, "Women Are Being Killed."

116. Quoted in Grant, "Who's Killing Us?," 148, emphasis added.

117. Caputi, *The Age of Sex Crime,* 116.

118. Javier Duarte resigned as governor in 2016 and was later arrested in Guatemala and charged with corruption and money laundering. In 2018, Duarte was found guilty of embezzling billions of dollars and sentenced to nine years in prison.

119. Driver, "Four Women Were Also Raped."

120. Driver, "Four Women Were Also Raped."

121. Goldman, "Who Killed Rubén Espinosa and Nadia Vera?"

122. Goldman, "Who Killed Rubén Espinosa and Nadia Vera?"

CHAPTER 3: THE ARTIST AND WITNESS

An earlier (and abridged version) of this chapter was published as "The Art of Witness in Lourdes Portillo's *Señorita Extraviada,*" in *Border Cinema: Reimagining Identity through Aesthetics,* edited by Monica Hanna and Rebecca A. Sheehan (New Brunswick: Rutgers University Press, 2019), 62–80.

1. Portillo, "Filming *Señorita Extraviada*," 234.

2. Portillo, "Filming *Señorita Extraviada*," 234.

3. Portillo, "Filming *Señorita Extraviada*," 234.

4. Lourdes Portillo, interview with the author, 2003.

5. Tercer Cine is also known as the new Latin American cinema movement.

6. Birri, "For Nationalist, Realist, Critical and Popular Cinema," 96.

7. See Fregoso and Bejarano, *Terrorizing Women*; *Feminicidio en América Latina*; Fregoso, "'We Want Them Alive!'"; Fregoso, *meXicana Encounters*; Fregoso, "Voices without an Echo."

8. Villaseñor, "An Interview with Lourdes Portillo," 170. In a recent conversation (September 16, 2021), Portillo reminded me that she first read about the cases of feminicide in the Juárez newspapers, prior to Nathan's article.

9. Lourdes Portillo, interview with the author, 2011.

10. Portillo, "Filming *Señorita Extraviada*," 233.

11. Portillo, "Filming *Señorita Extraviada*, 229; Lourdes Portillo, interview with the author, 2007.

12. Villaseñor, "An Interview with Lourdes Portillo," 174.

13. Lourdes Portillo, interview with the author, 2002.

14. Portillo, interview with the author, 2002.

15. See Renov, "Towards a Poetics of Documentary."

16. Felman and Laub, *Testimony*, 5.

17. Felman and Laub, *Testimony*, 204.

18. Gómez-Peña and Novaro's comments are from the interview I conducted with Portillo in 2004. On July 19, 2002, the documentary was screened in a public plaza, El Jardín Hidalgo in Coyoacán (Mexico City), followed by a panel talk with notable Mexican intellectuals, including the late Carlos Monsiváis, Elena Poniatowska, and María Novaro. Lourdes Portillo, interview with the author, 2004.

19. Felman and Laub, *Testimony*, 204.

20. Derrida, "A Self-Unsealing Poetic Text," 194.

21. Portillo, interview with the author, 2004.

22. Derrida, "A Self-Unsealing Poetic Text," 194.

23. Guerin and Hallas, "Introduction," 12.

24. Cubilié, *Women Witnessing Terror*, 11.

25. Derrida, "A Self-Unsealing Poetic Text," 188.

26. Derrida, "A Self-Unsealing Poetic Text," 199.

27. Oliver, *Women as Weapons*, 161.

28. Portillo, interview with the author, 2004.

29. Portillo, interview with the author, 2004.

30. See Fregoso, "Sacando los Trapos al Sol," for further discussion of these techniques, as they apply to *The Devil Never Sleeps*.

31. Portillo, interview with the author, 2003.

32. "Death Comes to the Maquilas: A Border Story," proposal to the Soros Documentary Fund for a preproduction grant of US$25,000 (on file with the author).

33. Portillo, interview with the author, 2007.

34. Guerin and Hallas, "Introduction," 2.

35. Sontag, *On Photography*, 19–20.

36. Sontag, *On Photography*, 20.

37. Taylor, *Disappearing Acts*, 157.

38. See de la Mora, "Terrorismo de género en la frontera," for further discussion of Mexican popular culture's obsession with the pornography of sexualized violence, or what he terms the "spectacle of the gendered practices of sexualized violence."

39. See my complete analysis of Bowden's abjection of the murdered women of Juárez in Fregoso, *meXicana Encounters*, chapter 1.

40. See Portillo, "Filming *Señorita Extraviada*."

41. Portillo, interview with the author, 2007.

42. Writing in another context about the production of presence, I consider the language of the ephemeral as a way to animate the unseen but felt presences, the memories of las desaparecidas. *Señorita Extraviada* is part of a new politics of the body taking shape around poetic, ethereal representations that animate an alternative sense of presence or a "*praesentia*," the manifestation of "an absence" within the "material presence of social life" (Fregoso, "'We Want Them Alive!,'" 127). Originally concerned with the manifestation of the holy dead (saintly relics) in "insignificant fragment[s] of ordinary material" or saintly relics, *praesentia* is "concerned with performance and presence . . . with the experience of mingling: distance and proximity; presence and absence; secular and divine; human and non-human; subject and object; time and space; vision and touch." In "making those discursive categories appear uncertain and blurred," it brings to the surface the unseen but felt presence, the memories of the subject no longer living, the socially haunting forces. *Praesentia* points to the centrality of alternative cosmologies for understanding

and imagining subjectivity, and in particular the subject of human rights. See Fregoso, "'We Want Them Alive!'" For a compelling analysis of the allegorical elements in *Señorita Extraviada*, see Carroll, "'Accidental Allegories,'" 357–96.

43. Berger, *Ways of Seeing*, 7.

44. See Fregoso, "California Dreaming," 257–74.

45. Marks, *The Skin of the Film*, xvi.

46. Marks, *The Skin of the Film*, 168.

47. Marks, *The Skin of the Film*, xi.

48. Marks, *The Skin of the Film*, 172.

49. Marks, *The Skin of the Film*, 2.

50. Portillo, interview with the author, 2007.

51. Paraphrasing Marks, *The Skin of the Film*, 164.

52. Portillo, interview with the author, 2002.

53. Villaseñor, "An Interview with Lourdes Portillo," 171.

54. See Fregoso, *meXicana Encounters*, chapter 1.

55. Portillo, interview with the author, 2003.

56. Writing in another context, I note that *Señorita Extraviada* is an example of the inscription of normative gender identities. The exclusive focus on the murder and disappearance of young women has had a similar effect of normalizing traditional gender identities, in this case, by coding the murdered women as virgins. As I have argued elsewhere, the film's emphasis on the purity and innocence of the victims is strategic, designed to counter the state and the media's campaign of blaming the victim by attributing female nonnormative sexuality as the cause for their murders and disappearances. Yet the title of the film, *Señorita*, is problematic from a feminist perspective for its failure to unsettle traditional meanings about women's sexuality, especially the assumptions regarding the patriarchal regulation of women's sexual behavior implicit in the word *señorita*. The Spanish use of the term *señorita* refers to several things. It translates into "young woman" (Missing Young Woman); an unmarried woman (in contrast to a señora); and, most telling, it refers to a woman's virginity ("es señorita"), derived from Catholic prohibitions on premarital sex and patriarchal valorization of a woman's purity (read "virginity"). The documentary privileges young and innocent victims at the expense of the other, older (less pure) victims of feminicide (single, divorced mothers, sex workers, etc.), which can in turn leave viewers with the impression that violence against women is somehow more egregious if the victim is young and innocent. See Fregoso, "'We Want Them Alive!'"

57. Theresa Delgadillo characterizes the film as a form of "spiritual mestizaje," and Portillo's identification as "mother" with the mothers of the murdered and disappeared women. See Delgadillo, *Spiritual Mestizaje*, 128–36.

58. de la Mora, "Terrorismo de género en la frontera."

59. Portillo, interview with the author, 2003.

60. Cubilié, *Women Witnessing Terror*, 187.

61. Butler, *Precious Life*, 44–45.

62. Portillo, interview with the author, 2002.

63. Birri, "For Nationalist, Realist, Critical and Popular Cinema," 96.

64. Portillo, interview with the author, 2002.

INTERLUDE 2: REDRESSING INJUSTICE

This interlude was originally published in the article "For a Pluriversal Declaration of Human Rights," 595–97.

1. Kester, *The One and the Many*, 96.

2. These and subsequent quotes are from Irene Simmons, interview with the author, March 18, 2007, in Tucson, Arizona.

3. Drawing from Levinas and Gandhi, Baxi similarly writes about an alternative language of human rights rooted in a spiritual ethic of human responsibility. See Baxi, *The Future of Human Rights*, 210–12.

CHAPTER 4: THE ART OF WITNESS

A version of this chapter first appeared in *Chiricú Journal* 2, no. 1 (Fall 2017): 118–36. I'm deeply grateful to Linda Watanabe McFerrin of Left Coast Writers, whose workshops have enabled my incursions into a different type of writing. I also thank fellow participants of these workshops for their invaluable feedback.

1. "Feminicide = Sanctioned Murder: Gender, Race and Violence in a Global Context," conference at Stanford University, Stanford, CA, March 16–19, 2007.

2. Elena Poniatowska, opening remarks at "Feminicide = Sanctioned Murder."

3. Tomlinson and Lipsitz, *Insubordinate Spaces*, 32.

4. Paula Flores, personal conversation with author, June 2007.

5. Henderson, "Citizenship in the Line of Fire," 973.

6. Mahony and Eguren, *Unarmed Bodyguards*, 2.

7. Henderson, "Citizenship in the Line of Fire," 974.

8. Henderson, "Citizenship in the Line of Fire," 970.

9. Tomlinson and Lipsitz, *Insubordinate Spaces*, 24.

10. Paula Flores, interview with the author, August 5, 2007.

11. Flores, interview with the author.

12. Pérez, *Chicana Art*, 93.

13. Pineda-Madrid, *Suffering and Salvation*, 115.

14. Mesa-Baines, "The Interior Life," 9.

15. Pineda-Madrid, *Suffering and Salvation*, 119.

16. Isabel Velásquez, personal phone conversation with the author, September 1999.

17. Flores, interview with the author.

18. Quintana, "Mujeres en éxodo por la vida."

19. Pineda-Madrid, *Suffering and Salvation*, 93.

20. The cross remained in front of the *Umbral* for eight years and was removed sometime in 2015, according to Paula Flores.

21. Walker, *The Way Forward*, 200.

CHAPTER 5: WITNESSES TO MEXICO'S "LIVING DEAD"

A version of this chapter first appeared in *Kalfou* 3, no. 2 (Fall 2016): 185–206.

1. This and all subsequent quotes are from my notes during the hearings. All translations from the original Spanish into English are mine.

2. During the 1960s and 1970s, the Mexican government launched a Dirty War against the civil society groups on the left who opposed the state's repressive policies. The Dirty War, which continues to this day, includes enforced disappearances, assassinations, and criminalization of human rights defenders, women's rights activists, communitarian leaders, and Indigenous and environmental activists.

3. See Santos, *Places Left Unfinished*.

4. To view this image, see Fundar: Centro de Análisis e Investigación, "Audiencia de feminicidio y violencia de género," September 18, 2014, https://fundar.org.mx/audiencia-de-feminicidio-y-violencias-de-genero/.

5. Testimony presented before the tribunal.

6. Organization of American States, "Inter-American Convention on Forced Disappearances."

7. This was Videla's response during a news conference with journalists in 1979. See *El Día*, "No están muertos ni vivos."

8. Testimony presented before the tribunal.

9. Human Rights Watch, *Mexico's Disappeared*.

10. Guevara Rosas, "Surveying the Damage."

11. See GIEI, *Informe Ayotzinapa*. The members of the independent commission were Alejandro Valencia Villa, Ángela María Buitrago, Carlos Martín Beristaín, Claudia Paz y Paz Baile, and Francisco Cox Vial.

12. Franzblau, "Why Is the US Still Spending Billions?"

13. Quoted in Global Alliance for the Rights of Nature, "People's Tribunal versus Judicial Tribunal."

14. The PPT issued its final ruling on Mexico on November 15, 2014. Permanent Peoples' Tribunal, "Final Ruling." See also SubVersiones, "Feminicidio y violencias contra las mujeres."

INTERLUDE 3: FLOR DE ARENA

This interlude was originally published in the article "For a Pluriversal Declaration of Human Rights," 599–602.

1. Alexander, *Pedagogies of Crossing*, 317.

2. Miller, "Native America Writes Back," 12. Writing in another context, Talal Asad addresses the "destabilization of the concept of the rights-bearing human subject" through "interventions by genetic engineering" and adds, "Because the concept of the natural is now being reconfigured, we may now have to rethink the supernatural" (*Formations of the Secular*, 157–58).

3. This and all other quotes are from an interview I conducted with Verónica Leiton in September 2012, Ciudad Juárez, Chihuahua.

4. Marcos, "The Borders Within," 91. Marcos draws from Calixta Guiteras-Holmes's (1961) superb ethnography on Indigenous peoples of Chiapas, *Perils of the Soul*.

CHAPTER 6: STOLEN LIVES AND FUGITIVITY

An earlier version of this chapter first appeared in *Death Studies* 44, no. 11 (2020): 736–45, DOI: 10.1080/07481187.2020.1771856.

1. See Human Rights First, "Delivered to Danger."

2. Chomsky, "Prospects for Survival," 629.

3. Evans, "The Death of Humanitarianism."

4. For further discussion of the criminalization of migrants, see Inda, "Fatal Prescriptions," 699–708.

5. Cacho, *Social Death*, 4.

6. Refugees are persons who apply for refuge while outside the United States, whereas asylum seekers currently reside in the United States or arrive at an official point of entry.

7. Weheliye, *Habeas Viscus*, 2

8. Lifton uses the concept of death in life to describe the profound death-life disruption conveyed by survivors of Hiroshima: "the widespread sense that life and death were out of phase with one another, no longer properly distinguishable" (*Death in Life*, 23).

9. Mackey, *Paracritical Hinge*, 187; originally published as Mackey, "Cante Moro."

10. Guerrero, "Sessions Says 'Zero Tolerance' Policy for Border Crossers."

11. Center for Gender and Refugee Studies, "*Matter of A-B-*," 2.

12. Center for Gender and Refugee Studies, "*Matter of A-B-*."

13. Center for Gender and Refugee Studies, "*Matter of A-B-*," 5.

14. Cházaro, Casey, and Kuhl, "Getting Away with Murder."

15. Cházaro, Casey, and Kuhl, "Getting Away with Murder," 34.

16. Cházaro, Casey, and Kuhl, "Getting Away with Murder," 17.

17. From June 12 to November 30, 2018, immigration courts in the United States approved twenty-nine petitions for asylum in domestic violence cases and seventeen grants in cases of gang violence.

18. Chishti, Pierce, and Jacks, "Trump Administration's Unprecedented Actions."

19. Grillo, "Mexican Border as Refugee Camp."

20. Department of Homeland Security, Migrant Protection Protocols.

21. Egelbo, "UN Official."

22. In 2018, the Trump administration announced a new policy that bars people from petitioning for asylum if they travel to the United States through a third country, other than the one they fled. This policy is known as the Transit Asylum Ban. See Margulies, "The Ninth Circuit's Asylum Ban."

23. Note that the recent ruling by the Ninth Circuit differs from an earlier ruling by the Court of Appeals for the Third Circuit and forms the basis of an appeal to the Supreme Court.

24. Weheliye, *Habeas Viscus*, 2.

25. Weheliye, *Habeas Viscus*, 2.

26. Weheliye, *Habeas Viscus*, 4.

27. Weheliye, *Habeas Viscus*, 14.

28. Patterson, *Slavery and Social Death*.

29. Kanstroom, *Deportation Nation*, 77–78. My thanks to Catherine Ramírez for suggesting Kanstroom's book.

30. Minian, "America Didn't Always Lock Up Migrants."

31. My translation of "sin bañarse uno ni cepillarte los dientes nos tratan tan pesimo a uno como si fueramos animales. A veces nos castigaban y no nos daban agua ni comida . . . Dormiamos tirados en el suelo, nos daban papel de aluminio para taparnos . . ." Grassroots Leadership, "These Letters from Migrant Women." This letter is available at https://www.cnn.com/2018/07/03/us/detention-center-letters-grassroots-leadership/index.html?sr=fbCNNp070418detention-center-letters-grassroots-leadershipo822AMStory&CNNPolitics=fb. First accessed on July 20, 2018; accessed again on July 29, 2022. It does not have a number like the subsequent letters published by Grassroots Leadership (see below).

32. Inda, "Fatal Prescriptions," 699.

33. Weheliye, *Habeas Viscus*, 37.

34. Durkin, "The Migrants Who Have Died."

35. Durkin, "The Migrants Who Have Died." For an examination of the necropolitics of uncare in migrant detention facilities, see Inda's case study of Juan Carlos Baires in "Fatal Prescriptions." See also American Immigration Lawyers Association, "Deaths at Adult Detention Centers."

36. Egelbo, "UN Official."

37. Alexander, "Reckoning with Violence," A21.

38. The Corrections Corporation of America (CCA/CoreCivic, formerly CCA) is the oldest private prison corporation, with over sixty facilities nationwide. Freedom for Migrants, *Persecuted in U.S. Migrant Detention*.

39. Stinger and Valdés, "Divest from Private Prisons."

40. My translation of "8 dias sin bañarme ni mi medicamiento pensaba que me enfermaria. Luego nos llevaron a la corte y nos esposaron de pies y mano como si fueramos delincuentes como por 8 horas sin desayunar ni almorsar. No es justo como nos tratan como si fueramos animales." Grassroots Leadership, "These Letters from Migrant Women," letter #20.

41. Southern Poverty Law Center, *No End in Sight*.

42. Freedom for Migrants, *Persecuted in U.S. Migrant Detention*.

43. Law, "Forced to Work for Pennies."

44. Law, "Forced to Work for Pennies."

45. My translation of "Yo soy una de las madres que viene uyendo de su paiz porq nos amenasaron con matarnos a mi y a mis niños. Por eso uyimos del paiz pero aqui nos mataron en vida quitandonos a nuestros hijos. Por favor ayudenme." Grassroots Leadership, "These Letters from Migrant Women," letter #14.

46. Haraway, *Staying with the Trouble*, 145.

47. For a similar category, see "life-in-death" in Holland, *Raising the Dead*, 18.

48. Martínez, "Living Dead, 721." See also Kobelinsky's use of "living dead" as "border beings," which is more akin to Agamben's notion of "bare life."

49. Martínez, "Living Dead," 721.

50. Weheliye, *Habeas Viscus*, 39.

51. Weheliye, *Habeas Viscus*, 56.

52. Malkki, "Refugee and Exile," 519. Also see Freedman's discussion regarding the notion of vulnerability as reproducing gendered stereotypes in "The Uses and Abuses of 'Vulnerability.'"

53. Malkki, "Refugee and Exile," 500.

54. Arendt, *The Origins of Totalitarianism*.

55. See also Inda's discussion of the growth of migrant incarceration and criminalization in the aftermath of the passage of new immigration laws in the 1980s and 1990s in "Fatal Prescriptions."

56. Minian, "America Didn't Always Lock Up Migrants."

57. Following Malkki, the refugee as a social category refers to its usage in the academic disciplines of the social sciences; the "political" refers to its use as a category in geopolitical discourse, which generally overlaps with its intelligibility as a legal category in international law. See Malkki, "Refugee and Exile," 497–98.

58. Malkki, "Refugee and Exile," 501; United Nations Human Rights, Office of the High Commissioner, "Convention Relating to the Status of Refugees," emphasis added.

59. The definitions are culled from various internet sources.

60. For a comprehensive analysis of the gendered construction and norms behind the notion of vulnerability in EU asylum and refugee policies, see Freedman, "Uses and Abuses of 'Vulnerability.'"

61. Cacho, *Social Death*, 5.

62. Freedman, "The Uses and Abuses of 'Vulnerability,'" 7.

63. *The American Heritage Dictionary of the English Language*, 5th ed.

64. See *The American Heritage Dictionary of the English Language*, 5th ed.

65. Weheliye, *Habeas Viscus*, 12.

66. My translation, Mezzadra, *Derecho de Fuga*, 17. In *Assimilation: An Alternative History*, Catherine Ramírez argues that the emphasis on migrants' "contributions" to the host society "ends up reinforcing the logic of deservingness and bolstering the image of the host country as an egalitarian meritocracy. The argument that immigrants contribute to the host society also reifies them as bearers of human capital, not bearers of rights." Email conversation with author.

67. Mezzadra, *Derecho de Fuga*, 51.

68. Kanstroom, *Deportation Nation*, 78.

69. Gruesz, "'Poor Eliza' on the Border," 183. I'm indebted to Catherine Ramírez for referring me to Gruesz's article.

70. Mackey, *Paracritical Hinge*, 187.

71. Moten, *In the Break*, 305. On epistemic disobedience, see Mignolo, *The Darker Side of Western Modernity*.

72. Von Gleich, "Fugitivity against the Border," 204.

73. Campt, *Image Matters*, 80.

74. Von Gleich, "Fugitivity against the Border," 210.

75. Von Gleich, "Fugitivity against the Border," 211.

76. Martínez, "Living Dead," 724.

77. The narrative details are factual and taken from actual declarations by asylum seekers who petitioned for gender asylum in the United States.

Bibliography

Ackerley, Brooke A. *Universal Human Rights in a World of Difference.* Cambridge: Cambridge University Press, 2008.

Aikin Araluce, Olga. *Activismo Social Trasnacional: Un Análisis en Torno a los Feminicidios en Ciudad Juárez.* Guadalajara: ITESO; Tijuana: El Colegio de la Frontera Norte; Ciudad Juárez: Universidad Autónoma de Ciudad Juárez, 2011.

Alexander, M. Jacqui. *Pedagogies of Crossing: Meditations on Feminism, Sexual Politics, Memory, and the Sacred.* Durham, NC: Duke University Press, 2005.

Alexander, Michelle. *The New Jim Crow: Mass Incarceration in the Age of Colorblindness.* New York: New Press, 2010.

Alexander, Michelle. "Reckoning with Violence." *New York Times*, March 1, 2019.

Allen-Ebrahimian, Bethany. "China's Domestic Violence Epidemic." *Axios*, March 7, 2020. https://www.axios.com/china-domestic-violence -coronavirus-quarantine-7b00c3ba-35bc-4d16-afdd-b76ecfb28882.html.

American Immigration Lawyers Association. "Deaths at Adult Detention Centers." AILA Doc. No. 16050900, December 4, 2018; updated to July 11, 2022. https://www.aila.org/infonet/deaths-at-adult-detention -centers.

Amnesty International. "Mexico: Intolerable Killings: 10 Years of Abductions and Murders of Women in Ciudad Juárez and Chihuahua: Summary Report and Appeals Cases." August 10, 2003. https://www .amnesty.org/en/documents/AMR41/027/2003/en/.

Archibold, Randal C. "Rights Groups Contend Mexican Military Has Heavy Hand in Drug Cases." *New York Times*, August 3, 2011.

Arendt, Hannah. *The Origins of Totalitarianism.* San Diego: Harcourt, 1968.

Asad, Talal. *Formations of the Secular: Christianity, Islam, Modernity.* Stanford, CA: Stanford University Press, 2003.

Ashuri, Tamar, and Amit Pinchevski. "Witnessing as a Field." In *Media Witnessing: Testimony in the Age of Mass Communication,* edited by Paul Frosh and Amit Pinchevski, 113–56. London: Palgrave Macmillan, 2009.

Associated Press. "Twenty Die in Mexican Prison Fight Near US Border." *Guardian,* October 15, 2011. http://www.guardian.co.uk/world/2011/oct/16/mexican-prison-fight-matamoros.

Azaola, Elena. *Crimen, castigo y violencias en México.* Mexico City: FLACSO and CIESAS, 2009.

Baldwin, James. *The Evidence of Things Not Seen.* New York: Henry Holt and Company, 1995.

Ballinas, Victor, and Andrea Becerril. "Violencia contra mujeres, en grave incremento: CNDH." *La Jornada,* March 6, 2018. https://www.jornadabc.mx/tijuana/06-03-2018/violencia-contra-mujeres-en-grave-incremento-cndh.

Bautista, Nidia. "'The Other Ayotzinapa': Organizing against Feminicide in Mexico." Common Dreams, March 15, 2015. https://www.commondreams.org/views/2015/03/15/other-ayotzinapa-organizing-against-feminicide-mexico.

Baxi, Upendra. *The Future of Human Rights.* New Delhi: Oxford University Press, 2006.

Bejarano, Cynthia. "Las Super Madres de Latino America: Transforming Motherhood by Challenging Violence in Mexico, Argentina, and El Salvador." *Frontiers: A Journal of Women's Studies* 23, no. 1 (2002): 126–50.

Bejarano, Cynthia. "Memory of Struggle in Ciudad Juárez." *Aztlán: A Journal of Chicano Studies* 38, no. 1 (Spring 2013): 189–203.

Benítez, Rohry, Adriana Candia, Patricia Cabrera, Guadalupe de la Mora, Josefina Martínez, Isabel Velázquez, and Ramona Ortiz. *El Silencio que la voz de todas quiebra.* Chihuahua, Mexico: Ediciones Azar, 1999.

Benner, Katie, and Caitlin Dickerson, "Sessions Says Domestic and Gang Violence Are Not Grounds for Asylum." *New York Times,* June 11, 2018. https://www.nytimes.com/2018/06/11/us/politics/sessions-domestic-violence-asylum.html

Berger, John. *Bento's Sketchbook.* New York: Pantheon, 2011.

Berger, John. *Ways of Seeing.* New York: Penguin Books, 1977.

Bernstein, Elizabeth. "Carceral Politics as Gender Justice? The 'Traffic in Women' and Neoliberal Circuits of Crime, Sex, and Rights." *Theory and Society* 4, no. 3 (2012): 233–59.

Bernstein, Elizabeth. "Militarized Humanitarianism Meets Carceral Feminism: The Politics of Sex, Rights, and Freedom in Contemporary Anti-trafficking Campaigns." *Signs: Journal of Women in Culture and Society* 36, no. 4 (2010): 45–71.

Bernstein, Elizabeth. "The Sexual Politics of the 'New Abolitionism.'" *Differences* 18, no. 3 (2007): 128–51.

Bettinger-Lopez, Caroline, Davida Finger, Meetali Jain, JoNel Newman, Sarah Paoletti, and Deborah Weissman. "Redefining Human Rights Lawyering through the Lens of Critical Theory: Lessons for Pedagogy and Practice." *Georgetown Journal on Poverty Law and Policy* 18 (2011). http://ssrn.com/abstract=1768167.

Birri, Fernando. "For Nationalist, Realist, Critical and Popular Cinema." In *New Latin American Cinema.* Vol. 1, *Theory, Practices, and Transnational Articulations,* edited by Michael T. Martin, 95–98. Detroit: Wayne State University Press, 1997.

Brown Childs, John. *Transcommunality: From the Politics of Conversion.* Philadelphia: Temple University Press, 2003.

Bulawayo, NoViolet. *We Need New Names.* New York: Back Bay, 2013.

Bumiller, Kristin. *In an Abusive State: How Neoliberalism Appropriated the Feminist Movement against Sexual Violence.* Durham, NC: Duke University Press, 2008.

Butler, Judith. *The Force of Nonviolence: An Ethico-Political Bind.* New York: Verso, 2020.

Butler, Judith. "Introduction." In *Vulnerability in Resistance,* edited by Judith Butler, Zeynep Gambetti, and Leticia Sabsay, 1–11. Durham, NC: Duke University Press, 2016.

Butler, Judith. *Precious Life: The Power of Mourning and Violence.* New York: Verso, 2006.

Butler, Judith. "Rethinking Vulnerability and Resistance." In *Vulnerability in Resistance,* edited by Judith Butler, Zeynep Gambetti, and Leticia Sabsay, 12–27. Durham, NC: Duke University Press, 2016.

Cacho, Lisa Marie. *Social Death: Racialized Rightlessness and the Criminalization of the Unprotected.* New York: New York University Press, 2012.

Camacho Servín, Fernando. "Al menos 44 mujeres periodistas y activistas han sido asesinadas en el país." *La Jornada,* May 13, 2017. https://www.jornada.com.mx/2017/05/13/politica/009n1pol.

Campt, Tina M. *Image Matters.* Durham, NC: Duke University Press, 2012.

Cantalupo, Nancy Chi. "Using Law and Education to Make Human Rights Real in Women's Lives." In *Confronting Global Gender Justice: Women's Lives, Human Rights,* edited by Debra Bergoffen, Paula Ruth Gilbert, Tamara Harvey, and Connie L. McNeely, 200–12. New York: Routledge, 2011.

Caputi, Jane. *The Age of Sex Crime.* Bowling Green, OH: Bowling Green University Press, 1987.

Carroll, Amy Sally. "'Accidental Allegories' Meet 'the Performative Documentary': *Boystown, Señorita Extraviada,* and the Border-Brothel Maquiladora Paradigm." *Signs* 31, no. 2 (Winter 2006): 357–96.

Castañeda Salgado, María Patricia. "Feminicide in Mexico: An Approach through Academic, Activist and Artistic Work." *Current Sociology* 64, no. 7 (2016): 1054–70.

Cavareno, Adriana. *Horrorism: Naming Contemporary Violence.* New York: Columbia University Press, 2011.

CEDEM. "El feminicidio de Marisela Escobedo: un Crimen de Estado." Centro de los Derechos Humanos de las Mujeres, February 2011.

Centenera, Mar. "Feminicidios: Una mujer asesinada cada 30 horas en Argentina por violencia machista." *El Pais*, April 1, 2016. https://elpais .com/internacional/2016/03/31/argentina/1459457396_981225.html.

Center for Gender and Refugee Studies. "Matter of A-B-. Practice Advisory." July 6, 2018. Practice advisory, available upon request at https:// uchastings.edu/assistance/request.

Cházaro, Angélica, Jennifer Casey, and Katherine Kuhl. "Getting Away with Murder: Guatemala's Failure to Protect Women and Rodi Alvarado's Quest for Safety." In Fregoso and Bejarano, *Terrorizing Women*, 93–115.

Chishti, Muzaffar, Sarah Pierce, and Hannah Jacks. "Trump Administration's Unprecedented Actions on Asylum at the Southern Border Hit Legal Roadblock." Migration Policy Institute, November 29, 2018. https://www.migrationpolicy.org/article/trump-administrations -unprecedented-actions-asylum-southern-border-hit-legal -roadblock.

Chomsky, Noam. "Prospects for Survival." *Massachusetts Review* (Winter 2017): 621–34.

Combahee River Collective. "Why Did They Die?" *Radical America,* no. 6 (November–December 1979). Also published as "Twelve Black Women: Why Did they Die?" In *Fight Back,* edited by Frédérique Delacoste and Felice Newman. Minneapolis: Cleis Press, 1981.

Comisión Nacional de Derechos Humanos en México. "Informe Especial sobre el tema de los homicidios y desapariciones de mujeres occurridos en el municipio de Juárez, Chihuahua." November 25, 2003. https:// www.cndh.org.mx/sites/default/files/documentos/2019–10/172.pdf.

Committee on the Elimination of Discrimination against Women. "Concluding Observations on the Ninth Periodic Report on Mexico." July 20, 2018. https://digitallibrary.un.org/record/1642447.

Connolly, William E. *A World of Becoming.* Durham, NC: Duke University Press, 2012.

Cubilié, Anne. *Women Witnessing Terror: Testimony and the Cultural Politics of Human Rights.* New York: Fordham University Press, 2005.

Darling, Marsha. "In the Realm of Responsibility: A Conversation with Toni Morrison." In *Conversations with Toni Morrison,* edited by Fanille Taylor-Guthrie, 246–54. Jackson: University Press of Mississippi, 1994.

Davis, Angela Y. *Are Prisons Obsolete?* New York: Seven Stories Press, 2003.

Davis, Angela Y. *Freedom Is a Constant Struggle: Ferguson, Palestine, and the Foundations of a Movement*. Chicago: Haymarket, 2016.

Davis, Angela Y. *Women, Race and Class*. New York: Vintage, 1981.

Davis, Angela Y., Gina Dent, Erica R. Meiners, and Beth E. Richie. *Abolition. Feminism. Now*. Chicago: Haymarket, 2022.

De Casas, Michelle. "Protecting Hispanic Women: The Inadequacy of Domestic Violence Policy." *Chicano-Latino Law Review* 24, no. 56 (2003): 56–78.

de la Mora, Sergio. "Terrorismo de género en la frontera México-EUA." *The Thinking Eye/El Ojo que piensa*. http://www.elojoquepiensa.udg.mx/ingles/. Accessed November 3, 2004. Article no longer available online; printout on file with author.

Delgadillo, Theresa. *Spiritual Mestizaje: Religion, Gender, Race and Nation in Contemporary Chicana Narrative*. Durham, NC: Duke University Press, 2011.

de Lima Costa, Claudia. "Introduction to Debates about Translation/Lost (and Found?) in Translation/Feminisms in Hemispheric Dialogue." In *Translocalities/Translocalidades*, edited by Sonia Alvarez, Claudia de Lima Costa, Verónica Feliu, Rebecca Hester, Norma Klahn, and Millie Thayer, 19–36. Durham, NC: Duke University Press, 2012.

Department of Homeland Security. "Migrant Protection Protocols." January 14, 2019. https://www.dhs.gov/news/2019/01/24/migrant-protection-protocols.

Derrida, Jacques. "A Self-Unsealing Poetic Text and the Politics of Witnessing," translated by Rachel Bowlby. In *Revenge of the Aesthetic: The Place of Literature in Theory Today*, edited by Michael P. Clark, 180–207. Berkeley: University of California Press, 2000.

Domínguez Ruvalcaba, Héctor. *Nación criminal*. Mexico City: Ariel, 2015.

Domínguez Ruvalcaba, Héctor, and Patricia Ravelo Blancas. *Desmantelamiento de la ciudadanía*. Mexico City: Ediciones y Gráficos Eón, 2011.

Driver, Alice. "Four Women Were Also Raped and Killed in Mexico Journalist Murder—but Media Calls Them Promiscuous." Women's Media Center, August 19, 2015. https://womensmediacenter.com/women-under-siege/women-raped-killed-mexico-espinosa-journalist-murder-media-promiscuous.

Durkin, Erin. "The Migrants Who Have Died in US Custody in 2018." *Guardian*, December 29, 2018. https://www.theguardian.com/us-news/2018/dec/29/immigrant-deaths-us-custody-felipe-gomez-alonzo-jakelin-caal.

Egelbo, Bob. "UN Official: Asylum Ban May Be Illegal." *San Francisco Chronicle*, December 7, 2018.

El Día (Argentina). "No están muertos ni vivos, están desaparecidos." May 17, 2003. Article is no longer available online.

Eng, David, and Jasbir Puar. "Introduction: Left of Queer." *Social Text* 38, no. 4 (December 2020): 1–23.

Escocer Perulero, Marisol. "Assassinatos de mulheres negras no México: Análise desde a conceitualização de feminicídio e racialização. In *Racismo e Neoliberalismo na América Latina: Descolonização e desracializaçã,* edited by Cristina Gomes. Curitiba: Ed. CRV, 2021. https://www.academia.edu/49177862/Assassinatos_de_mulheres_negras_no_M%C3%A9xico_An%C3%A1lise_desde_a_conceitualiza%C3%A7%C3%A3o_de_feminic%C3%ADdio_e_racializa%C3%A7%C3%A3o.

Esteva, Gustavo, and Makhuri Suri Prakash. *Grassroots Postmodernism.* London: Zed, 1998.

Euronews. "Domestic Violence Cases Jump 30% during Lockdown in France." March 28, 2020. https://www.euronews.com/2020/03/28/domestic-violence-cases-jump-30-during-lockdown-in-france.

Evans, Brad. "The Death of Humanitarianism." *Los Angeles Review of Books,* November 26, 2018. https://lareviewofbooks.org/article/the-death-of-humanitarianism/.

Federici, Sylvia. *Witches, Witch-Hunting, and Women.* Oakland, CA: PM Press, 2018.

Felman, Shoshana, and Dori Laub. *Testimony: Crises of Witnessing in Literature, Psychoanalysis, and History.* New York: Routledge, 1992.

Ferreyra, Christian. *The Risks of Defending Human Rights.* OXFAM International, October 2016. https://www.oxfam.org/en/research/risks-defending-human-rights.

Flores Contreras, Ezequiel. "Asesina a activista contra la violencia de género en Guerrero." *Proceso,* March 6, 2018. https://www.proceso.com.mx/nacional/2018/3/6/asesinan-activista-contra-la-violencia-de-genero-en-guerrero-201107.html.

Foucault, Michel. *"Society Must Be Defended": Lectures at the Collège de France, 1975–1976.* Translated by David Macey. New York: Picador, 2003.

Franco, Jean. *Cruel Modernity.* Durham, NC: Duke University Press, 2013.

Franzblau, Jesse. "Why Is the US Still Spending Billions to Fund Mexico's Corrupt Drug War?" *Nation,* February 15, 2015. https://www.thenation.com/article/archive/us-connection-mexicos-drug-war-corruption/.

Freedman, Jane. "The Uses and Abuses of 'Vulnerability' in EU Asylum and Refugee Protection." Papeles del CEIC. *International Journal on Collective Identity Research,* no. 1 (2019): 1–15. https://www.redalyc.org/journal/765/76566924004/html/.

Freedom for Migrants. *Persecuted in U.S. Migrant Detention: A National Report on Abuse Motivated by Hate.* 2018. https://www.freedomforimmigrants.org/report-on-hate.

Fregoso, Rosa-Linda. *The Bronze Screen: Chicana and Chicano Film Culture.* Minneapolis: University of Minnesota Press, 1993.

Fregoso, Rosa-Linda. "California Dreaming: Reimagining the Nation." In *Art/Women/California 1950–2000: Parallels and Intersections,* edited by Diana Burgess Fuller and Daniella Salvioni, 257–74. Berkeley: University of California Press, 2003.

Fregoso, Rosa-Linda. "For a Pluriversal Declaration of Human Rights." Special issue, *American Quarterly: Las Américas Quarterly* 66, no. 3 (September 2014): 583–608.

Fregoso, Rosa-Linda. *meXicana Encounters: The Making of Social Identities on the Borderlands.* Berkeley: University of California Press, 2003.

Fregoso, Rosa-Linda. "Sacando los Trapos al Sol (Airing Dirty Laundry) in Lourdes Portillo's Melodocumystery, *The Devil Never Sleeps.*" In *Redirecting the Gaze: Gender, Theory, and Cinema in the Third World,* edited by Diana Robin and Ira Jaffe, 307–29. Albany: State University of New York Press, 1999.

Fregoso, Rosa-Linda. "Violencia de género ante el derecho y los derechos humanos." In *Vidas y territorios en busca de justicia,* edited by Julia Estela Monárrez Fragoso, Rosalba Robles Ortega, Luis Ernesto Cervera Gómez, and César Mario Fuentes Flores, 237–61. Tijuana: El Colegio de la Frontera Norte; Ciudad Juárez: Universidad Autónoma de Ciudad Juárez, 2015.

Fregoso, Rosa-Linda. "Voices without an Echo: The Global Gendered Apartheid." *Emergence* 10, no. 1 (May 2000): 137–55.

Fregoso, Rosa-Linda. "'We Want Them Alive!': The Politics and Culture of Human Rights." *Social Identities* 12, no. 2 (March 2006): 109–38. Spanish translation: "'¡Las queremos vivas!' La política y cultura de los derechos humanos." *Debate Feminista* 39 (2009): 209–43.

Fregoso, Rosa-Linda. "Coming to Grips with Feminicide." *Truthout,* January 13, 2012. https://truthout.org/articles/coming-to-grips-with-feminicide/

Fregoso, Rosa-Linda, and Cynthia Bejarano, eds. *Terrorizing Women: Feminicide in the Américas.* Durham, NC: Duke University Press, 2010.

Fregoso, Rosa-Linda, coordinator; Rosa-Linda Fregoso and Cynthia Bejarano, eds. *Feminicidio en América Latina.* Mexico City: Centro de Investigaciones Interdisciplinarias en Ciencias y Humanidades, 2011.

Frías, Sonia M. "Between Agency and Structure: Advocacy and Family Violence in Mexico." *Women's Studies International Forum* 33 (2010): 542–51.

Frías, Sonia M. "Strategies and Help Seeking Behavior among Mexican Women Experiencing Partner Violence." *Violence against Women* 19, no. 1 (2013): 1–26. https://doi.org/10.1177/1077801212475334.

Friedman, Elizabeth Jay, and Constanza Tabbush. "#NiUnaMenos: Not One Woman Less, Not One More." NACLA, November 1, 2016. https://nacla

.org/news/2016/11/01/niunamenos-not-one-woman-less-not-one
-more-death.

Front Line Defenders. *Annual Report on Human Rights Defenders at Risk in 2016*. Dublin: Front Line, the International Foundation for the Protection of Human Rights Defenders, 2016.

Fumega, Silvana. "Tracking Latin America's Other Pandemic: Violence against Women." *Americas Quarterly*, April 13, 2020. https://www .americasquarterly.org/content/tracking-latin-americas-other -pandemic-violence-against-women.

Gago, Veronica. "La tierra tiembla." *Critical Times* 1, no. 1 (2018): 178–83.

Gallón, Natalie. "Women Are Being Killed at Record Rates in Mexico, but the President Says Most Emergency Calls Are 'False.'" CNN World, July 16, 2020. https://www.cnn.com/2020/06/05/americas/mexico -femicide-coronavirus-lopez-obrador-intl/index.html.

García-Del Moral, Paulina. "The Murders of Indigenous Women in Canada as Feminicides: Toward a Decolonial Intersectional Reconceptualization of Feminicide." *Signs: Journal of Women in Culture and Society* 43, no. 4 (2018): 929–54.

GIEI. *Informe Ayotzinapa: Investigación y primeras conclusions de las desapariciones y homicidios de los normalistas de Ayotzinapa*. Grupo Interdisciplinario de Expertos Independientes, CASEDE, 2015. https://www .casede.org/index.php/bibliotecacasede/derechos-humanos/461 -informe-ayotzinapa-investigacio-n-y-primeras-conclusiones-de-las -desapariciones-y-homicidios-de-los-normalistas-de-ayotzinapa.

Gilmore, Ruth Wilson. *Golden Gulag: Prisons, Surplus, Crisis, and Opposition in Globalizing California*. Berkeley: University of California Press, 2007.

Glassman, Bernie. *Bearing Witness: A Zen Master's Lessons in Making Peace*. New York: Bell Tower, 1998.

Global Alliance for the Rights of Nature. "People's Tribunal versus Judicial Tribunal—Rights of Nature Tribunal." April 26, 2014. http:// therightsofnature.org/peoples-tribunal-vs-judicial-tribunal/.

Goldman, Francisco. "Who Killed Rubén Espinosa and Nadia Vera?" *New Yorker*, August 14, 2015. https://www.newyorker.com/news/news-desk /who-killed-ruben-espinosa-and-nadia-vera.

Gómez-Barris, Macarena. *Beyond the Pink Tide: Art and Political Undercurrents in the Americas*. Berkeley: University of California Press, 2018.

González Rodríguez, Sergio. *The Femicide Machine*. Translated by Michael Parker-Stainback. Cambridge, MA: MIT Press, 2012.

Grant, Jaime M. "Who's Killing Us?" In *Femicide: The Politics of Women Killing*, edited by Jill Radford and Diana E. H. Russell, 145–60. New York: Twayne, 1992.

Grassroots Leadership. "These Letters from Migrant Women in Detention Centers Are Gut-Wrenching to Read." July 4, 2018. http://

grassrootsleadership.org/in-the-news/2018/these-letters-migrant
-women-detention-centers-are-gut-wrenching-read.

Grillo, Ioan. "Mexican Border as Refugee Camp." *New York Times*, December 21, 2018.

Gruesz, Kirsten Silva. "'Poor Eliza' on the Border." *Journal of Nineteenth Century Americanists* 6, no. 1 (Spring 2018): 182–89.

Guerin, Frances, and Roger Hallas. "Introduction." In *The Image and the Witness*, edited by Frances Guerin and Roger Hallas, 1–22. London: Wallflower, 2007.

Guerrero, Jean. "Sessions Says 'Zero Tolerance' Policy for Border Crossers May Split Families." *City News Service,* May 7, 2018. https://www.kpbs
.org/news/midday-edition/2018/05/07/attorney-general-jeff-sessions
-to-visit-san-diego

Guevara Rosas, Erika. "Surveying the Damage: Enrique Peña Nieto." *Amnesty International News*, November 30, 2018. https://www.amnesty
.org/en/latest/news/2018/11/enrique-pena-nieto-el-recuento-de-los
-danos/.

Guiteras-Holmes, Calixta. *Perils of the Soul*. New York: Free Press of Glenco, 1961.

Haney, Craig. "The Perversions of Prison: On the Origins of Hypermasculinity and Sexual Violence in Confinement." *American Criminal Law Review* 48 (2011): 121–41.

Haraway, Donna J. *Staying with the Trouble: Making Kin in the Chthulucene*. Durham, NC: Duke University Press, 2016.

Henderson, Victoria. "Citizenship in the Line of Fire: Protective Accompaniment, Proxy Citizenship, and Pathways for Transnational Solidarity in Guatemala." *Annals of the Association of American Geographers* 99, no. 5 (2009): 969–76.

Holder, Cindy L., and Jeff J. Corntassel. "Indigenous Peoples and Multicultural Citizenship: Bridging Collective and Individual Rights." *Human Rights Quarterly* 24, no. 1 (2002): 126–51.

Holland, Sharon P. *Raising the Dead: Readings of Death and (Black) Subjectivity*. Durham, NC: Duke University Press, 2010.

Hong, Grace Kyungwon, and Roderick A. Ferguson, eds. *Strange Affinities: The Gender and Sexual Politics of Comparative Racialization*. Durham, NC: Duke University Press, 2011.

Huacuz Elías, María Guadalupe. "Introducción: Reflexiones sobre el concepto de violencia falocéntrica desde el método de la complejidad." In *La bifucación del caos*, edited by María Guadalupe Huacuz Elías, 9–29. Mexico City: Editorial Itaca, 2011.

Human Rights Watch. *Mexico's Disappeared: The Enduring Costs of a Crisis Ignored*. February 20, 2013. https://www.hrw.org/report/2013/02/20
/mexicos-disappeared/enduring-cost-crisis-ignored.

Hurtado, Aida. *Intersectional Chicana Feminisms.* Tucson: University of Arizona Press, 2020.

Inda, Jonathan Xavier. "Fatal Prescriptions: Immigration Detention, Mismedication, and the Necropolitics of Uncare." *Death Studies* 44, no. 11 (2020): 699–708.

Iturralde, Christina. "Searching for Accountability on the Border." In Fregoso and Bejarano, *Terrorizing Women,* 243–62.

Kanstroom, Daniel. *Deportation Nation: Outsiders in American History.* Cambridge, MA: Harvard University Press, 2007.

Kapur, Ratnar. *Erotic Justice: Law and the New Politics of Postcolonialism.* New York: Routledge-Cavendish, 2005.

Kester, Grant H. *The One and the Many: Contemporary Collaborative Art in a Global Context.* Durham, NC: Duke University Press, 2011.

Kobelinsky, Carolina. "The Living, the Dead, and the Living Dead: Presences at the Spanish Moroccan Border." *Death Studies* 44, no. 11 (2020): 709–17.

Lagarde de los Rios, Marcela. "Preface." In Fregoso and Bejarano, *Terrorizing Women,* xi–xxv.

Laporta, Elena Hernández. "El Feminicidio como categoría jurídica. De la regulación en América Latina a su inclusion en España." In *Feminicidio: De la categoría político-jurídica a la justicia universal,* edited by Graciela Atencio. Madrid: Los Libros de la Catarata.

Laqueur, Thomas W. "The Dead Body and Human Rights." In *The Body,* edited by Sean Sweeney and Ian Hodder, 75–93. London: Cambridge University Press, 2002.

Law, Victoria. "Forced to Work for Pennies." *New York Times,* December 30, 2018.

Lifton, Robert Jay. *Death in Life: Survivors of Hiroshima.* Reprint, Chapel Hill: University of North Carolina Press, 1991.

López, Oscar. "Number of Journalists Killed for Their Reporting Doubled in 2020." *New York Times,* December 22, 2020. https://www.nytimes.com/2020/12/22/world/americas/mexico-journalists-killings-double.html.

López, Oscar. "President of Mexico Speaks Up for Reporter." *New York Times,* August 11, 2021.

López Medellín, Marta Olivia. *Tamaulipas: La construcción del silencio.* Dokumen, February 2015. https://dokumen.tips/reader/f/tamaulipas-la-construccion-del-silencio-freedomhouseorg.

Lugones, María. "Reading the Coloniality of Gender." Talk presented at the Annual Meeting of the American Studies Association, 2012.

Lugones, María. "Toward a Decolonial Feminism." *Hypatia* 25, no. 4 (Fall 2010): 742–59.

Mackey, Nathaniel. "Cante Moro." In *Sound States: Innovative Poetics and Acoustical Technologies,* edited by Adalaide Morris, 194–212. Chapel Hill: University of North Carolina Press, 1997.

Mackey, Nathaniel. *Paracritical Hinge: Essays, Talks, Notes, Interviews*. Des Moines: University of Iowa Press, 2013.

Mahoney, Liam, and Louis Eguren. *Unarmed Bodyguards: International Accompaniment for the Protection of Human Rights*. West Hartford, CT: Kumarian, 1997.

Malkki, Liisa. "Refugee and Exile: From 'Refugee Studies' to the National Order of Things." *Annual Review of Anthropology* 24 (1995): 495–523.

Mani, Lata. *The Integral Nature of Things: Critical Reflections on the Present*. New Delhi: Routledge, 2013.

Mani, Lata. *Myriad Intimacies*. Durham, NC: Duke University Press, 2022.

Marcos, Sylvia. "The Borders Within: The Indigenous Women's Movement and Feminism in Mexico." In *Dialogue and Difference: Feminisms Challenge Globalization*, edited by Marguerite Waller and Sylvia Marcos, 81–110. New York: Palgrave Macmillan, 2005.

Margulies, Peter. "The Ninth Circuit's Asylum Ban Ruling Is a Message to Trump." *Lawfare*, December 10, 2018. https://www.lawfareblog.com/ninth-circuits-asylum-ban-ruling-message-trump.

Marks, Laura U. *The Skin of the Film: Intercultural Cinema, Embodiment, and the Senses*. Durham, NC: Duke University Press, 2000.

Martínez, María. "Living Dead: Suspended Lives during/after Gender Violence." *Death Studies* 44, no. 11 (2020): 718–26.

Mbembe, Achille. "Necropolitics." Translated by Libby Meintjes. *Public Culture* 15, no. 1 (2003): 11–40.

Méndez, Enrique, and Néstor Jiménez. "Gertz: Aumentaron los feminicidios 137% en cinco años." *La Jornada*, February 11, 2020. https://www.jornada.com.mx/ultimas/politica/2020/02/11/gertz-aumentaron-los-feminicidios-137-en-cinco-anos-4329.html.

Menjívar, Cecilia. *Enduring Violence: Latina Women's Lives in Guatemala*. Berkeley: University of California Press, 2011.

Menjívar, Cecilia, and Shannon Drysdale Walsh. "The Architecture of Feminicide, the State, Inequalities, and Everyday Gender Violence in Honduras." *Latin American Research Review* 52, no. 2 (2017): 221–40.

Mesa-Baines, Amalia. "The Interior Life: The Works of Patssi Valdez." In *The Painted World of Patssi Valdez* (exhibition catalog). May 5–July 4, 1993. Los Angeles: Boathouse Gallery, Plaza de la Raza.

Meyer, Maureen. "Abuso y miedo en Ciudad Juárez: Un análisis de violaciones de los derechos humanos cometidas por militares en México." Centro de Derechos Humanos and Washington Office on Latin America, October 5, 2010. http://www.wola.org/es/noticias/violaciones_a_los_derechos_humanos_cometidas_por_el_ejercito_mexicano_descritas_en_el_nuevo.

Mezzadra, Sandro. *Derecho de fuga: Migraciones, ciudadania y globalización*. Translated by Miguel Santucho. Madrid: Traficantes de Sueños, 2005.

Mignolo, Walter D. *The Darker Side of Western Modernity: Global Futures, Decolonial Options*. Durham, NC: Duke University Press, 2011.

Mignolo, Walter D. *Local Histories/Global Designs: Coloniality, Subaltern Knowledges, and Border Thinking*. Princeton, NJ: Princeton University Press, 2000.

Miller, Susan A. "Native America Writes Back: The Origins of the Indigenous Paradigm in Historiography." *Wicazo Sa Review* 23, no. 2 (2008): 9–23.

Minian, Ana Raquel. "America Didn't Always Lock Up Migrants." *New York Times*, December 3, 2018.

Monárrez Fragoso, Julia. "Feminicidio: Muertes públicas, comunidades cerradas y Estado desarticulado." In *Vidas y territorios en busca de justicia*, edited by Julia Estela Monárrez Fragoso, Rosalba Robles Ortega, Luis Ernesto Cervera Gómez, and César Mario Fuentes Flores, 109–40. Tijuana: El Colegio de la Frontera Norte; Ciudad Juárez: Universidad Autónoma de Ciudad Juárez, 2015.

Monárrez Fragoso, Julia. "Feminicidio sexual sistémico: Impunidad histórica constante en Ciudad Juárez, víctimas y perpetradores." *Estado y communes, revista de políticas y problemas públicos* 1, no. 8 (January–June 2019): 85–110.

Monárrez Fragoso, Julia. "La cultura de feminicidio en Ciudad Juárez, 1993–99." *Frontera Norte* 12, no. 23 (January–June 2000): 87–117.

Monárrez Fragoso, Julia. "Serial Sexual Feminicide in Ciudad Juárez, 1993–2001." *Aztlán* 28, no. 2 (Fall 2003): 153–78.

Monárrez Fragoso, Julia. *Trama de una injusticia: Feminicidio sexual sistémico en Ciudad Juárez*. Tijuana: Colegio de la Frontera Norte, 2009.

Monárrez Fragoso, Julia, and Luis E. Cervera Gómez. "Spatial and Temporal Behavior of Three Paradigmatic Cases of Violence in Ciudad Juarez, Chihuahua México: Feminicide, Homicide and Involuntary Disappearances of Girls and Women (1993–2013)." El Colegio de Frontera Norte, April 26, 2013. https://www.academia.edu/4342188/Spatial_and_temporal_behavior_of_three_paradigmatic_cases_of_violence_in_Ciudad_Juarez_Chihuahua_M%C3%A9xico_feminicide_homicide_and_involuntary_disappearances_of_girls_and_women_1993_2013_.

Morrison, Toni. *Burn This Book*. New York: Harper Collins Publisher, 2009; 2012.

Moten, Fred. *In the Break*. Minneapolis: University of Minnesota Press, 2003.

Muñoz, José Esteban. *Dis-identifications: Queers of Color and the Performance of Politics*. Minneapolis: University of Minnesota Press, 1999.

Nathan, Debbie. "Death Comes to the Maquilas." *Nation* 264, no. 2 (January 1997): 18–22.

Ni Una Menos. "Nosotros paramos." *Critical Times* 1, no. 1: 184–88.

Nuñez Rebolledo, Lucia. "Contribución a la crítica del feminismo punitivo."
In *La bifucación del caos*, edited by María Guadalupe Huacuz Elía,
181–203. Mexico City: Editorial Itaca, 2011.

Observatorio Ciudadano Nacional de Feminicidio. *Informe Implementación
del Tipo Penal del Feminicidio en México*. Coyoacán, Mexico: Católicas
por el Derecho a Decidir, 2018.

Observatorio Ciudadano Nacional de Feminicidio. "Informe Implementación del Tipo Penal en México: Deasfíos para acreditar las razones de
género 2014–2017." Mexico City: Católicas por el Derecho a Decidir,
2018. https://www.observatoriofeminicidiomexico.org/_files/ugd
/ba8440_66cc5ce03ac34b7da8670c37037aae9c.pdf.

Oliver, Kelly. "Witnessing and Testimony." *Parallax* 10, no. 1 (2004): 79–88.

Oliver, Kelly. *Witnessing: Beyond Recognition*. Minneapolis: University of
Minnesota Press, 2001.

Oliver, Kelly. *Women as Weapons of War: Iraq, Sex, and the Media*. New
York: Columbia University Press, 2007.

ONU Mujeres/SEGOB/INMUJERES. "La violencia feminicida en México,
aproximaciones y tendencias 1985–2016." Mexico: Entidad de las
Naciones Unidas para la Igualdad de Género y el Empoderamiento
de las Mujeres, 2017. https://mexico.unwomen.org/es/digiteca
/publicaciones/2017/12/violencia-feminicida.

Organization of American States. "Inter-American Convention on Forced
Disappearances of Persons." Department of International Law, 1994.
https://oas.org/juridico/English/treaties/a-60.html.

Orsi, Peter. "Mexico: Thousands Stay in to Protest Violence against
Women." Associated Press, March 9, 2020. https://apnews.com/article
/a0af573598d3fec88bda6149d2e35644.

Paredes, Julieta. *Hilando fino: Desde el feminism comunitario*. La Paz, Bolivia:
Comunidad Mujeres Creando Comunidad, 2010.

Paterson, Kent. "The Border's COVID-19 Pandemic: Crisis upon Crisis."
Americas Program, June 24, 2020. https://www.americas.org/the
-borders-covid-19-pandemic-crisis-upon-crisis/.

Paterson, Kent. "Mexico's New Dirty War." Americas Program, April 30,
2010. https://www.americas.org/mexicos-new-dirty-war/.

Paterson, Kent. "The Silencing of Women's Voices." *Frontera Norte-Sur*,
March 7, 2011. The server is decommissioned. Article on file with author. See: http://newmexicomercury.com/author/103.

Patterson, Orlando. *Slavery and Social Death: A Comparative Study*. Cambridge, MA: Harvard University Press, 1982.

Peláez Ferrusca, Mercedes. "Derechos humanos y prisión: Notas para el
acercamiento." *Boletin Mexicano de Derecho Comparado*. Instituto
de Investigación Jurídica de la Universidad Nacional Autónoma de

México. May–August 1999. https://revistas.juridicas.unam.mx/index
.php/derecho-comparado/article/view/3594/4334#P6.

Pérez, Laura E. *Chicana Art: The Politics of Spiritual and Aesthetic Altarities.*
Durham, NC: Duke University Press, 2007.

Pérez, Laura. "Enrique Dussel's *Etica de la liberación*: U.S. Women of Color
Decolonizing Practices, and Coalitional Politics amidst Difference." *Qui
Parle* 18, no. 2 (Spring/Summer 2010): 121–46.

Permanent Peoples' Tribunal. "Final Ruling: Permanent Peoples' Tribunal
Chapter Mexico (Dictamen final TPP México en inglés)." November 15,
2015. http://www.tppmexico.org/final-ruling-permanent-peoples
-tribunal-chapter-mexico/.

Pineda-Madrid, Nancy. *Suffering and Salvation in Ciudad Juárez.* Minneapolis: Fortress Press, 2011.

Pola, Susi. *Femi(ni)cidio en República Dominicana 2000–2006.* San José:
CEFEMINA.

Portillo, Lourdes. "Filming *Señorita Extraviada*." *Aztlán* 28, no. 2 (2003):
229–34.

Quintana S., Víctor M. "Mujeres en éxodo por la vida." *La Jornada,* November 13,
2009. https://www.jornada.com.mx/2009/11/13/opinion/021a2pol.

Ramírez, Catherine. *Assimilation: An Alternative History.* Berkeley: University of California Press, 2020.

Ramos, Jorge. *Stranger: The Challenge of a Latino Immigrant in the Trump
Era.* New York: Vintage, 2018.

Ravelo Blancas, Patricia. *Miradas etnológicas.* Mexico City: Ediciones y
Gráficos Eón, 2011.

Renov, Michael. "Towards a Poetics of Documentary." In *Theorizing Documentary,* edited by Michael Renov, 12–36. New York: Routledge, 1993.

Richardson, Allissa V. *Bearing Witness While Black: African Americans,
Smartphones, and the New Protest #Journalism.* New York: Oxford University Press, 2020.

Richie, Beth E. *Arrested Justice: Black Women, Violence, and America's Prison
Nation.* New York: New York University Press, 2012.

Rivera Cusicanqui, Sylvia. "The Notion of Rights and the Paradoxes of Post-
colonial Modernity: Indigenous Peoples and Women in Bolivia." *Qui
Parle* 18, no. 2 (Spring/Summer 2010): 29–54.

Rivera Garza, Cristina. *Grieving: Dispatches from a Wounded Country.* Translated by Sarah Booker. New York: Feminist Press, 2020.

Rivera Garza, Cristina. *The Restless Dead: Necrowriting and Disappropria-
tion.* Translated by Robin Myers. Nashville, TN: Vanderbilt University
Press, 2020.

Rojas Blanco, Clara E. "The V-Day March in Mexico: Appropriation and
(Mis)Use of Local Women's Activism." *National Women's Studies
Association Journal* 17 (2005): 217–27.

Rosas, Erika Guevara. "Surveying the Damage: Enrique Peña Nieto." *Amnesty International*, November 30, 2018. https://www.amnesty.org/en/latest/news/2018/11/enrique-pena-nieto-el-recuento-de-los-danos/

Russell, Diana E. H. "Femicide: Politicizing the Killing of Females." In *Strengthening Understanding of Femicide*, 26–31. Program for Appropriate Technology in Health, InterCambios, Medical Research Council of South Africa, and World Health Organization, 2009. https://path.azureedge.net/media/documents/GVR_femicide_rpt.pdf.

Russell, Diana E. H. "Preface." In *Femicide: The Politics of Woman Killing*, edited by Jill Radford and Diana E. H. Russell, xi–xv. New York: Twayne, 1992.

Russell, Diana E. H., and Roberta A. Harmes, eds. *Feminicide in a Global Perspective*. New York: Teachers College Press, 2001.

Sanford, Victoria. "From Genocide to Feminicide: Impunity and Human Rights in the Twenty-First Century." *Journal of Human Rights* 7, no. 2 (2008): 104–22.

Sanford, Victoria. *Guatemala: Del genocidio al feminicidio*. Guatemala City: F & G Editorial, 2008.

Santos, John Phillip. *Places Left Unfinished at the Time of Creation*. New York: Penguin, 1999.

#Save Asylum. "Delivered to Danger." February 19, 2021. https://deliveredtodanger.org/.

Secretaría de Gobernación. "Búsqueda e Identificación de Personas Desaparecidas: Reporte Semestral 1 de enero al 30 de junio, 2021." Gobierno de México, 2021. https://www.gob.mx/segob/documentos/busqueda-e-identificacion-de-personas-desaparecidas.

Sekkgya, Margaret. *Report of the Special Rapporteur on the Situation of Human Rights Defenders*, 2010. https://digitallibrary.un.org/record/678641?ln=es.

Sheridan, Mary Beth. "The Search for Mexico's Disappeared Points to Mexico's Darkest Secrets." *Washington Post*, December 3, 2020. https://www.washingtonpost.com/graphics/2020/world/mexico-losing-control/mexico-disappeared-drug-war/.

Solnit, Rebecca. "In Patriarchy No One Can Hear You Scream: Rebecca Solnit on Jeffrey Epstein and the Silencing Machine." *Literary Hub*, July 10, 2019. https://lithub.com/in-patriarchy-no-one-can-hear-you-scream-rebecca-solnit-on-jeffrey-epstein-and-the-silencing-machine/.

Solnit, Rebecca. "The Longest War." *Tom Dispatch*, January 24, 2013. https://tomdispatch.com/rebecca-solnit-the-longest-war/.

Sontag, Susan. *On Photography*. London: Penguin, 1977.

Southern Poverty Law Center. *No End in Sight*. 2018. https://www.splcenter.org/20181003/no-end-sight.

Spivak, Gayatri Chakravorty. *Death of a Discipline*. New York: Columbia University Press, 2003.

Stinger, Scott M., and Javier H. Valdés. "Divest from Private Prisons." *New York Times*, July 31, 2018.

SubVersiones. "Feminicidio y violencias contra las mujeres." September 26, 2014. http://subversiones.org/archivos/85204.

Sudbury, Julia. "Introduction: Feminist Critiques, Transnational Landscapes, Abolitionist Visions." In *Global Lockdown: Race, Gender, and the Prison-Industrial Complex*, edited by Julia Sudbury, xi–xxviii. New York: Routledge, 2005.

Sutton, Barbara. *Bodies in Crisis: Culture, Violence, and Women's Resistance in Neoliberal Argentina*. New Brunswick, NJ: Rutgers University Press, 2010.

Szymanek, Angelique. "Elina Chalet: Decolonizing Disappearance." *Latin American and Latinx Visual Culture* 4, no. 1 (2022): 58–74.

Tabuenco Córdova, María Socorro. "Día V-Permanente en Ciudad Juárez." *El Diario*, March 2, 2003, 21A.

Taylor, Chloë. *Foucault, Feminism, and Sex Crimes: An Anti-carceral Analysis*. New York: Routledge, 2018.

Taylor, Diana. *Disappearing Acts: Spectacles of Gender and Nationalism in Argentina's Dirty War*. Durham, NC: Duke University Press, 2003.

Tomlinson, Barbara, and George Lipsitz. *Insubordinate Spaces: Improvisation and Accompaniment for Social Justice*. Philadelphia: Temple University Press, 2019.

Trinh T. Minh-ha, *Lovecidal: Walking with the Disappeared*. New York: Fordham University Press, 2016.

UDGTV.com. "Presentó informe 2020 el Observatorio Ciudadano Nacional del Feminicidio en México de manera virtual." December 9, 2020. https://udgtv.com/radio/presento-informe-2020-observatorio -ciudadano-nacional-del-feminismo-mexico-manera-virtual/.

United Nations Human Rights, Office of the High Commissioner. "Convention Relating to the Status of Refugees." July 28, 1951. https://www .ohchr.org/en/professionalinterest/pages/statusofrefugees.aspx.

UN Women. "COVID-19 and Ending Violence against Women and Girls." March 2020. https://www.unwomen.org/en/digital-library /publications/2020/04/issue-brief-covid-19-and-ending-violence -against-women-and-girls.

V-Day. "2004 Spotlight: Women in Juarez." Accessed June 27, 2022. https:// www.vday.org/2004-spotlight-women-in-juarez/.

Villaseñor, Maria Cristina. "An Interview with Lourdes Portillo." *Risk/Riesgo* 2, no. 3 (2003): 170–78.

von Gleich, Paula. "Fugitivity against the Border: Afro-pessimism, Fugitivity and the Border to Social Death." In *Critical Epistemologies to Global Politics*, edited by Marc Woons and Sebastian Weier, 203–14. Bristol, UK: E-International, 2017.

Walker, Alice. *The Way Forward Is with a Broken Heart*. New York: Ballantine, 2000.

Washington Valdez, Diana. *Cosecha de Mujeres*. Mexico City: Editorial Oceano, 2005.

Weheliye, Alexander G. *Habeas Viscus: Racializing Assemblages, Biopolitics, and Black Feminist Theories of the Human*. Durham, NC: Duke University Press, 2014.

Weissman, Deborah. "The Personal Is Political—and Economic: Rethinking Domestic Violence." *Baylor University Law Review* 387 (2007): 387–450.

Weissman, Deborah, and Marsha Weissman. "The Moral Politics of Social Control: Political Culture and Ordinary Crime in Cuba." *Brooklyn Journal of International Law* 35, no. 2 (2010): 312–67.

Weiwei, Ai. *Humanity*. Edited by Larry Warsh. Princeton, NJ: Princeton University Press, 2019.

World Health Organization. "Violence against Women." November 29, 2017. http://www.who.int/news-room/fact-sheets/detail/violence-against-women.

Wright, Melissa. "Mujeres de Negro." In Fregoso and Bejarano, *Terrorizing Women*, 312–30.

Wright, Melissa W. "Necropolitics, Narcopolitics and Femicide: Gender Violence on the Mexico-U.S. Border." *Signs* 36, no. 3 (March 2011): 707–31.

Index

Villamizar, Mónica, 94

Villa Mojica, Juventina, 89

Villaseñor, María Cristina, 100

La ville qui tue les femmes. See The city that
murders women

violence, against women, 17, 79; culture
sexualizing, 201; family changed by,
189n41; government ignoring, 63–65;
against journalists, 88–90, 93–95; legislation not diminishing, 80–81; neoliberalism increasing, 65–66; neoliberalism
pathologizing, 83; as personal contrasted
with political, 23; as private contrasted
with public matter, 56, 73; against rights
defenders, 63–64, 88–89; social media
showing, 107; state and, 23, 42, 49, 73,
76–77, 88; as structural, 57; as systemic,
23, 42, 74; transnational corporations
aggravating, 155. *See also* domestic
violence; feminicide

Violence against Women Act (VAWA), 41, 80

"La Violencia de género y los límites del
sistema estadounidense" (talk), 191n59

La Virgen de Guadalupe, 58, 60–62

visuality, 109–13

Voices without an Echo (*Voces sin Eco*)
(organization), 19, 24, 32, 123–24

"Voices without an Echo" (Fregoso), 15

Von Gleich, Paula, 180

vulnerability, 208n52, 208n60; activist-
mothers sharing, 31; of activists, 88; of
asylum seekers, 177; domestic violence
and, 54; of refugees, 175; testimony
determining, 9; of women, 87

Walker, Alice, 137

Wall of Memories (exhibition), 58–62

Walsh, Shannon Drysdale, 73, 86

war on drugs, 50, 66–68, 86

war on women, Catholic Inquisition
launching, 93

Washington Valdez, Diana, 84

Weheliye, Alexander, 166, 170, 175

Weissman, Deborah, 42

Weissman, Marsha, 42

"Why Did They Die?" (manifesto), 40, 93

witness. *See* specific topics

women: crosses memorializing, 123–24, 137;
hierarchies separating, 75; kidnappings
of, 13, 77; murder blamed on, 47–48,
95; photography memorializing, 126;
shelters for, 91, 156, 183–84; Simmons
remembering, 117–18; on strike in Argentina, 45–46; vulnerability of, 87. *See also*
mothers, of victims; violence, against
women; women of color

Women Dressed in Black (*Mujeres de
Negro*) (coalition), 25, 30–31, 130, 188n26,
189n29

Women in Black (movement), 188n26

women of color: feminism by, 74; hypersexuality conflated with, 77; as untrans-
latable concept, 71

workers, assembly plants recruiting, 66

Wright, Melissa, 31, 188n26

YGB (survivor), asylum sought by, 55–57

Zamora, Martha, 16

www.ingramcontent.com/pod-product-compliance
Lightning Source LLC
Chambersburg PA
CBHW071737270326

41928CB00013B/2712